PublicServicePrep Comprehensive Guide to Canadian Public Service Exams

Copyright © 2019 Dekalam Hire Learning Incorporated

COMPREHNSIVE GUIDE TO CANADIAN PUBLIC SERVICE EXAMS, published by:

PublicServicePrep
http://www.publicserviceprep.com
info@publicserviceprep.com

Authors:
Deland Jessop, Kalpesh Rathod, and Adam Cooper.

All rights reserved. PublicServicePrep. No part of this book may be reproduced in any form, by photostat, microfilm, xerography, or any other means, or incorporated into any information retrieval system, electronic or mechanical, without the written permission of the copyright owner.

Note that any resemblance of descriptions to people living or dead, or incidents past or present, is coincidental.

ISBN 0-9735151-2-0

Printed and bound in Canada

Table of Contents

Introduction 5

Preparation Material 7

    Resume Building 8
    The Interview 17
    Hiring Process 25
    General Suggestions 28

Teaching Material
- Math 29
- English 72
- Situational Judgment Test 82
- Essay Writing 83
- General 87

Practice Exams

    Office Skills Test (OST) 101
    General Competency Test Level 1 (GCT 1) 123
    General Competency Test Level 2 (GCT 2) 141
    Graduate Recruitment Test (GRT) 175
    Situational Judgment Test (SJT) 191
    Written Communication Proficiency Test (WCPT) 227
    Grammar Spelling and Punctuation Test (GSPAT) 245
    Wonderlic Practice Test 263
    Writing Skills In English MCT (WSE-MCT) 283

Introduction

Welcome to PublicServicePrep. The application process for government jobs can be very competitive. We understand the situation you're in and the challenges that lie ahead for you. This study guide was developed to help you prepare for the public service exams used by government bodies across Canada.

By purchasing this guide, you have taken the most important step - you have moved from thinking about preparation to taking action. Your dedication to preparing for your entrance exams demonstrates that you are the motivated person government services want to hire.

If you are looking for more practice tests and further preparation materials, visit our website at WWW.PUBLICSERVICEPREP.COM. We offer a special discount of 25% for those who have purchased this guide. When signing up online input the following code in the referral code section to get the discount (note the code is case sensitive):

ppdc712

Please do not hesitate to contact us if you have any questions, concerns or comments about this book, our website, or the application and testing process. We will be happy to do anything we can to assist you.

Email: info@publicserviceprep.com
URL: http://www.publicserviceprep.com

Preparation Material

Resume Building

A resume is a tool you can use to demonstrate your fit for the job-specific requirements of a career. Few people have received instruction on building a resume, or had much experience writing them. They don't understand what should or should not be included to present themselves in the best manner they can.

Resume building does not start at the writing stage. If you are serious about applying for a government position, you should have a long list of volunteer experience, academic achievements, languages, computer skills and other highlights to place on your resume. If you don't, begin today. Many organizations, including food banks, charity organizations and Children's Aid Societies are desperate for volunteer help. Languages, especially French are important for government agencies, as are computer skills and any other life skills.

The main purpose of your resume is to frame your experiences, skills and knowledge in a manner relevant to the position to which you are applying. You have to not only demonstrate what you've done, but also show that you have done it well. It is crucial to present information clearly and concisely so the person reviewing your resume can quickly find what they require. Three principles should be followed:

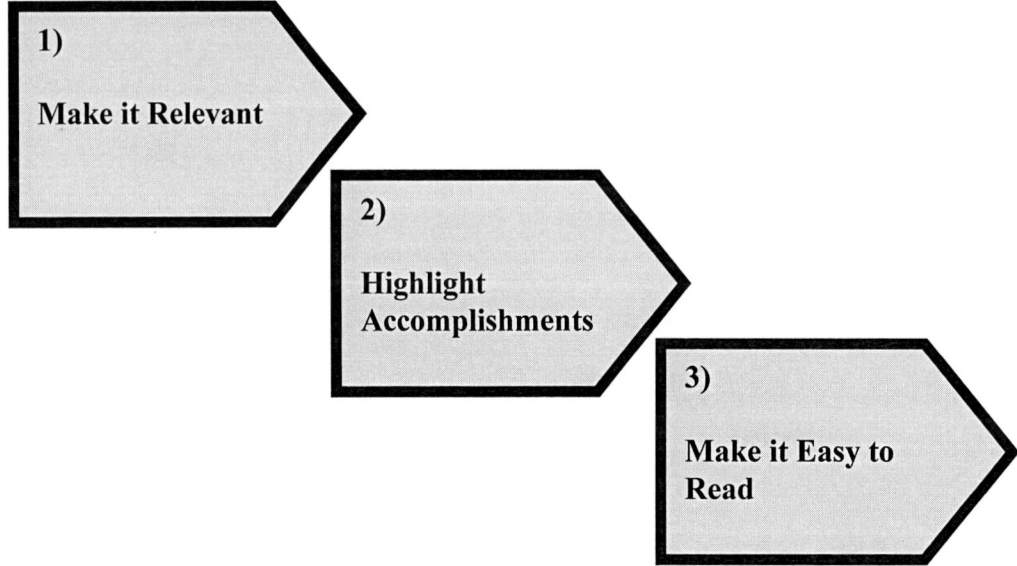

Principle One: Make it Relevant

Government agencies want to fill positions with people who fit their needs. It is important to determine what competencies are required for the job. Below is a sample list of competencies that may be useful for many government jobs.

Analytical Thinking	The ability to analyze situations and events in a logical way, and to organize the parts of a problem systematically.
Self – Confidence	A belief in your capabilities and recognition of personal limitations.
Communication	You must have the skills to effectively communicate using listening skills and verbal and written communications skills.
Flexibility / Valuing Diversity	With government jobs, you will have to work with a wide cross-section of the community with diverse backgrounds, cultures and socio-economic circumstances. You must have the ability to adapt your approach to each situation.
Self - Control	You must establish that you can control your emotions and actions when provoked.
Relationship Building	Developing contacts and relationships both within and outside your area of employment is extremely valuable.
Achievement Orientation	You must demonstrate a desire for continuous improvement in service and accomplishments.
Information Seeking	The ability to seek out and consider information from various sources before making decisions.
Assertiveness	The capacity to use authority confidently and to set and enforce rules appropriately.
Initiative	Demonstrated proficiency to be self-motivated and self-directed in identifying and addressing important issues.
Cooperation	Willing to act with others by seeking their input, encouraging their participation and sharing information.

Negotiation / Facilitation	The ability to influence and persuade others by anticipating and addressing their interests and perspectives.
Work Organization	The ability to develop and maintain systems for organizing information and activities.
Community Service Orientation	Proven commitment to helping or serving others.
Commitment to Learning	Demonstrated pattern of activities that contribute to personal and professional growth.
Organization Awareness	A capacity for understanding the dynamics of organizations, including the formal and informal cultures and decision-making processes.
Developing Others	Commitment to helping others improve their skills.

Many people squeeze everything into a resume hoping that something will click. Any material on your resume that does not exhibit traits from the list of core competencies the specific department is looking for is a waste of space.

Do not include every employer on your resume unless you are specifically asked to provide that information. Many government agencies require an employment history application. Pick out the most relevant positions you have had and focus on demonstrating the qualities. Any additional information such as Activities, Volunteer Experience, Education, or Special Skills should also demonstrate your competencies.

Principle Two: Highlight Accomplishments

Accomplishment statements should give your potential employer an indication of how well you performed. It should reveal not only what you did, but also how well you did it. Each statement should include the following:

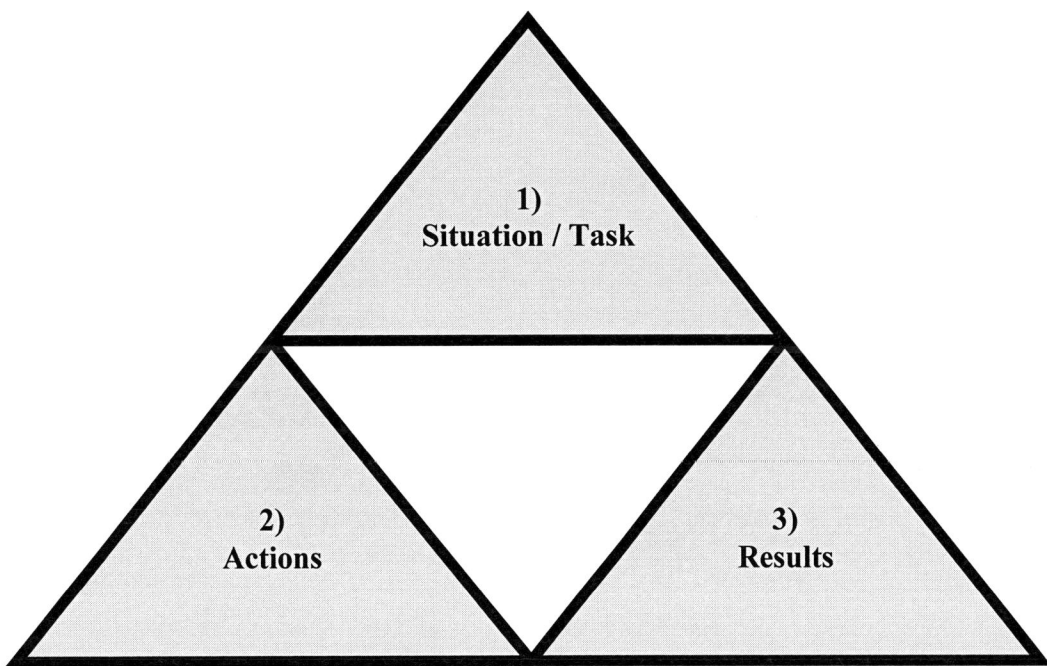

Each accomplishment should describe skills relevant to the job you're applying for. Practice writing these statements. Typically, accomplishment statements fall under the Work Experience, Volunteer Experience, or Education sections of your resume.

Example Action Statements

1) Day Camp Counsellor

Core Competency	Situation / Task	Action	Result
Developing Others, Cooperation, Assertiveness, Community Service, Communication.	Field trips as a day camp counsellor.	Instruction and supervision.	Ensured safety of 60 children with fellow counsellors.

"Supervised and instructed 60 young children on field trips ensuring their safety and enjoyment with a team of fellow counsellors."

2) Retail / Grocery

Core Competency	Situation / Task	Action	Result
Work Organization, Communication, Negotiation / Facilitation	Controlling Inventory.	Organized units and placed orders (quantified)	Diverse customer's needs anticipated and satisfied.

"Organized shelving units and placed orders in excess of $20,000 ensuring diverse customer needs were anticipated and satisfied."

3) Post-Secondary Education

Core Competency	Situation / Task	Action	Result
Initiative, Achievement Orientation, Analytical Thinking, Commitment to Learning, Communication	Attending post-secondary education.	Studied sociology (or any other major)	Graduated with a strong standing, developing a core set of skills.

"Developed analytical, presentation, computer and XXXX skills, studying sociology and graduating with a 75% average."

4) Volunteer Work

Core Competency	Situation / Task	Action	Result
Initiative, Communication, Cooperation, Work Organization, Developing Others, Self-Confidence, Flexibility / Valuing Diversity, Negotiation / Facilitation, Community Service Orientation	Food drive at work.	Organized and implemented.	Raised $2,000 for needy people in the community.

"Organized and implemented a Food Drive with a team of volunteers, effectively raising $2,000 for needy people in the community."

Action Verbs to be used for your Accomplishment Statements

Accelerated	Displayed	Negotiated	Saved
Accumulated	Documented	Ordered	Scheduled
Accomplished	Effected	Organized	Selected
Acquired	Enforced	Performed	Separated
Analyzed	Engineered	Perpetuated	Served
Applied	Evaluated	Planned	Set
Arranged	Facilitated	Prepared	Shared
Assessed	Filed	Prescribed	Showed
Authorized	Financed	Presented	Solved
Approved	Founded	Problem-solved	Strengthened
Began	Generated	Processed	Succceded
Bought	Hired	Produced	Supplied
Budgeted	Identified	Promoted	Taught
Coached	Implemented	Provided	Team-built
Collected	Invented	Questioned	Trained
Combined	Launched	Raised	Translated
Communicated	Learned	Read	Tutored
Conducted	Made	Realized	Uncovered
Convinced	Maintained	Reorganized	Unified
Coordinated	Managed	Repaired	Utilized
Developed	Marketed	Researched	Vitalized
Directed	Minimized	Revised	Won
Discovered	Monitored	Risked	Wrote

Principle 3 - Make it Easy to Read

Recruiters may look at thousands of resumes each year. They do not necessarily spend a lot of time on each one. This means your resume has only a few minutes to prove that you are a good fit for the job. The information presented has to be immediately pertinent and easy to read. Key things you should be mindful of when finishing up your resume are:

- use high quality bond paper
- incorporate as much white space as possible so the reader is not overwhelmed
- highlight only key words or positions to attract attention
- use bullet points rather than paragraphs
- keep font sizes between 10 and 12 pt

Language and grammar are very important to a resume and the following should be observed:

- make every word count
- use short, simple and concrete words that are easily understood
- use strong nouns and vital verbs to add action, power and interest
- avoid personal pronouns
- spell check the document and always have someone proof read the material
- double check the meaning of easily confused words, i.e.:

    affect (influence) vs. effect (result)
    personal (private) vs. personnel (staff)
    elicit (draw forth) vs. illicit (unlawful)
    discreet (showing good judgement) vs. discrete (distinct or separate)
    allude (indirect reference) vs. elude (to evade)

A few rules-of-thumb

- months do not need to be included in dates when the length of employment is greater than six months
- part-time and full-time descriptors are generally not included
- do not include names of supervisors
- check with the government service to which you are applying to about disclosing full employment history

Review the copy of the sample resume below.

Resume Components

Name	Address Telephone Number E-mail
Education Educational Institution Location Degree Educational Institution Location Degree	 Date Date
Work Experience Company, Geographic Location Position title - Descriptive Statement if needed - Relevant Accomplishment Statement - Relevant Accomplishment Statement Company, Geographic Location Position title - Descriptive Statement if needed - Relevant Accomplishment Statement - Relevant Accomplishment Statement Company, Geographic Location Position title - Descriptive Statement if needed - Relevant Accomplishment Statement - Relevant Accomplishment Statement	 Date Date Date
Examples of Optional Section Headings - Professional Development - Awards - Computer Skills - Summary of Qualifications - Languages - Functional Skills - Activities and Interests - Publications - Volunteer Experience - Academic Achievements	

Jane / John Doe (EXAMPLE)
2 / 2 Wellington Crescent, Winnipeg, Manitoba   Phone: (204) 555-1212
jdoe@xxx.ca

Education

CITY COLLEGE, Winnipeg, Manitoba   (2002 -2006)
B.A. in Political Studies
- Elected Class President and managed a budget of $5,000 and a team of 15 volunteers to deliver class social activities and educational assistance programs.

MAIN STREET COLLEGIATE, Brandon, Manitoba   (1998-2002)
OSSD, OAC Certificate, Honour Roll, Senior English Award

Professional Experience

Bank of Canada, Vancouver, British Columbia   (2006-present)
Customer Representative
- Solved customer problems by providing individual solutions to specific customer needs.
- Assisted the implementation of a new deposit procedure to reduce customer wait times.
- Responsible for daily cash deposits and withdrawals.

Toronto Parks Department, Toronto, Ontario   (1995-1999)
Assistant Activity Implementer
- Scheduled and implemented a variety of after school activities for 50 – 60 children with fellow co-workers.
- Used a needs-based approach to assist children from diverse cultural backgrounds with a variety of problems such as schoolwork, bullying and loneliness.

Volunteer
- Thanksgiving Food Drive - annually delivering food to needy people throughout the community
- Children's Aid Society – Special Buddy Program   (1995-1998)
- City College Orientation Leader   (1999)

Interests
- Shodan Black Belt in Jiu Jitsu, running, weight training, snowboarding, rock climbing, white water rafting, sport parachuting, water skiing and SCUBA diving.
- Piano – Royal Conservatory Grade 5. Guitar - Introductory lessons.

Computer Skills
- Excel, WordPerfect, PowerPoint
- Internet development, Outlook

The Interview

It is important to recognize that government agencies are looking for the best people for the job and will not try to consciously confuse you.

At this stage it is your interpersonal and communication skills that will help you land a job. The interviewer is looking for someone who is competent, likeable and who fits in with the organization's culture, goals, beliefs and values.

What Interviewers Tend to Look For

Friendly Personality

With many government jobs, you spend a great deal of time with co-workers. Every interviewer will ask themselves whether or not they would enjoy working with you. You must prove that you are likeable enough to do this.

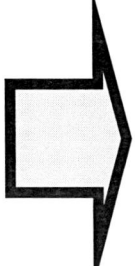

Organizational Fit

Many organizations may have a very particular culture and it is important for interviewers to ensure that job applicants will fit that culture. Suitability may include the willingness to work shift work and overtime if required, give up days off if required, or an ability to function well as a member of a team.

It is important not to pretend to be something you're not. If you feel you wouldn't fit in with an organization's culture, then it is probably best for both you and the organization that you seek another career. It is important to ask these questions of yourself. Once in the interview stage, you should be confident that you would fit in with the culture.

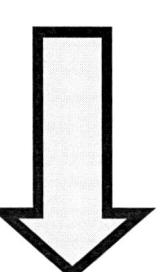

Capable and Professional

Government organizations want competent personnel. You must demonstrate that you are capable of handling responsibility and that you can perform the required tasks. It would be prudent to review any core competencies required for the job to which you are applying.

Handling Pre-Interview Stress

Feeling nervous before an interview is perfectly normal. Politicians, entertainers and media personalities feel nervous prior to performances as well. The best way to handle the stress is to be well prepared. Once again, interviewers are not trying to trick you. They want you to succeed; it makes their job easier. Some things you should do before the interview include:

- Get a good night's sleep (this goes without saying, but bears repeating).
- Practice interviewing with friends, using the behavioural questions below.
- Wear professional clothing (suits or business dress).

You should bring all of the documents that are requested from you (transcripts, copy of your resume, portfolio) to the interview along with a pad of paper, a pen, a list of references and a list of questions you may have. Interviewers are often impressed if you have intelligent and researched questions about the job.

How to Influence the Hiring Decision

Understand the Organization – Local Focus Interviews

It is important to have at least a rudimentary understanding of the organization to which you are applying. This information is available on most websites, or at employment offices where you are applying. Some information you should know would include:

- Rough size of the organization or group with which you will work.
- Name of the managers or politicians in charge of departments. (example: Ralph Goodale – Minister of Finance 2005.)
- The challenge that all government services are facing (asked to do more with less, budget constraints, intense scrutiny, etc.)

Before any interview, make a habit of reading the newspaper and checking the internet for news about the department you are applying to, so that you are aware of the local issues and concerns of the area.

Understand the Job

You have to understand the job to which you are applying. Gather as much information about the job as you can, including typical tasks, where your office would be, career paths, etc. To prove that you understand the job, make sure that you include the less glamorous duties that it might entail (filing reports, answering phones, dealing with the public, etc.).

Understand Yourself

When you are involved with an interview, it is extremely important to be very familiar with your resume and past situations in your life. You will more than likely encounter questions about your past acts, goals and emotions. The list below includes a number of questions you should be familiar with prior to any interview.

- How have you prepared for this position and what are your qualifications?
- What are your greatest strengths and weaknesses?
- How do you get along with co-workers?
- Why are you pursuing a career with this department?
- What motivates you to perform well?
- What are your three greatest accomplishments in life?
- How would you work under pressure?

First Impressions

First impressions are extremely important. Many judgements are made about a person within the first 30 seconds of an encounter (fairly or unfairly). It is your job to impress the interviewer(s). Three basic steps you can take to ensure that you make a great first impression are:

Look Professional	Be Confident	Break the Ice
Interviewers want to see an applicant who respects them enough to wear the appropriate attire.	Greet the interviewer(s) with a smile, a firm handshake, a relaxed manner and a friendly "Hello".	Engage in small talk. It can be about anything, (weather, traffic, etc). It doesn't have to be profound. It's meant to put both parties at ease.

Communication and Interpersonal Effectiveness

The interview process is a situation that tests your communication skills. You should be aware of the following:

Eye Contact	Maintain eye contact with the person you are addressing. This means looking at the person who is speaking to you. In interviews with more than one interviewer spend an equal amount of time on each person.
Body Language	Be aware of your position in your seat and your breathing pattern. Attempt to relax by taking steady breaths. Make sure you sit up straight in an interview. This will exhibit self-confidence and professionalism.
Gestures and Speech	Be aware of any gestures you use. Nod and maintain eye contact to indicate that you understand interview questions. Smile when appropriate, and be vocally expressive by alternating your tone where necessary. Be natural and avoid filler words such as "umm" and "like".

During the Interview

Make an effort to read the interviewers. Ask yourself whether they appear to be straining to follow you, if you are talking too fast (breathe more deeply), or too softly (speak louder). If they are writing frantically, that is usually a good sign, but make occasional pauses so that they can keep up. If you do not understand a question, ask them to repeat or clarify it. If you do not know the answer to one of their questions, admit it. Do not lie during the interview.

Prepare Stories Prior to the Interview

Interviewers may have some questions regarding your resume, or your past experiences. Make sure you are familiar with the content in your resume, and any tasks that you mention in it.

Many government agencies will use a behavioural-based interview method. This means that they will ask you questions about yourself and will ask you to describe events that have actually occurred in your past (usually the last two years). Some examples of questions you should be prepared to answer include:

Give an example in your life when you:

- were involved in a stressful situation and how you dealt with it.
- were extremely angry and how you dealt with it.
- had to take the role of a leader, and how was the situation resolved.
- had to work as part of a team and explain what happened.
- had to resolve a conflict with other parties and how did you handled it.
- were up against an important deadline and how you handled the work.
- had a conflict with a supervisor and how you handled it.

There are many other behavioural questions, but these are some of the most common examples.

How to Answer Behavioural Based Questions

Each behavioural question is a story about your past. Make sure that the story you tell is relevant, clear, and even interesting (interviewers are only human). Each story should have:

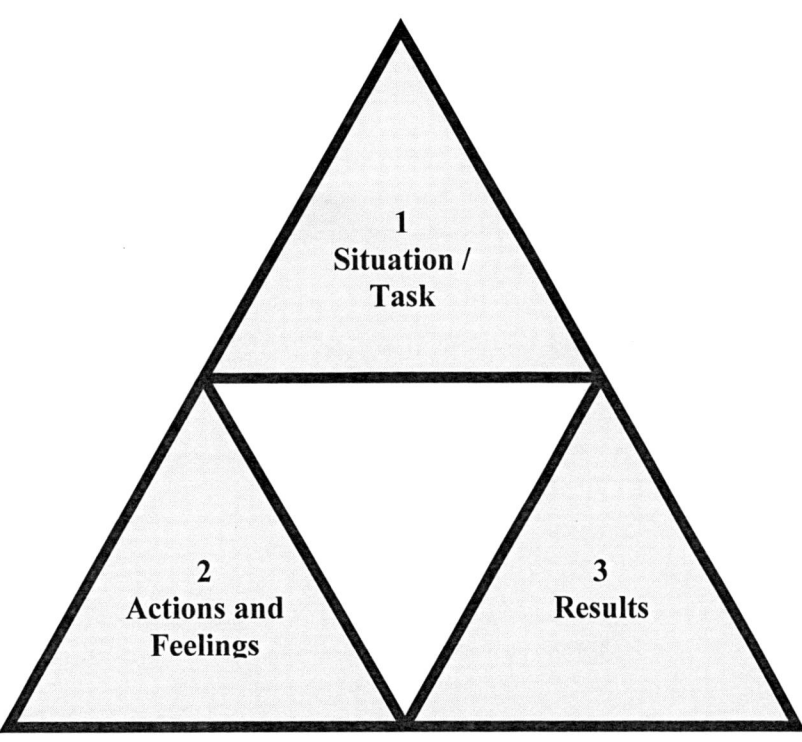

Step One - Understand the Question

This is vital. If you do not understand the question or what the interviewer is asking for, ask them to repeat it or explain it. There is no point giving a very effective answer to the wrong question. For example: one interviewee, asked about Ethnicity, spoke a great deal about Ethics during an interview. The interviewers probably thought he was an idiot, but he was probably just nervous and didn't hear the question properly.

Step Two - Brief Synopsis

Let the interviewers know what you plan to talk about with a brief outline of the situation, with little detail. This will give you some time to organize your thoughts and the interviewers will understand where you are going. This should take no longer than a couple of sentences.

> **Example:**
>
> "I am going to tell you about a conflict I had with my boss while I was working as a personal trainer. It involved a situation where I was told to bill a client at a rate I didn't feel was justified. We dealt with it away from the customer and resolved it in a manner that satisfied myself, the manager, and the client."

Step Three - Full Story

A retelling of the story will demonstrate to the interviewers your competencies in dealing with the situation and your communication capabilities. Interviewers want a clear story, preferably in a chronological sequence. They are most concerned with your feelings during the situation, the actions you took, and the result of your actions. Always finish the story with the results of your actions. Keep these points in mind both while you are preparing for the interview, and when you are participating in it:

- Answer the question asked.
- Pause and think – don't rush in with an answer.
- Pay attention to the pronouns you are using. Interviewers want to know what "YOU" did. Use the pronoun "I" for your actions and "Us" for team actions. **DO NOT ALWAYS USE "WE".** You will fail the interview.

> **Bad Example:**
>
> "We formed a team to solve the problem. We brainstormed an idea to solve the problem. We then decided on a course of action and began to implement it. We handled task "A" while others handled task "B". We all had individual assignments."

> **Good Example**:
>
> "I formed a team to solve a problem. We brainstormed an idea to solve the problem. I then had to decide the course of action and we began to implement. My friend John and I were responsible for task "A" while another group handled task "B". My particular assignment was to do "X".

- Ensure you effectively explain the situation, your feelings, your actions and the result.
- If necessary take pauses to collect your thoughts. There is no need to be constantly talking.
- Relax and enjoy telling the story. You should know it well, as you actually did it.
- Give focused and fluid answers.
- Avoid run-on answers.
- Give support for claims that are made, if possible.
- Show evidence of preparation work.

Other Interviewing Methods

You should be aware that you could be asked technical or "what if" questions or questions about your past. Some agencies may ask:

- What would you do if you caught a co-worker stealing?
- Have you ever smoked marijuana?
- Have you ever stolen anything?
- Have you ever committed an illegal act?

It is important to give these questions careful consideration and answer honestly. If you tried smoking marijuana when you were in high school, admit it and tell the interviewer why you didn't continue to use it. For example, you found it hurt the academic performance of your friends, or something along those lines.

"What if" questions are intended to challenge you, to see if you are the type of person who will immediately back down. This is not a trait agencies are looking for. Once you have made up your mind on an issue, stand by it. Interviewers may challenge you but this is part of the process. Just ensure that you give careful thought to the question to avoid defending a weak position. It is acceptable to credit the other opinion, but do not change your decision.

On top of these questions, you may receive some technical questions when applying to specific positions

Completing the Interview

Just like the first impression, it is important to give a positive impression during the last few moments of an interview. If you have any questions for the interviewers, the end of the interview is when they should be asked. It is acceptable to have prepared questions written down. As you are leaving the room, smile at the interviewer(s) individually, walk up to each one, look into their eyes, shake their hands and personally thank them for their time.

Hiring Process

Applying for a position with the government is a major commitment and can often take up to two years to be successful. It can be a discouraging process because governments can go for long periods of time without hiring at all. Conversely, depending on budgets, government agencies can hire a bulk of people all at once. When applying you will encounter the following three stages.

1) **Applying for the Job**
   - Once they receive your application, it can take approximately one month for a response.

2) **Invited to Interview**
   - If successful you will be required to take tests relevant to the position to which you have applied.

3) **Invited to Take a Test**
   - Tests may include Language Tests, Situational Judgment Tests, Written Communication Proficiency Tests, as well as others.

Applying for the Job

Every year the Public Service Commission receives thousands of applicants for positions. You can apply for these jobs online through the following link:

www.jobs.gc.ca

This website contains two areas you need to monitor closely. Once you are on the site, click on an area marked "Jobs Open to the Public". This contains a list of currently available jobs, which are broken down by category or region. You are required to provide information, create a cover letter and build a resume specific to the job to which you are applying.

It is also possible to create a Job Alert in this area. You need to provide the information for a position you would like to have, and you will be alerted by email when this position becomes available. At this point you would have to apply to it.

Post Secondary Recruitment

A second area you should monitor, provided you have the qualifications, is the Post Secondary Recruitment area. This area contains job listings that are different than those in the "Jobs Open to the Public" area. To access these jobs, create a "Job File" containing the following information:

- Personal Information
- Address Information

- Education
- Work Locations
- Languages
- Employment Equity
- Resume
- Completed Courses
- Employment Tenure
- Job Categories and Salary

You will be able to match your profile to jobs that are currently available in the public service. Once you have selected a currently available job, you should complete all of the requirements prior to the closing date. Please note that you can only post one resume on this system, and therefore can't tailor it toward specific postings.

Key Information

There is standard information that must be input into the applications. The screening tools used to filter job applicants are very specific. Often they perform word search filters to determine if applicants possess the requisites for the job. When applying for positions, make sure you use the specific words for which they ask in their job descriptions. Being overly creative could cause your application to be overlooked.

> For example, if the position for which you are applying requires accounting experience, state very clearly that you have "Accounting Experience". Adding detail is fine, but make sure you don't obscure the key requisites for which they are searching.

First you have to select the job for which you are interested in applying. It is important to make sure you have the relevant experience and education. You can post your information, resume, cover letter and career objective online. Once you have officially applied for a position, it normally takes a month until you are notified. If you have the relevant experience and are selected, you will be invited for an interview. If you are successful at this stage you will then be invited to perform the relevant test.

Contract Work

Term or contract work is another strategy you can use to secure a position with the government. The difference with these jobs is that they are not permanent, and they are not union positions. They are often a foot in the door and a chance to prove your abilities in a government position. These jobs are not intended to lead to permanent positions, but the experience and contacts that you can develop with them can often lead to permanent positions.

www.Jobset.ca

Jobset.ca is a resource that you should use to be notified of government positions as they become available. There are four searchable criteria that you can use for finding out information on these jobs.

1) Government Jobs
2) Contract / permanent positions
3) Non-Profit / Companies working with the government
4) All hiring agencies

Personal Statement of Interest for PSR

For some positions, the government requires specific personality types to fill certain positions that can be stressful, emotionally challenging, or potentially dangerous.

Personal Statements of Interest should be structured so that each quality for which the government is looking is addressed. Words should be chosen carefully and the statement should be concise. The government receives thousands of applications for these positions and any examples that you use to build your statement should be relevant and timely. This can be a subjective, rather than an objective, task. It would be best to play up strengths and be honest about any shortcomings.

Once again, it is important to use a language similar to that which is used in the posting. For example:

"We are looking for people with experience driving red cars."

Your statement should contain:

"I have experience driving red cars."
I obtained this experience...
I have 100 hours of....
My record...

You should keep emotionally charged statements out of the application and replace them with more relevant objectives.

Poor Examples:
"I want to save the world."
"I want to make a difference."

Better Examples:
"Canada has established itself as an international leader in peace keeping... as a Canadian citizen, I can…"

General Suggestions

Preparation Prior to Testing

Check out the websites and contact the government agency to ensure that you are familiar with the testing procedures and the content of the exams. It is important to get as much information as possible from the department to which you are applying.

Practice on numerous tests to ensure that you are familiar with the content of the testing material.

Before Testing

Get enough sleep before the tests and enough food and water even if you are nervous prior to entering the test. Try to remain relaxed and comfortable. Wear clothing that is professional, but also comfortable to work in. Arrive early and ready to begin.

During the Test

Don't waste time on a question you are unable to answer; take a guess and move onto the next question. Make a note of answers you are not certain of, and review them if you have time after answering the remaining questions.

Pay attention to the answer sheet and the question number. Many applicants have failed as the result of an error on the scoring card. Every time you respond to a question, look at the answer card carefully and make sure that the number you are answering on the card matches the number of the question.

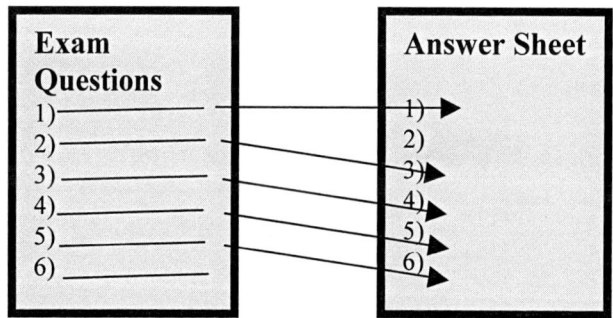

In the above example, even if the applicant answered the questions correctly, the applicant would only get one out of the six questions right because of the errors on the scoring card. Keep this in mind when taking the test. You will not be able to correct or explain yourself if you make a mistake on the score card because they are computer scored. This mistake is more common if you if you decide to skip a particular question. In the event that you decide to skip questions, a tactic to avoid making an order error is to cross off the question you skipped on the answer card.

Teaching Material Math

Addition

$$\begin{array}{r} 7 \\ +5 \\ \hline 12 \end{array}$$

$7 + 5 = 12$

The above two equations have the same value and are very straightforward. It is important to know that the order of numbers does not make a difference in addition (or multiplication). For example:

$$\begin{array}{r} 6 \\ +3 \\ \hline 9 \end{array} \quad \text{same} \quad \begin{array}{r} 3 \\ +6 \\ \hline 9 \end{array}$$

$$243 + 716 = 959$$
same
$$716 + 243 = 959$$

Some complications arise when larger numbers are used and you need to carry numbers.

Note: When you see a math problem laid out horizontally, as in the box immediately above, rearrange the numbers so that they are vertical (on top of each other) to make the addition easier to do.

Example:

$$\begin{array}{r} 3\;5\;1 \\ 6\;9\;9 \\ +4\;5\;7 \\ \hline \end{array}$$

(A)
$$\begin{array}{r} 3\;5\;1 \\ 6\;9\;9 \\ +\;4\;5\;7 \\ \hline 17 \end{array}$$

(B)
$$\begin{array}{r} 1 \\ 3\;5\;1 \\ 6\;9\;9 \\ +\;4\;5\;7 \\ \hline 20\;7 \end{array}$$

(C)
$$\begin{array}{r} 2 \\ 3\;5\;1 \\ 6\;9\;9 \\ +\;4\;5\;7 \\ \hline 1\;5\;0\;7 \end{array}$$

(A)
Start by adding up the numbers in the right most column. The result is 17. The seven remains but the one is carried over to be added to the next column of numbers.

(B)
The same rules apply to the sum 20 in the second column. The 0 remains in the second row, while the 2 is carried over to the column to the left to be added.

(C)
The final column is then added and the answer is recorded.

Subtraction

$$\begin{array}{r} 8 \\ - 3 \\ \hline 5 \end{array}$$

$8 - 3 = 5$

The above two equations have the same value and are very straightforward. It is important to know that the order of numbers is significant in subtraction (and division). Different ordering will result in different answers. For example:

$$\begin{array}{r} 18 \\ - 3 \\ \hline 15 \end{array} \quad \text{different} \quad \begin{array}{r} 3 \\ - 18 \\ \hline -15 \end{array}$$

$$712 - 245 = 467$$
different
$$245 - 712 = -467$$

Some complications arise when larger numbers are used and you need to carry numbers.

Example:

$$\begin{array}{r} 7\,4\,3 \\ -\,5\,8\,9 \end{array}$$

(A)
$$\begin{array}{r} 3 \\ 7\,\cancel{4}\,13 \\ -\,5\,\,8\,\,9 \\ \hline 4 \end{array}$$

(B)
$$\begin{array}{r} 6\ \ 13 \\ \cancel{7}\,\cancel{4}\,\,3 \\ -\,5\,\,8\,\,9 \\ \hline 1\,\,5\,\,4 \end{array}$$

(A)
The first task is to subtract the right most column. Because 9 is larger than 3, a unit has to be borrowed from the column to the left. The 4 in the middle column is reduced to 3, and the one is added to the right column, making the first row 13 - 9 = 4.

(B)
The second task is to subtract the second column. The same process is repeated. Borrow a 1 from the left column to allow the subtraction. The top number in the left column becomes 6, while the top number in the centre column becomes 13. 13 - 8 = 5. The left column would then be subtracted. 6 - 5 = 1.

Note: If subtracting more than 2 numbers, you cannot stack the numbers as you would in addition. Instead, work from the first subtraction to the last, two numbers at a time.

Multiplication

$$\begin{array}{r} 8 \\ \times 6 \\ \hline 48 \end{array} \qquad 8 \times 6 = 48$$

The above two equations have the same value and are very straightforward. It is important to know that the order of numbers makes no difference in multiplication (or addition). For example:

$$\begin{array}{r} 7 \\ \times 8 \\ \hline 56 \end{array} \qquad \text{same} \qquad \begin{array}{r} 8 \\ \times 7 \\ \hline 56 \end{array}$$

$$245 \times 233 = 57,085$$
$$\text{same}$$
$$233 \times 245 = 57,085$$

Multiplication, simply put, is adding groups of numbers. For instance, in the above example, the number 8 is being added six times.

$8 \times 6 = 48$	$7 \times 7 = 49$
$8 + 8 + 8 + 8 + 8 + 8 = 48$	$7 + 7 + 7 + 7 + 7 + 7 + 7 = 49$
$9 \times 5 = 45$	$6 \times 3 = 18$
$9 + 9 + 9 + 9 + 9 = 45$	$6 + 6 + 6 = 18$

It will be difficult to pass an exam if you have to calculate all simple multiplication in this manner. You should memorize the basic multiplication tables for 1 through 12. Review the multiplication table in this book.

Some complications arise when larger numbers are used and you need to carry numbers.

Example:

```
  2 6 7
x 1 5 6
```

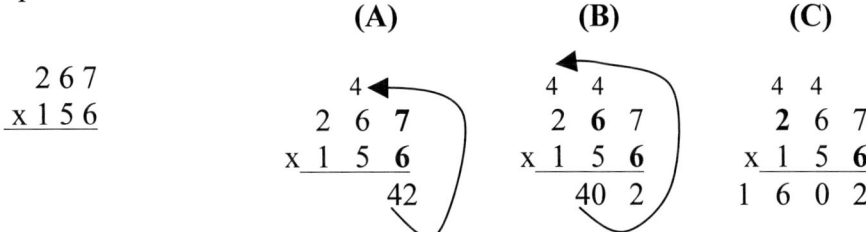

(A)
Begin by multiplying out the right row. The 2 is recorded in the right column and the 4 is transferred to the middle column and recorded as above.

(B)
The second step is to multiply the 6 in the middle column. 6 x 6 = 36. The 4 that was carried over from step A has to be added to the 36. The result is 40 and the 0 is recorded in the middle column. The four is then carried forward to left column as in step A.

(C)
The 6 then has to be multiplied to the left digit on the top number. 6 x 2 = 12. The four that was carried over from step B is added to the 12. The result is 16 and recorded as shown.

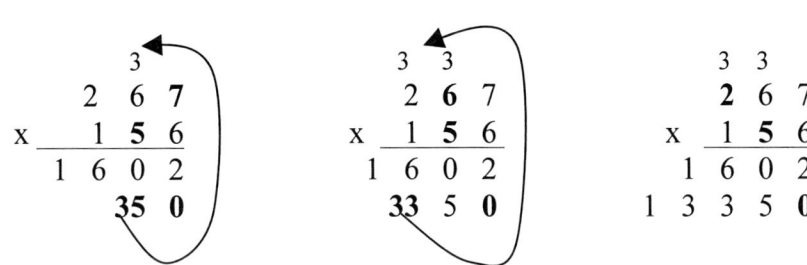

(D-F)
The next steps are to multiply the second digit in the bottom row (the 5) to each of the top digits. The 5 is multiplied to the 7, the 6 and the 2. The process is the same as steps A - C. If the number is 10 or larger the number is carried over, as above, and added to the next multiplication.

It is important to remember that the next multiplication set has to be recorded on the line below and lined up starting in the next column. Place a zero in the right column to ensure the digits line up properly

```
         (G)            (H)             (I)

         2  6  7        2  6  7         2  6  7
    x    1  5  6    x   1  5  6     x   1  5  6
         1  6  0  2     1  6  0  2      1  6  0  2
    1  3  3  5  0   1  3  3  5  0   1  3  3  5  0
             7  0  0       6  7  0  0   2  6  7  0  0
```

The next steps are to multiply the left digit in the bottom number by each of the digits in the top number. The same process is used as outlined above if numbers have to be carried over.

Lining up of the digits is also necessary at this stage. Because you are multiplying from the hundreds column (the left most) you begin recording the answer in the hundreds column. Follow the same procedure as outlined above. Fill in the first two columns with zeros.

```
            2  6  7
      x     1  5  6
            1  6  0  2
         1  3  3  5  0
       + 2  6  7  0  0
         4  1  6  5  2
```

The final step is to add up the three numbers that were multiplied out. Treat the addition of these three numbers exactly as you would a regular addition problem. If you failed to line the numbers up properly, you will wind up with an incorrect answer. 41,652 is the final answer.

Note: Because complex multiplication questions (like the one above) involve addition, make sure you have a firm grasp of the addition section before trying to tackle multiplication.

Things to Watch For

Watch out for a multiplication question where the first digit in the bottom number is a zero, or where there are zeros in the equation. You still have to properly line up the digits. Note the highlighted zeros.

```
      3 4 5
    x     5 0
    1 7 2 5 0
```

Remember that zero multiplied by any other number is zero. In this situation you begin multiplying with the 10's column (the 5). Because you are multiplying from the 10's column, you begin recording your answer there. Place a zero in the first column.

```
        3
      6 0 9
    x       4
    2 4 3 6
```

When the four is multiplied to the 0, the result is 0. The number, which is carried over from multiplying 9 x 4 has to be added to 0, which results in the highlighted answer - 3.

```
          4 5 2
      x   3 0 9
          4 0 6 8
    + 1 3 5 6 0 0
      1 3 9 6 6 8
```

In this situation there is no need to multiply the bottom ten's digit out, as the result will equal 0. You must, however, properly line up the numbers. Because the 3 is in the hundred's column, you must begin recording your answer in the hundred's column. That is why there are two highlighted zeros.

Multiplication Tables

	1	2	3	4	5	6	7	8	9	10	11	12
1	1	2	3	4	5	6	7	8	9	10	11	12
2	2	4	6	8	10	12	14	16	18	20	22	24
3	3	6	9	12	15	18	21	24	27	30	33	36
4	4	8	12	16	20	24	28	32	36	40	44	48
5	5	10	15	20	25	30	35	40	45	50	55	60
6	6	12	18	24	30	36	42	48	54	60	66	72
7	7	14	21	28	35	42	49	56	63	70	77	84
8	8	16	24	32	40	48	56	64	72	80	88	96
9	9	18	27	36	45	54	63	72	81	90	99	108
10	10	20	30	40	50	60	70	80	90	100	110	120
11	11	22	33	44	55	66	77	88	99	110	121	132
12	12	24	36	48	60	72	84	96	108	120	132	144

Use of the Table

To use this table, take a number along the top axis and multiply it by a number along the side axis. Where they intersect is the answer to the equation. An example of this is 7 x 3. If you find 7 on the side axis and follow the row until you reach the 3 column on the top axis, you will find the answer – 21.

Look for simple patterns to assist your memorization efforts. For example:

Whenever 10 is multiplied to another number, just add a zero.
    10 x 3 = 30   10 x 7 = 70
    10 x 10 = 100   10 x 12 = 120

Whenever 11 is multiplied by a number less than 9, just double the digit 11 is multiplied by.
    11 x 3 = 33   11 x 5 = 55
    11 x 7 = 77   11 x 9 = 99

One multiplied by any other number is always equal to that number.
    1 x 1 = 1   1 x 4 = 4
    1 x 8 = 8   1 x 12 = 12

Zero multiplied to any number is always zero.
    0 x 10 = 0   0 x 3 = 0

Nine multiplied by any number less than 11 adds up to 9.
    9 x 3 = 27   (2 + 7 = 9)
    9 x 9 = 81   (8 + 1 = 9)

Division

$$6 / 3 = 2 \qquad\qquad 6 \div 3 = 2$$

$$\frac{6}{3} = 2 \qquad\qquad 3\overline{)6}^{\,2}$$

The above equations have the same values and are very straightforward. It is important to know that the order of the numbers is significant in division (and subtraction). Different ordering of numbers will result in different answers. For example:

$10 / 5 = 2$	different	$5 / 10 = 0.5$
$15 \div 5 = 3$	different	$5 \div 15 = 0.33$
$\frac{100}{10} = 10$	different	$\frac{10}{100} = 0.1$
$10\overline{)50}^{\,5}$	different	$50\overline{)10}^{\,0.2}$

Simply put, division determines how many times a number will fit into another. Picture an auditorium with 100 chairs available. Several schools want to send 20 students to see a play in the auditorium. Now you need to determine how many schools can attend the play. This will require division.

By dividing 100 by 20 (100 ÷ 20) you come up with the number 5. Five schools can send 20 students to attend the play.

Long Division

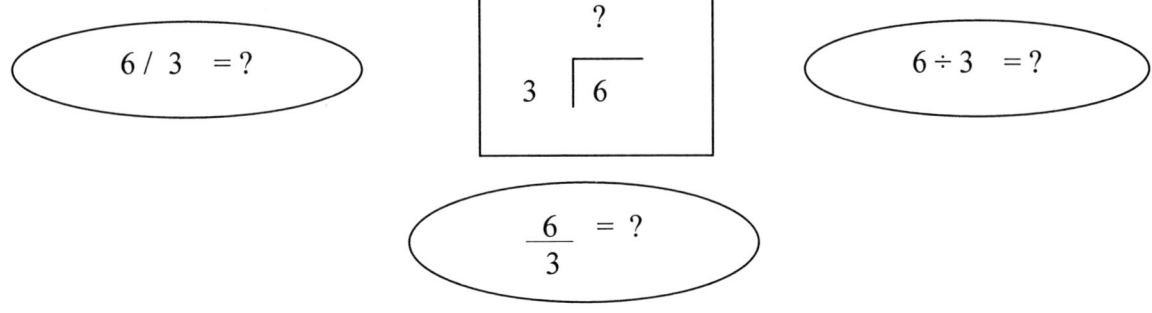

When performing long division, it is important to organize the information as is seen in the centre square. You have to understand how the different formats for division are transferred into the format seen above.

Example

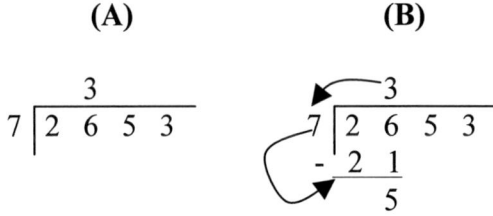

In order to answer a division question on paper, you must place the equation in the proper format. After this is accomplished you can begin to solve the problem.

(A)

The first step is to focus on the highlighted area of the number under the bracket. You have to work with a number that is larger than the dividing number (7). Because 2 is smaller than 7, you have to work with 26. Ask yourself how many times you can multiply 7 without going over 26. If you count by 7's (7, 14, 21, 28) you'll realize that 3 is the most times that 7 will fit into 26.

(B)

With the information you have in section A, you now have to perform a simple multiplication. Take the top number (3) and multiply it by the dividing number (7). The answer is placed below 26 and then subtracted from the digits you were working with. (26 - 21 = 5) Make sure you keep the numbers in the proper columns. (If, after subtracting, the answer is greater than the dividing number, you need to start again using a larger top number.)

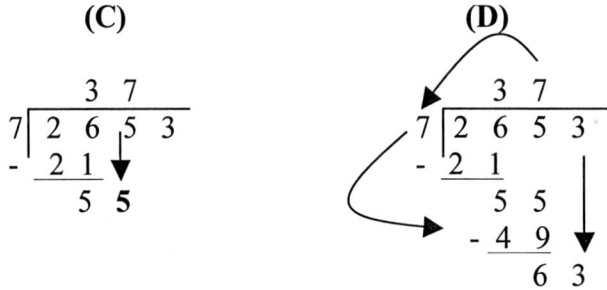

(C)
After subtraction, bring down the next digit to sit beside the solution. This becomes your new number to work with (55). Then repeat step A using this number. Determine how many times you can multiply 7 without exceeding 55. Place this digit above the next digit in the question on top of the bracket.

(D)
Next repeat step B. Multiply out the 7's and record your answer below the 55. Subtracting the numbers results in 6. Continue to work the same pattern, and bring down the next digit in the question to determine a new number to work with.

(E)

```
           3 7 9
      ┌─────────
   7  │ 2 6 5 3
      - 2 1
        ─────
          5 5
        - 4 9
          ─────
            6 3
          - 6 3
            ─────
              0
```

(E)
The final steps in the process are to repeat the process. Determine how many times you can multiply 7 without going over 63. You can do this 9 times. When you multiply it out and subtract the result is 0. The answer to the question is shown above.

$$2653 \div 7 = 379$$

Decimals

There are times when you are dividing a number and, after the final subtraction, there is a value left over. This is a remainder. When this happens, you can choose whether or not to continue calculating the number. If you continue, 1 or more decimal points will be introduced.

Example:

```
        331                           331.625
    8 | 2653                      8 | 2653.000
       -24                           -24
        25                            25
       -24                           -24
        13                            13
       -08                           -08
         5                            50
                                     -48
                                      20
                                     -16
                                      40
                                     -40
                                       0
```

You must follow the same procedure with decimal places as you would with regular long division. Ensure that the digits are properly lined up, and continue adding 0's after the decimal places in the equation.

Decimals and Whole Numbers

You may be required to solve division problems with decimals already in place. Below are two examples of decimals occurring in division questions.

Example 1

```
                              7.17
   5 | 35.85           5 | 35.85
```

To answer the question correctly, you have to place the decimal point in the answer directly above the decimal point in the question.

Example 2

```
                               1060.0
   2.7 | 2862          27 | 28620.0
```

When a decimal point is found in the denominator (the number of parts into which the whole is divided – bottom number of a fraction), then you must eliminate it before answering the question. This is achieved by shifting the decimal point however many spaces to the right it takes to create a whole number, in this example one space. This has to be matched by shifting the decimal place in the numerator (the number to be divided – top number of a fraction) by one space as well. If the numerator is a whole number, shift the decimal point right by adding a zero, as in the example above.

Example 3

$$3.5 \overline{)46.55} \qquad 35 \overline{)465.5}^{\,13.3}$$

When a decimal point is found in both the numerator and the denominator you must combine both steps. First, you must eliminate the decimal place in the denominator, as in example 2. Then you have to ensure that the new decimal place lines up, as in example 1.

Hints

Long division becomes more complicated with higher numbers, especially higher denominators.

$$67 \overline{)3015}^{\,0045}$$
$$\underline{-268}$$
$$335$$
$$\underline{-335}$$
$$0$$

Using 0's to Line up Numbers

67 will not fit into 3, or 30. You will therefore have to work with 301. By placing 0's above the 3 and the 0, (highlighted), you will not make any errors with improperly aligned numbers.

Rounding Up

Determining how many times 67 will fit into 301 can be a difficult task. It may help to round 67 up to 70. By counting 70 four times, you will reach 280. Five times equals 350, which exceeds 301. Four is the best guess, and by multiplying it out, using 67 you are proven correct.

Disregarding Decimals

The majority of the answers on a test will not require decimals. If your calculation of an equation gives you an answer with decimals, but none of the optional answers have decimals, stop calculating. Make a selection from the available options, or consider that you made a mistake. Quickly check your work, but don't spend too much time on one question that's causing you problems. Move onto the next question.

Zeros and Ones

Any time zero is divided by any other number the answer is 0.

$0 / 3 = 0$ $\qquad$ $0 \div 25 = 0$ $\qquad$ $\dfrac{0}{99} = 0$ $\qquad$ $0 \overline{\smash{)}99}$ gives 0

It is impossible for a number to be divided by 0. It is indefinable.

$9 / 0 =$ undefined $\qquad$ $77 \div 0 =$ undefined $\qquad$ $\dfrac{66}{0} =$ undefined

Any number divided by 1 is equal to itself.

$3 / 1 = 3$ $\qquad$ $55 \div 1 = 55$ $\qquad$ $\dfrac{1{,}297}{1} = 1{,}297$ $\qquad$ $1 \overline{\smash{)}38}$ gives 38

Place Value

It is important to maintain proper place value of digits when performing mathematical calculations. You must be able to convert written numbers into digits. For example:

Two million, forty thousand and two	2,040,002
One and a half million	1,500,000
Ten thousand and ten	10,010

You can practice place value questions by answering questions such as the ones below:

a) Write a number that is 100 more than 4,904.
b) Write a number that is 1000 less than 478,243.
c) What number is one more than 9,999?
d) What is the value of 5 in the number 241,598?
e) What figure is in the ten thousands place in 4,365,243?
f) What number is 30,000 less than 423,599?

The answers are listed below.

Place value is important when lining up numbers for addition and subtraction questions. For example:

$$15 + 1043 + 603 + 20{,}602 = \begin{array}{r} 20{,}602 \\ 1{,}043 \\ 603 \\ \underline{15} \\ 22{,}263 \end{array}$$

$$13.09 + 0.4 + 206 + 0.002 = \begin{array}{r} 206.000 \\ 13.090 \\ 0.400 \\ \underline{0.002} \\ 219.492 \end{array}$$

One of the most common errors is failing to place digits correctly under one another, which often occurs when trying to calculate these problems in your head.

Answers to practice questions.

a) 5,004   b) 477,243

c) 10,000   d) 500

e) 6   f) 393,599

Make sure you are comfortable with the proper names for the location of digits in a number.

$$1,234,567.890$$

1 = millions column   2 = hundred thousands column

3 = ten thousands column   4 = thousands column

5 = hundreds column   6 = tens column

7 = ones column   8 = tenths column

9 = hundredths column   0 = thousandths column

Order of Operations

The following rules have to be obeyed while working with mathematical equations. There is an order to how numbers are manipulated and worked on.

BEDMAS

You should memorize this acronym, as it tells you how to proceed with an equation.

1) **B** – Brackets

   You must perform all mathematical calculations that occur within brackets before any other calculation in the equation.

2) **E** – Exponents

   After calculations within brackets are handled, you have to perform any calculations with exponents next.

3) **D / M** – Division and Multiplication

   Division and multiplication components are next. These are handled in the order they appear reading from left to right.

4) **A / S** – Addition and Subtraction

   The final calculations are individual addition and subtraction questions, which are performed in the order they appear reading from left to right.

The best way to understand this process is to work through several problems.

Example 1:		
6 + 5 x 3 – 7	Step 1: Multiplication	5 x 3 = 15
6 + 15 – 7	Step 2: Addition	6 + 15 = 21
21 – 7	Step 3: Subtraction	21 - 7 = 14
Example 2:		
14 – 7 + 18 ÷ 3	Step 1: Division	18 ÷ 3 = 6
14 – 7 + 6	Step 2: Subtraction	14 – 7 = 7
7 + 6	Step 3: Addition	7 + 6 = 13

Example 3:

7 + (15 – 6 x 2)	Step 1: Brackets Remember to follow the order of operation within the brackets. (Multiply before subtracting.)	6 x 2 = 12
7 + (15 – 12)		15 – 12 = 3
7 + 3	Step 2: Addition	7 + 3 = 10

Example 4:

$2(2+5)^2$	Step 1: Brackets	2 + 5 = 7
$2(7)^2$	Step 2: Exponents	$7^2 = 7 \times 7 = 49$
2 (49)	Step 3: Multiplication	2 x 49 = 98

Remember that two numbers separated only by brackets are multiplied together (a bracket = x.)   2 (6) = 6 x 2

Practice Questions

Try these practice questions to see if you are comfortable with mathematical order of operation. The final answers are listed below.

a) 7 – 4 + 6 x 8 ÷ 2

b) 14 + 8 (6 – 3)

c) $30 - 3(5-2)^2$

d) (5 – 1) (4 + 7)

e) $75 - (6 \div (2+1))^2$

f) $10^2 - 10 + 3^2$

g) (10 + 3) x 2 + 6(5-2)

h) $17 + 6^2 (18 \div 9)$

i) 4 (5+2-3+6)

j) 10 (6 + (15 – (10-5)))

Answers

a) 27   b) 38   c) 3   d) 44

e) 71   f) 99   g) 44   h) 89

i) 40   j) 160

Grouping Like Terms

You will come across mathematical problems where you have to group like terms together. Examples of this are very common with money. Whenever you are adding sums of money, there is no need to continually restate the same denominations. Below is an example of an equation adding up a suspect's money:

Denomination	# of Bills
$50	4
$20	3
$10	4

One means of calculating the total value of money seized is to individually add up all of the bills.

$$50 + 50 + 50 + 50 + 20 + 20 + 20 + 10 + 10 + 10 + 10$$

However, there is an easier and more orderly way of writing and working with this equation. Here is the statement rewritten separating the like terms.

$$(50 + 50 + 50 + 50) + (20 + 20 + 20) + (10 + 10 + 10 + 10)$$

Instead of adding all of the $50 bills together you can count the number of 50's and multiply that number by the value.

$50 + 50 + 50 + 50$	=	4×50 or $4(50)$
$20 + 20 + 20$	=	3×20 or $3(20)$
$10 + 10 + 10 + 10$	=	4×10 or $4(10)$

The statement can then be written more clearly as: $\quad 4(50) + 3(20) + 4(10)$

Remember that it doesn't matter what order the terms are in, so long as they remain together. The above equation could be restated any of the following ways:

$3(20) + 4(50) + 4(10)$ $\qquad$ $20(3) + 50(4) + 10(4)$

$20(3) + 10(4) + 50(4)$ $\qquad$ $4(10) + 3(20) + 4(50)$

Like terms can occur in any addition question. It doesn't have to be a monetary question. Any time you see two or more of the same number in an addition problem, they can be combined.

$5 + 6 + 3 + 5 + 2 + 6 + 5$	=	$3(5) + 2(6) + 3 + 2$
$75 + 63 + 75 + 63 + 75$	=	$3(75) + 2(63)$
$5 + 5 + 5 + 5 + 5 + 4$	=	$5(5) + 4$

Fractions

A fraction is simply a part of a whole thing. The example below is of a circle divided into four pieces. Each segment represents ¼ of the circle.

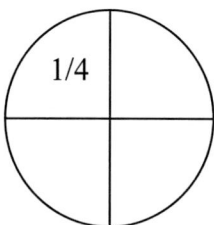

In each of the circles below, the same area is represented, but the area is divided into different numbers of equal parts.

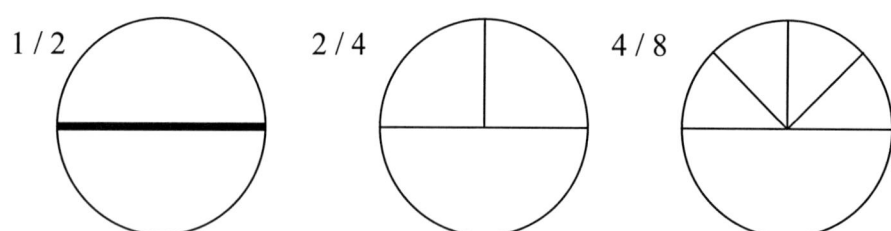

This diagram demonstrates that the fractions 1/2, 2/4 and 4/8 represent the same quantity.

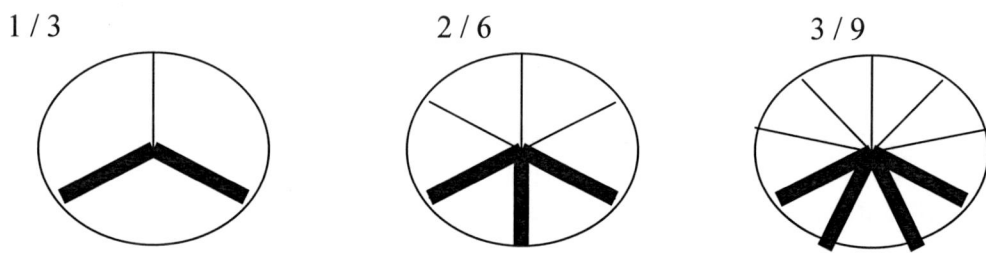

The fractions 1/3, 2/6 and 3/9 are equivalent. You can determine fractions of equivalent value by multiplying both the numerator and the denominator of the fraction by the same number.

$$\frac{1 \times 7}{3 \times 7} = \frac{7}{21} \quad \text{thus} \quad \frac{7}{21} = \frac{1}{3}$$

A similar rule holds when dividing the numerators and denominators of fractions. This is necessary to reduce fractions to their lowest form.

$$\frac{5 \text{ divided by } 5}{15 \text{ divided by } 5} = \frac{1}{3}$$

Improper Fractions

When a fraction has a larger numerator than denominator then the fraction is larger than one. The diagram below illustrates an example of improper fractions.

3 / 2 = 1 1/2

Adding and Subtracting Fractions

Whenever you are adding or subtracting fractions, you have to ensure that the denominators of the fractions are the same. For example:

$\frac{1}{2}$ + $\frac{6}{8}$ does not equal $\frac{7}{10}$

By multiplying both the denominator and the numerator of 1/2 by 4, you will be able to add the fractions together. 1 / 2 becomes 4 / 8.

$\frac{4}{8}$ + $\frac{6}{8}$ = $\frac{10}{8}$ = $\frac{5}{4}$

When you are adding and subtracting fractions, you also maintain the same denominator, and add or subtract the numerator.

$\frac{3}{4} - \frac{1}{4} = \frac{2}{4} = \frac{1}{2}$ $\frac{3}{18} + \frac{12}{18} = \frac{15}{18} = \frac{5}{6}$

$\frac{5}{10} - \frac{3}{10} = \frac{2}{10} = \frac{1}{5}$ $\frac{7}{8} + \frac{5}{8} = \frac{12}{8} = 1\frac{1}{2}$

Multiplying Fractions

When multiplying fractions, there is no need to find a common denominator. Simply multiply the two top numbers and then multiply the two bottom numbers. Multiplying two fractions together (other than improper) will result in a fraction that is smaller than the original numbers.

$\frac{4}{5} \times \frac{3}{4} = \frac{12}{20} = \frac{3}{5}$ $\frac{1}{2} \times \frac{1}{5} = \frac{1}{10}$

$\frac{3}{4} \times \frac{7}{18} = \frac{21}{72} = \frac{7}{24}$ $\frac{3}{2} \times \frac{4}{5} = \frac{12}{10} = 1\frac{1}{5}$

Dividing Fractions

Division with fractions is very similar to multiplying with fractions.

12 divided by 12 = 1	12 goes into 12 once
12 divided by 6 = 2	6 goes into 12 twice
12 divided by 4 = 3	4 goes into 12 three times
12 divided by 3 = 4	3 goes into 12 four times
12 divided by 2 = 6	2 goes into 12 six times
12 divided by 1 = 12	1 goes into 12 twelve times
12 divided by 1/2 = 24	1/2 goes into 12 twenty four times

This is logical when you think about the statement on the right. Whenever you are dividing by a fraction you have to multiply one fraction by the reciprocal of the other. That is, when you divide one fraction by another, you have to multiply one fraction by the inverse of the other. For example:

$$\frac{1}{2} \div \frac{6}{7} = \frac{1}{2} \times \frac{7}{6} = \frac{7}{12}$$

$$\frac{3}{4} \div \frac{4}{5} = \frac{3}{4} \times \frac{5}{4} = \frac{15}{16}$$

$$1\frac{3}{4} \div \frac{4}{5} = \frac{7}{4} \times \frac{5}{4} = \frac{35}{16} = 2\frac{3}{16}$$

Whenever dividing mixed fractions (1 1/2, 2 3/4 etc) you must use improper fractions (3/2, 11/4 etc).

Percentages

It is important to have a solid background in decimals and fractions before you try to handle percentage questions. Percentages are simply fractions. Per means "out of" and cent means "a hundred". Percentages are fractions with 100 as a denominator. They are often noted with this sign: %.

    10 % means 10 out of 100 or $\frac{10}{100}$

    13 % means 13 out of 100 or $\frac{13}{100}$

    100 % means 100 out of 100 or $\frac{100}{100}$

100% means everything. 100% of your salary is your whole salary. You simply follow the same rules of conversion from fractions to decimals for calculating percentages. Simply move the decimal points two places to the left to convert percents to decimals. This is essentially dividing the percentage by 100.

Example:
- 75% = 0.75
- 8% = 0.08
- 53.5% = 0.535
- 208% = 2.08

Any percent larger than 100% indicates more than the whole. For example:

A man's stock portfolio is worth 125% of what it was a year ago. This means that the stocks are now worth 25% more. If his stocks were worth $500 last year, they would be worth:

$500 x 125% =
```
   500
 x 1.25
 $ 625
```

Percentages with Fractions

Some questions you encounter may incorporate percentages and fractions. Examples include 2 1/2 % or 33 1/3 %. In order to deal with these problems, you must first convert the percentages to improper fractions.

$$2\ 1/2 = 5/2 \qquad\qquad 33\ 1/3 = 100/3$$

After this step you simply carry out the division question.

$$\begin{array}{r} 2.5 \\ 2\overline{\smash{)}5.0} \\ \underline{4} \\ 10 \\ \underline{10} \\ 0 \end{array} \qquad\qquad \begin{array}{r} 33.33 \\ 3\overline{\smash{)}100.00} \end{array}$$

Once you have the decimal equivalent of the percentage, you then follow the same rules that apply to a regular percentage. Divide the number by 100 or, more simply, move the decimal to the left twice. Thus:

$$2\ 1/2\% = 0.025 \qquad\qquad 33\ 1/3\% = 0.3333$$

Percentages You Should Memorize

25%	=	1/4	=	0.25
50%	=	1/2	=	0.5
75%	=	3/4	=	0.75
100%	=	4/4	=	1.00
33 1/3 %	=	1/3	=	0.333
66 2/3 %	=	2/3	=	0.666
10%	=	1/10	=	0.1
20%	=	1/5	=	0.2
40%	=	2/5	=	0.4
60%	=	3/5	=	0.6
80%	=	4/5	=	0.8

Decimal / Fraction Conversion Instruction

Fraction to Decimal

There are many situations where you will have to convert fractions to decimals. Decimals are often easier to work with. Changing fractions to decimals is simply a division problem. All you have to do is take the numerator and divide it by the denominator.

Examples:

$$1/2 = 2\overline{)1.0} = 0.5$$
$$\underline{-1.0}$$
$$0$$

$$4/5 = 5\overline{)4.0} = 0.8$$

$$1/3 = 3\overline{)1.000} = 0.333$$
$$\underline{-0.9}$$
$$0.10$$
$$\underline{-09}$$
$$010$$
$$\underline{-09}$$
$$1$$

Mixed Fractions

Mixed fractions have to first be converted to improper fractions before they can be converted to decimals. Multiplying the whole number by the denominator and adding the numerator will achieve this. As soon as the improper fraction is found, you calculate the decimal in the same way as above.

Example 1 $3\frac{1}{2} = \frac{7}{2}$ $2\overline{)7.0} = 3.5$

Multiply 3 by 2, and then add 1. This is the new numerator, and the denominator remains the same.

Example 2 $2\frac{5}{6} = \frac{17}{6}$ $6\overline{)17.000} = 2.833$

Decimal to Fraction

When converting decimals to fractions, place value is extremely important. The first decimal point to the right of the decimal point is the tenths, followed by the hundredths, thousandths, etc. All you have to do is properly line up the place value with the proper denominator.

    0.1   is a way of writing $\dfrac{1}{10}$

    0.01   is a way of writing $\dfrac{1}{100}$

and

    0.6   is a way of writing $\dfrac{6}{10}$

    0.78   is a way of writing $\dfrac{78}{100}$

There is one zero in the denominator for every place to the right of the period in the original decimal.

Exponents

Exponents indicate how many times a number should be multiplied by itself. If a number is raised to the power of 2, the number should be multiplied by itself twice. If the number is raised to the power of 6, the number should be multiplied by itself 6 times.

$$2^2 = 2 \times 2 = 4$$

$$2^3 = 2 \times 2 \times 2 = 8$$

$$2^4 = 2 \times 2 \times 2 \times 2 = 16$$

$$2^5 = 2 \times 2 \times 2 \times 2 \times 2 = 32$$

$$7^2 = 7 \times 7 = 49$$

$$5^4 = 5 \times 5 \times 5 \times 5 = 625$$

Positive and Negative Integers

You must have an understanding of positive and negative integers and how they react when they are added, subtracted, multiplied and divided by each other. Look at the number line below. Positive integers exist to the right of the zero and negative integers exist to the left of the zero.

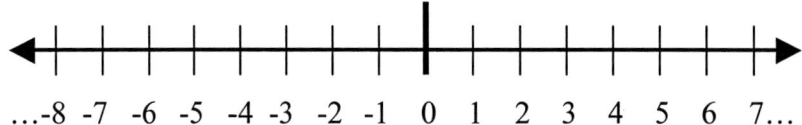

Adding Positive and Negative Integers
1) -7 + 5 = -2   2) -6 + 3 = -3
3) -2 + 7 = 5   4) -4 + 11 = 7

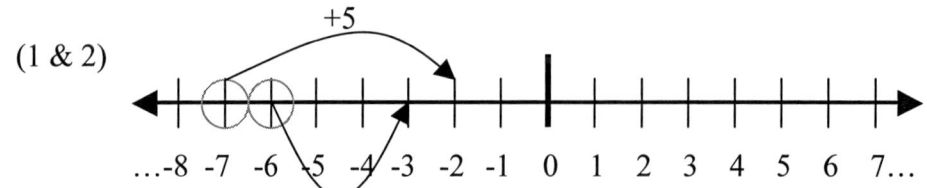

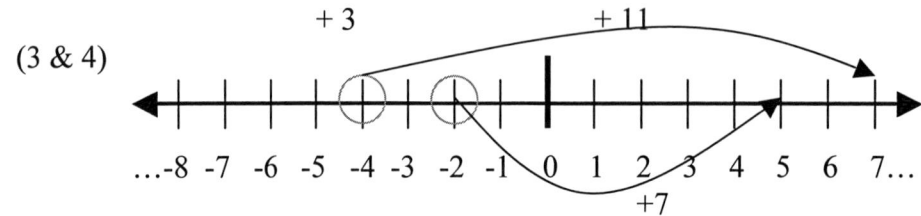

Subtracting Positive and Negative Integers
1) -2 – 5 = -7   2) -4 – 8 = -12
3) 4 – 7 = -3   4) 2 – 5 = -3

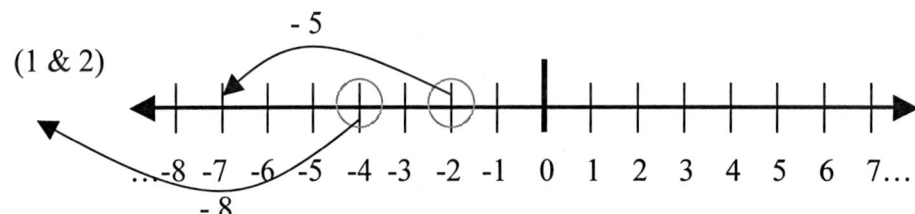

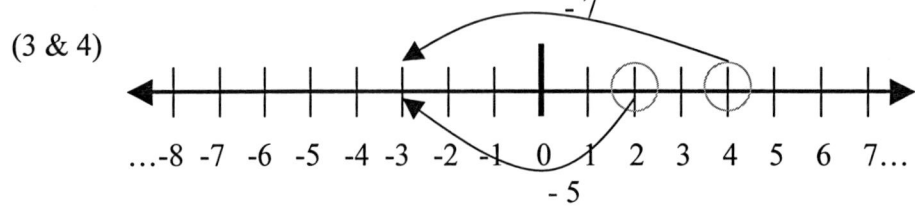

When adding and subtracting positive and negative integers you must know what to do when two signs are directly beside each other.

<u>2 Positives</u>   <u>2 Negatives</u>   <u>Opposite Signs</u>

+ + = +   - - = +   + - = -

For instance: 6 + (+3)   6 + (-3)   6 - (-3)
                = 6 + 3   = 6 – 3   = 6 + 3
                = 9   = 3   = 9

Try these sample questions. The answers are below.

1) 5 – 9 =   2) –4 + 6 =   3) –5 – 2 =   4) 2 – 7 =

5) –2 + 5 =   6) 1 – 9 =   7) 4 – (+6) =   8) –2 –(-4) =

9) + 3 – (-6) =   10) 6 + (-4) =   11) 6 + (+2) =   12) -3 + (-2) =

Multiplying and Dividing Positive and Negative Integers

While multiplying and dividing positive and negative integers, remember the rules that apply to adding and subtracting integers with two signs directly beside each other.

<u>2 Positives</u>   <u>2 Negatives</u>   <u>Opposite Signs</u>

+ + = +   - - = +   + - = -

You should break questions like this into two steps.

Step 1: Solve the equation ignoring the signs.

   6 x (-3) = 18   - 5 x 4 = 20
   5 x (-7) = 35   - 3 x (-4) = 12
   -12 ÷ (-4) = 3   -21 ÷ 3 = 7
   36 ÷ (-9) = 4   -64 ÷ (-8) = 8

If you ignored the + and – signs in front of the numbers you would end up with the answers above.

Step 2: Determine the + / - sign. The rules about + / - integers come into play. If there are two + signs, then the equation is positive. If there are two – signs, then the equation is also positive. If there is one + and one – sign, then the equation is negative.

    6 x (-3) = **-18** (+ / -)   - 5 x 4 = **-20** (- / +)
    5 x (-7) = **- 35** (- / +)   - 3 x (-4) = **12** (- / -)
    -12 ÷ (-4) = **3** (- / -)   -21 ÷ 3 = **- 7** (- / +)
    36 ÷ (-9) = **- 4** (+ / -)   -64 ÷ (-8) = **8** (- / -)

The final answers are displayed in bold above.

Try these sample questions. The answers are posted below.

a) 3 x (– 6) =   b) – 2 x (-9) =   c) – 18 ÷ (–9) =

d) 7 x 7 =   e) –72 ÷ 8 =   f) –12 x (– 9) =

g) 7 x (-6) =   h) –28 ÷ (-4) =   i) 16 ÷ (-4) =

j) 3 x (-4) =   k) -45 ÷ (-15) =   l) -3 x (2) =

Answers to Sample Questions

1) 5 – 9 = **- 4**   2) – 4 + 6 = **2**   3) – 5 – 2 = **- 7**

4) 2 – 7 = **-5**   5) –2 + 5 = **3**   6) 1 – 9 = **-8**

7) 4 – (+6) = **-2**   8) –2 –(-4) = **2**   9) + 3 – (-6) = **9**

10) 6 + (-4) = **2**   11) 6 + (+2) = **8**   12) -3 + (-2) = **-5**

_____

a) 3 x (– 6) = **-18**   b) – 2 x (-9) = **18**   c) – 18 ÷ (–9) = **2**

d) 7 x 7 = **49**   e) –72 ÷ 8 = **-9**   f) –12 x (– 9) = **108**

g) 7 x (-6) = **-42**   h) –28 ÷ (-4) = **7**   i) 16 ÷ (-4) = **-4**

j) 3 x (-4) = **-12**   k) -45 ÷ (-15) = **3**   l) -3 x (2) = **-6**

Perimeters

Perimeter is defined as the border around an object, or the outside edge of an object.

 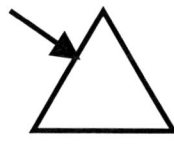

Perimeter is calculated by adding the sides of the object together.

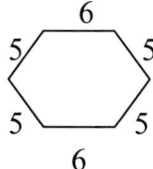   Perimeter = 6 + 5 + 5 + 5+ 5 + 6
              = 32

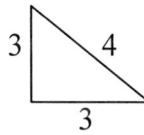   Perimeter = 4 + 4 + 4 + 4
              = 16

Perimeter = 3 + 3 + 4
          = 10

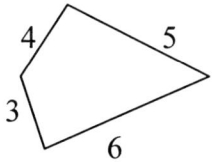   Perimeter = 3 + 4 + 5 + 6
              = 18

Circumferences

Circumference is also defined as the border around a shape, but is always associated with a circle.

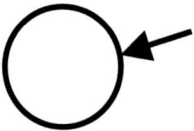

In order to determine the circumference of a circle, you must use a formula. You need to be familiar with some definitions.

$$\pi = 3.14 \text{ (pi)}$$

You are going to have to remember that pi is equal to 3.14.

Diameter (d)

Diameter is the distance from one edge of the circle, through the middle, to the opposite side of the circle.

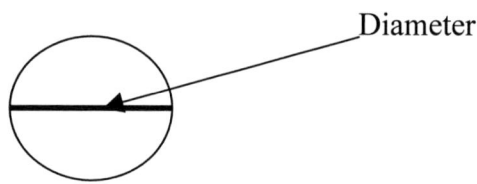

Radius (r)

Radius is defined as ½ of the diameter, or the distance from the mid-point of a circle to its outer edge.

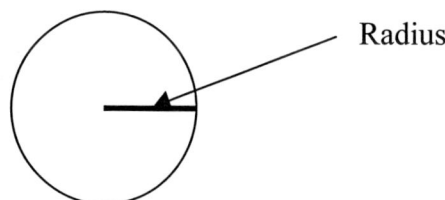

Formula for Calculating Circumference

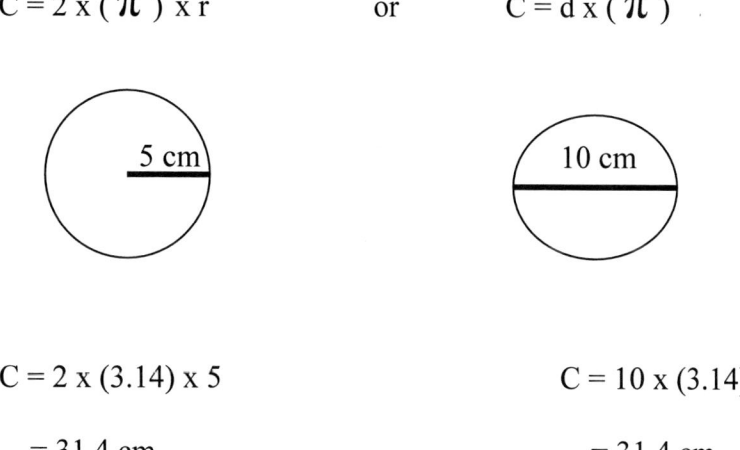

$C = 2 \times (\pi) \times r$ or $C = d \times (\pi)$

$C = 2 \times (3.14) \times 5$ $C = 10 \times (3.14)$

$= 31.4$ cm $= 31.4$ cm

The information you are given in a question will dictate the formula you should use to calculate the circumference. If you are given the radius, calculate the diameter by multiplying by two. Dividing the diameter by two will give you the radius.

Areas

Area is space that is occupied within the borders of a shape. It is measured in units squared and is represented by the area shaded in the shapes below.

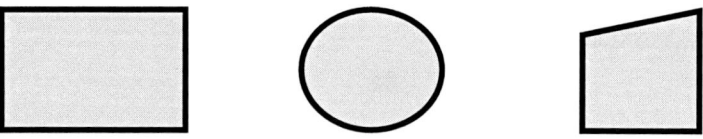

The three shapes you should know how to calculate area for are the triangle, rectangle and circle.

Area of a Rectangle or Square

To calculate the area of a square or rectangle, multiply the base of the object by its' height.

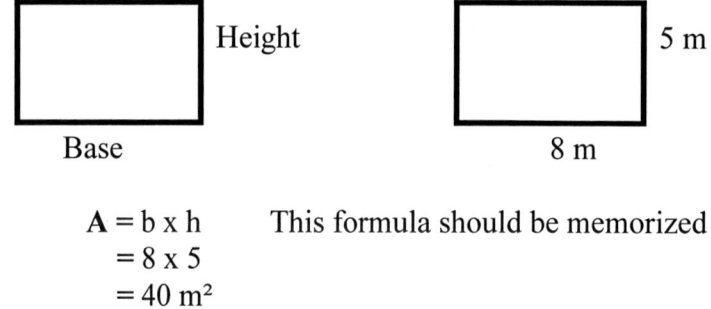

$A = b \times h$ This formula should be memorized
$= 8 \times 5$
$= 40 \text{ m}^2$

Area of a Triangle

To calculate the area of a triangle, follow the formula below.

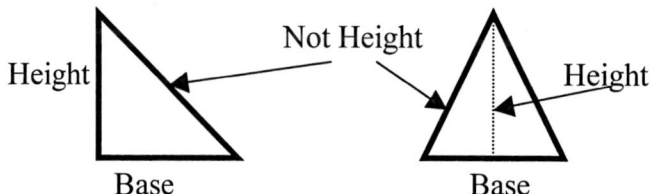

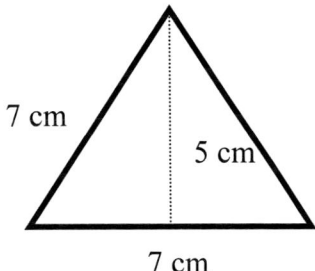

A = ½ x b x h   **This formula should be memorized.**
 = ½ x 7 x 5
 = 17.5 cm²

Remember that height is not necessarily an edge of the triangle, but the distance from the base to the top of the triangle.

Area of a Circle

To calculate the area of a circle, follow the formula below.

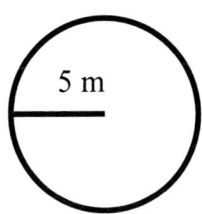

A = π (r)²   **This formula should be memorized.**
 = (3.14) (5)²
 = (3.14) (25)
 = 78.5 m²

Other Shapes

You may have to calculate the area of shapes other than basic squares, triangles and circles. You can attempt to break shapes into smaller components and use the formulas above. For example:

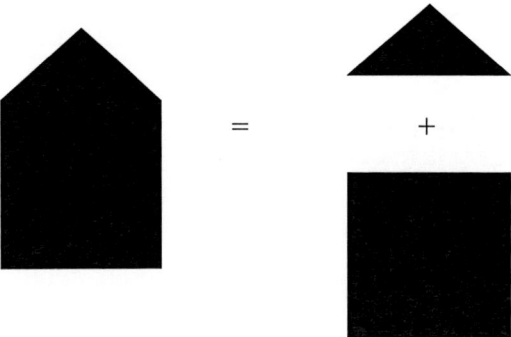

Calculate the area of the triangle and adding it to the area of the square results in the area of the whole shape.

You can divide the shape on the left into a square and a half circle. Calculate the area of the square and the area of the circle. Divide the area of the circle in half and add the two together.

Volumes

Volume is defined as the area occupied by a three dimensional shape. If you pictured an empty cup, volume is the amount of liquid it contains. Calculating volume for different objects can be very difficult and involves complex formulas. We will discuss how to calculate the volume of three simple objects. Volume is always discussed in units cubed (example $3m^3$.)

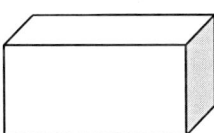  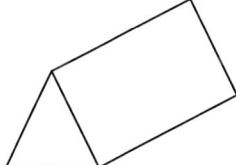

Volume of a Cube

You should memorize the formula for calculating the volume of a cube.

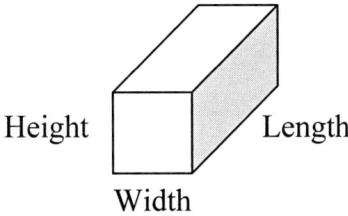 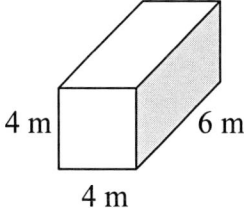

V = length x width x height
= 6 x 4 x 4
= 96 m^3

Volume of a Cylinder

To calculate the volume of a cylinder, determine the area of the circle and multiply it by the height of the cylinder.

Radius = 5 m

Height = 10 m

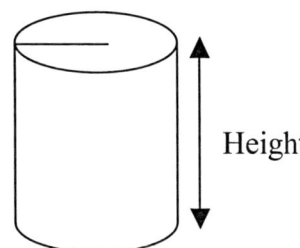

Height

V = π (r)^2 x height
= (3.14) (5)^2 (10)
= 785 m^3

Volume of a Triangular Shaped Object

To calculate the volume of an object like the one below, first calculate the area of the triangle and multiply it by the length of the object.

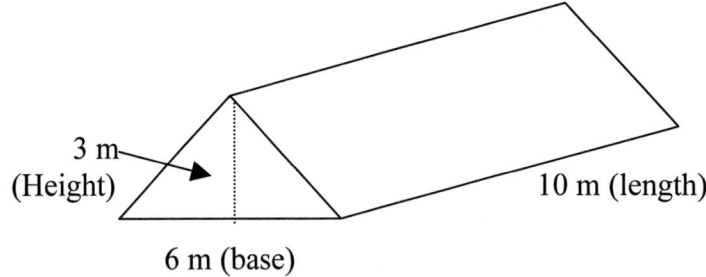

V = ½ (base) (height) (length)
 = ½ (6) (3) (10)
 = 90 m^3

Metric Conversions

The key to understanding metric conversions is to memorize the prefixes and roots to each word. The root of each word indicates the basic measurement (litre, metre, gram), while the prefixes determine the relative size of the measurement (larger or smaller units – milli, centi, kilo, etc,).

Prefixes

All units in the metric system are easily converted because they are all based on units of 10. When converting between different measurements of the same base unit, it is as easy as shifting the decimal point.

For example:

432,000 millimetres
43,200 centimetres   ALL EQUAL EACH OTHER
432 metres
0.432 kilometres

Length

Length is used to measure the distance between points. The base unit for length is the metre. The most common units you'll encounter with length include:

Millimetres – small units (25 millimetres in 1 inch)
Centimetres – small units (2.5 centimetres in 1 inch)
Metres – larger units (1 metre = 3.2 feet or 1.1 yards)
Kilometres – large units (1.6 kilometres in 1 mile)

Prefix	Example	Sign	Conversion
Milli	Millimetres	mm	1 m = 1000 mm
Centi	Centimetre	cm	1 m = 100 cm
Deci	Decigram	dm	1 m = 10 dm
-	Metre	m	1 m = 1 m
Kilo	Kilometre	km	1 km = 1000 m

Volume

Volume is defined as the capacity of a given container. It usually measures the amount of liquid or gas that an object can hold. For example, the volume of a pop can is 355 millilitres, or the volume of a milk carton is 1 litre. The base unit for volume in the metric system is the litre. A litre is roughly the amount of milk that will fit into a milk carton or roughly three glasses of milk.

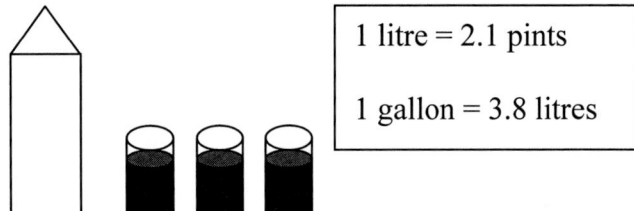

The most common prefix used with volume is the millilitre (used to measure small amounts, such as tablespoons.) The majority of the time when measuring volume you will be using the litre measurement itself.

Prefix	Example	Sign	Conversion
Milli	Millilitres	mL	1 L = 1000 mL
Centi	Centilitres	cL	1 L = 100 cL
Deci	Decilitres	dL	1 L = 10 dL
-	Litres	L	1 L = 1 L
Kilo	Kilolitres	kL	1 kL = 1000 L

Mass or Weight

The base unit for weight in the metric system is the gram. The most common units you'll encounter with weight are:

Milligrams – very small (1000 milligrams in 1 gram)
Grams – small units (28.3 grams in 1 ounce)
Kilograms – large units (1 kilogram = 2.2 pounds)

Prefix	Example	Sign	Conversion
Milli	Milligrams	mg	1 g = 1000 mg
Centi	Centigram	cg	1 g = 100 cg
Deci	Decigram	dg	1 g = 10 dg
-	Gram	G	1 g = 1 g
Kilo	Kilogram	kg	1 kg = 1000 g

Algebraic Equations

Before beginning this section, make sure that you are comfortable with the rules of order of operation in mathematical equations. It is necessary to know in what order you add, subtract, divide and multiply in an equation.

Algebraic equations involve using letters and symbols to represent unknown numbers. In order to solve these equations you must isolate the unknown variable. We will begin with a couple of simple examples.

When solving algebraic equations, it is important to know the opposite mathematical operations. For example, subtraction is the opposite of addition and division is the opposite of multiplication. Square roots are the opposite of squaring. We will not cover square roots in this section.

$6 + y = 12$ $6 + y - \mathbf{6} = 12 - \mathbf{6}$ $y = 6$	In order to isolate the "y", eliminate a + 6 on the left hand side of the equation. In algebraic equations, whatever you do to one side of the equation you must also do to the other side. Subtract 6 from both sides.
$y - 3 = 15$ $y - 3 + \mathbf{3} = 15 + \mathbf{3}$ $y = 18$	In order to isolate the "y", eliminate a - 3 on the left hand side of the equation. Add 3 to both sides.
$7y = 42$ $7y / \mathbf{7} = 42 / \mathbf{7}$ $y = 6$	In this case, "y" is multiplied by 7. To eliminate a number that is being multiplied, divide by the same number. Divide both sides by 7.
$y / 12 = 5$ $y / 12 \; \mathbf{x \; 12} = 5 \; \mathbf{x \; 12}$ $y = 60$	In this case, "y" is divided by 12. To eliminate a number that is being divided, multiply by the same number. Multiply both sides by 12.

Practice solving some of these simple equations:

1) y / 11 = 23   2) 15 + y = 63   3) – 5 + y = 10

4) 13 (y) = 130   5) 5 y = 15   6) 6 + 3 + y = 56

7) 2(y) = 56   8) y / 8 = 4   9) y (24) = 72

Answers are below.

More Advanced Algebraic Equations

When solving equations, follow the order of operations which dictate that you perform equations within brackets, followed by exponents, then division and multiplication, and finally addition and subtraction. When isolating unknown variables, use the opposite order. We will not cover solving equations with exponents at this level.

6 y + 12 = 84

6 y + 12 – **12** = 84 – **12**

6 y = 72

6 y / **6** = 72 / **6**

y = 12

| In order to isolate the "y", first eliminate a + 12 on the left hand side of the equation. Subtract 12 from both sides. You are left with 6y = 12. To isolate "y", now simply divide both sides of the equation by 6. |

y / 3 + 12 – 2 = **15 x 3 + 4**

y / 3 + 12 – 2 = **45 + 4**

y / 3 + 12 – 2 = 49

y / 3 + 12 – 2 + **2** = 49 + **2**

y / 3 + 12 = 51

y / 3 + 12 – **12** = 51 – **12**

y / 3 = 39

y / 3 **x 3** = 39 **x 3**

y = 117

You may encounter equations where one side has operations without an unknown variable. In cases like this, solve the side without an unknown variable FOLLOWING THE STANDARD ORDER OF OPERATION RULES.

After you have accomplished this, solve the equation in the standard manner. People more advanced in math will be able to consolidate portions of the left side as well, but unless you are comfortable you should proceed the way outlined to the left.

(6 − y) x 3 = 24

(6 − y) x 3 / **3** = 24 / **3**

(6 − y) = 8

6 − y − **6** = 8 − **6**

- y = 2

- y **x (-1)** = 2 **x (-1)**

y = − 2

> Perform this equation following the standard rules. Leave the brackets until the end. When only the brackets remain, you can get rid of them as they no longer serve a purpose.
>
> When you are left with an equation where the unknown is isolated, but negative, simply multiply both sides of the equation by − 1 to inverse the signs.
>
> The end result is that y = − 2.

18 / y = 2

18 / y **x (y)** = 2 **x (y)**

18 = 2 y

18 / **2** = 2 y / **2**

9 = y

> One other tricky situation you may encounter is when "y" appears on the bottom of a division equation. In order to solve for "y", move it from the bottom of the division sign by multiplying both sides of the equation by "y". The result is 18 = 2 y. Now solve the rest of the equation.

WHATEVER YOU DO TO ONE SIDE OF AN EQUATION YOU MUST ALSO DO TO THE OTHER SIDE.

More Practice Questions

a) 3 (y) + 6 − 10 = 89

b) (y) / 6 + 24 − 2 = 14

c) - y (3) +55 = 105

d) 5 y − 32 = 24 (3)

e) −32 + 6y/2 = 64

f) 22 y + 16 (8) = 6 y

Answers:

1) 253	2) 48	3) 15
4) 10	5) 3	6) 47
7) 28	8) 32	9) 3
a) 31	b) - 48	c) −16.7
d) 20.8	e) 32	f) − 8

Teaching Material English

Common Grammar Errors

It is beyond the scope of this book to cover all grammar errors that can occur during a government examination. Below are merely some examples you may come across. If you feel your grammar is a significant barrier to landing the job, it would be prudent to review a grammar textbook, or perhaps take an English grammar course.

The Use of "Then" and "Than"

Then is used to indicate time. It has the same meaning as "afterwards", "subsequently" or "followed by".

    Ex: I went to the play, *and then* I went home.

Than is used in comparison. It can be used with the word "rather". It has the same meaning as "as opposed to", or "instead of".

    Ex: I would rather play baseball *than* hockey.

The Use of "Is When"

This is not correct. Use the term "occurs when."

    Ex: The best part of the movie *occurs when* the killer is revealed.

Subordinate Clauses

Be careful with subordinate clauses. If one clause has less emphasis (less importance) in a sentence, it is subordinate or dependent on the other clause. When these clauses occur at the beginning of the sentence, they can be tricky.

    Ex: ***Since you began training,*** you have been unable to work an entire shift.

If you rearrange the sentence you can understand how "since" acts as the conjunction.

    Ex: You have been able to work an entire shift **since you began training.**

Forming Plurals

It is difficult to determine the plural form of many words. Examples include:

Goose	Geese	Man	Men
Woman	Women	Mouse	Mice
Mother-in-Law	Mothers-in-Law		

Comparative Adjectives and Adverbs

Single Syllable Words:

To form the comparative adjective or adverb for most single syllable words, add "*-er*" to the end of the word. If there are three or more parties to compare, use the ending "*-est*."

> Rafik was strong.
> Bill was *stronger* than Rafik.
> Pratik was the *strongest* of the three.
>
> Sean is fast.
> Sean is the faster of the two.
> Sean is the fastest of the three.

Be careful. There are always exceptions to the rule in the English language. You should be able to tell by the sound of the words when you should use an alternative method of comparison.

> I had a fun time at the party this year.
> I had *more fun* this year than last year.
> I had the *most fun* this year compared to all the other parties.
>
> The words "funner" and "funnest" do not exist.

Multiple Syllable Words:

As with the example "fun", multiple syllable words use linking words while making comparisons. When comparing two parties, use the word "*more*"; and while comparing three or more parties, use the word "*most*".

> He was *more eager* than her to finish the project.
> He was the *most eager* of the three to finish the project.
>
> Shelley was *more intelligent* than Michael.
> Lucy was the *most intelligent* of the group.

Subject / Verb Agreement

It is important to make sure that the verb agrees with the noun it relates to. There are six types of persons in the English language:

I	We
You (singular)	You (plural)
He / She / It	They

In English, there are several ways that subjects and verbs relate to each other. Here are a couple:

I	*run / do / was*	We	*run / do / were*
You	*run / do / was*	You	*run / do / were*
He / She / It	*runs / does / was*	They	*run / do / were*

Be careful of confusing the subject and verb agreement.

Example: I run fast.   I do well.   I **don't** understand.
           He run**s** fast.   He doe**s** well.   He **doesn't** understand.

This can be difficult if there is a clause between the subject and the verb. When analyzing a sentence, try to read the sentence without the clause to determine if there is subject / verb agreement.

Example: *Dheena*, along with the rest of us, *does* well.
Read aloud: *Dheena does well.* "Dheena do well" doesn't sound right.

The Use of "It's" and "Its"

This is often wrongly expressed.
"It's" is a contraction that translates into "it is".

> *It's* getting late. = *It is* getting late.
> I'm tired and *it's* time to go. = I'm tired and *it is* time to go.

"Its" refers to possession. It is the equivalent to an apostrophe "s".

The train and all *its* passengers were safe.
The train and all **the train's** passengers were safe.

The Use of "There", "Their" and "They're"

These are also often confused. Here are the definitions:

<u>There</u>: a location, nearby, in attendance, present
    The book is over **there,** on the table.

<u>Their</u>: a possessive pronoun implying ownership, belonging to them,
    I took **their** advice and followed through with the job.

<u>They're</u>: a contraction, meaning "they are"
    They're going to arrive late because of the snow.

The Use of "Two", "To", and "Too"

Make sure you follow these definitions. Use the correct "to/too/two" in the proper place.

To: in the direction, toward, near, in order to.
I went **to** the store **to** buy some bread.

Too: also, as well, in addition, besides, and excessively.
The teacher handed out an "A" to Bill and to Cindy, **too.**
Shayna and Jeff just left **too**.
The pizza deliverer took **too** long, so the pizza was free.

Two: the number
There were **two** beavers sitting on the log.

Verb Tenses

When reading a passage, ensure that the verbs in a sentence agree and that verbs discussing the same idea are in the same tense. For example, if you are speaking in the past in one sentence, you must remain consistent in the sentence following.

Incorrect
Bill **ran** to the store very quickly. He **is taking** Sally with him.
Sean **reads** at a fourth grade level and **studied** very hard.

Correct:
Bill **ran** to the store very quickly. He **took** Sally with him.
Sean **reads** at a fourth grade level and **studies** very hard.

Adverbs and Adjectives

Adverbs are used to modify or compliment verbs, adjectives or other adverbs. They generally explain how (gently), when (soon), or where (fully). A common trait of adverbs is to end in "-*ly*". However, this is not a reliable way to tell adverbs and adjectives apart.

Adjectives are used with nouns to describe a quality or modify a meaning. (old, tall, curly, Canadian, my, this...)

If the word you are describing or modifying is a noun, make sure you use the adjective form of the word. If the word is a verb, adjective, or adverb, use the adverb format.

He ran **quickly** down the street.   - Adverb quickly (how he runs)
He was a very **quick** thinker.   - Adjective quick (describing the thinker)

It was a **very large** house.   - Adverb very (describing large)
  - Adjective large (describing house)

It was a **loud** song. - Adjective loud (describing song)
She sang **loudly**. - Adverb loudly (modifying sang)

Uses of Commas in Lists

When a list is presented in a sentence, use commas between list items and a conjunction to separate the last two items on the list. It is not wrong to add an additional comma before the conjunction, but it is unnecessary.

He was going to bring his **toys, clothes, books and cookies** to class.

Angela was going to the Maritimes by **plane, train or boat**.

Uses of the Apostrophe

Apostrophes are used to indicate ownership.

Bill's school was one of the best in the country. (the school to which Bill went)
Martha's mirror was cracked. (the mirror belonging to Martha)

Meanings of "Fair" and "Fare"

People often confuse these two words. Definitions are listed below.

Fair: just, reasonable, light, fair haired, pale

He was a **fair** judge and handed down reasonable sentences.
The boy was very **fair**, and would burn easily in the sun.

Fare: charge, price, ticket, tariff, passenger

The **fare** for the plane was rather steep.

Subject / Object Noun Agreements

Depending on its role in the sentence, pronouns take on different forms. Below is a list.

Subject		Object	
I	We	Me	Us
You	You	You	You
He / She / It	They	Him / Her / It	Them

If the pronoun is acting as a subject, use a subject pronoun.

Subject	Object
Tim and I went to the baseball game.	Tim threw the ball to me.
He was the last one to leave.	Shayna surprised her at the party.
They will come later.	Alex passes the gravy to them.

The major distinction between a subject and an object is the manner in which the verb relates to the pronouns. A subject tends to perform the verb, while an object tends to have the verb performed on it. Read the examples above and see if you understand the difference. If not, you will have to check with a grammar textbook.

Double Negatives

Avoid using double negatives when both speaking and writing,. Examples include:

I do **not** want **no** gum.	I do **not** want **any** gum.
You ca**n't** go to **no** store.	You ca**n't** go to **any** store.
The sergeant has**n't no** time.	The sergeant has**n't any** time.

The uses of "From" and "Off"

When receiving objects, goods or information, remember that the word "from" is correct even though in common spoken language we often use the word "off".

The doctor received the X-rays **from** the technician.
She pulled the book **from** the cupboard.

The Uses of "Stayed" and "Stood"

This is similar to the "From" and "Off" problem mentioned above. You often hear the word "stood" used in spoken language, but "stayed" is the correct word to use.

Stood is the past tense of stand (position, place, locate). Stayed is the past tense of stay (remain, wait, reside.)

I should have stayed with my fellow officers in the tough times.
The nurse stayed by the patient all night long.

The Use of Amount and Number

Generally speaking, we use **"amount"** with something that is measured or can't be counted, such as weights or volumes. We use **"number"** to describe quantities that are countable.

She had a large **amount** of liquid in the test tube.
There was a large **amount** of chocolate used in the recipe.
There were a large **number** of soldiers in the army.
The **number** of signs on the highway is enormous.

Run-On Sentences

Watch out for run-on sentences when writing. When two or more separate independent clauses are incorrectly joined, this is a run-on sentence. An independent clause is the part of a sentence that could stand alone. If you put a period at the end of an independent clause, it could serve as a sentence.

Here is an example of a run-on sentence:

Jamie was extremely angry when he missed his final chemistry exam, he went back to his dormitory and yelled at his roommate for failing to wake him up.

There are several ways to deal with a run-on sentence.

1) Make two Separate Sentences.

This is the easiest way to correct the problem. Simply add a period and start the second sentence with a capital letter.

> Correct:
> Jamie was extremely angry when he missed his final chemistry exam. He went back to his dormitory and yelled at his roommate for failing to wake him up.

2) Use a semicolon to separate the independent clauses.

Semicolons can often replace periods, but a comma can't. Do not capitalize the word immediately after a semicolon.

> Correct:
> Jamie was extremely angry when he missed his final chemistry exam; he went back to his dormitory and yelled at his roommate for failing to wake him up.

3) Use a subordinating conjunction with one of the clauses.

A subordinating conjunction is used to turn one of the clauses from an independent clause to a dependent clause. Examples of subordinating conjunctions include "because" and "since".

> Correct:
> Since Jamie was extremely angry when he missed his final chemistry exam, he went back to his dormitory and yelled at his roommate for failing to wake him up.

4) Use a comma and a coordinating conjunction between the two clauses.

Coordinating conjunctions can connect two clauses. The most common coordinating conjunctions include "and", "or", "but", and "so".

> Correct:
> Jamie was extremely angry when he missed his final chemistry exam, so he went back to his dormitory and yelled at his roommate for failing to wake him up.

5) Use a semicolon, conjunctive adverb and comma to separate the clauses.

Conjunctive adverbs can connect clauses. Examples of these adverbs include: "therefore", "moreover", "however", and "nonetheless". In order to properly use these adverbs, place a semicolon before the adverb and a comma after the adverb.

> Incorrect:
> Jamie was extremely angry when he missed his final chemistry exam, therefore he went back to his dormitory and yelled at his roommate for failing to wake him up.

> Correct:
> Jamie was extremely angry when he missed his final chemistry exam; therefore, he went back to his dormitory and yelled at his roommate for failing to wake him up.

Sentence Fragments

A sentence fragment is an incomplete sentence. There are two ways to change a sentence fragment to a complete sentence.

1) Add Words

Incorrect:
> Justin, running across the front lawn and enjoying his childhood days.
> (incomplete sentence)

Correct:
> Justin was running across the front lawn and enjoying his childhood days.
> (complete sentence)

2) Take Away Words

Creating a complete sentence from a sentence fragment can also be achieved by removing words from the sentence fragment.

Incorrect:
> While Trevor was completing the exam but having difficulty coming up with the answer to question #51.

Correct:
> Trevor was completing the exam but having difficulty coming up with the answer to question #51.

Other Common Grammar Errors

Attend -	go to, be present at, concentrate
Tend -	be inclined, be likely, to have a tendency
Lose -	misplace, unable to find, to be defeated
Loose -	unfastened, wobbly, slack, movable
Threw -	hurled, tossed, past tense of "to throw"
Through -	from first to last, during, in the course of
Weather -	the seasons, elements, temperatures
Whether -	question of if, introducing an alternative possibility
Bear -	an animal in the woods, or to tolerate, stand, put up with
Bare -	to expose, naked, uncovered

The Situational Judgment Test

The Situational Judgment Test (SJT) is an attempt to test your ability to solve problems in situations that you will encounter at work. The primary competencies that are being evaluated are:

- **Teamwork** - Willing to act with others by seeking their input, encouraging their participation and sharing information. Commitment to helping others improve their skills.
- **Judgment** - The ability to analyze situations and events in a logical way, and to organize the parts of a problem systematically.
- **Interpersonal Relations** - Developing contacts and relationships both within and outside your area of employment is extremely valuable. With government jobs, you will have to work with a wide cross-section of the community with diverse backgrounds, cultures and socio-economic circumstances. You must have the ability to adapt your approach to each situation.

There are several points you should keep in mind when working through these scenarios.

- The government will want all inappropriate actions and behaviours discussed and acted upon. If the inappropriate behaviour continues, it must be reported to a higher authority.
- Instances of racism, sexism and discrimination cannot be tolerated.
- Customers and the public deserve to be treated fairly and professionally at all times.
- Managers expect orders to be followed with suitable judgment on the part of the employees.
- Cooperation and collaboration are vital to an organizations well being. Constructive criticism is acceptable but personal insults should not be tolerated.
- Employees must recognize and understand the dynamics of organizations, including the formal and informal cultures and decision-making processes.
- All people in the organization must act with integrity and honesty at all times.
- You will be answering the majority of questions (unless stated otherwise) with minimal authority and only have powers to persuade and influence.

Answering Questions

For the SJT you will be given a scenario and asked for the most effective and the least effective response. When selecting an answer choice for the most effective, first determine if there is a problem to solve and then disregard any options that do not contain important steps to solving the problem. When asked what the least effective solution to the problem would be, select the option that makes the situation worse or ignores the problem completely.

Essay Writing

There are several government agencies that may require you to submit an essay on a topic of their choice. You will be given a time limit (some are as little as 10 minutes) to compose your thoughts, organize a paragraph and write an essay or paragraph. If you are asked to do this, you will be marked on:

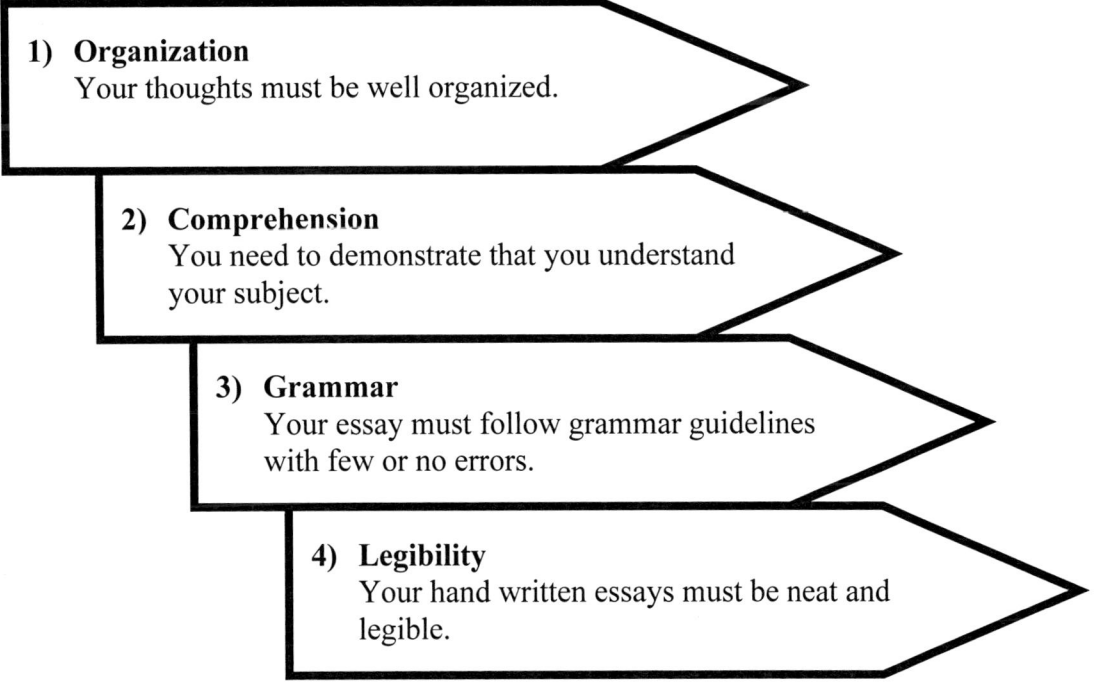

1) **Organization**
   Your thoughts must be well organized.

2) **Comprehension**
   You need to demonstrate that you understand your subject.

3) **Grammar**
   Your essay must follow grammar guidelines with few or no errors.

4) **Legibility**
   Your hand written essays must be neat and legible.

Possible Topics

Government agencies may ask you to write about anything, so there is very little you can do in terms of preparing for the content of the essay. There are, however, general topics tend to come up often.

- What challenges are government services facing in the future?
- Is diversity in the work force a good thing?
- What is the most important characteristic an employee should have?

You could be asked to answer one of these, or any another question in essay form.

Prior to Writing

Organize your thoughts in point form on a scrap of paper before you begin writing the essay.

Example: What challenges are government services facing in the future?

- Budget Cuts
- Terrorist Threats
- Racial Profiling and Race Relations
- Aging Personnel

No matter how long your list of points is, you should focus on three at most.

Structuring Your Essay

Write an essay appropriate for the time limit you are given. If the limit is 10 minutes, you will only have time to write a paragraph. If you are given thirty minutes or longer, structure your essay into multiple paragraphs. Break your paragraphs down in the following manner:

Single Paragraph

- Introductory Sentence
- Supporting Point # 1
- Supporting Point # 2
- Supporting Point # 3
- Concluding Sentence

Example:

There are many challenges facing government agencies that will require a great deal of personal commitment and dedication from all employees. Because of past instances of inappropriate spending and allegations of corruption, government employees will have to be extremely vigilant in order to perform their duties with the utmost integrity. The continual demand for services, accompanied by the public's demand for lower taxes, force government employees to do more with less. There is pressure to perform with fewer resources. Creative thinking will be required to approach problems in new ways. Demands for smaller, more accountable government agencies have led to cutbacks in the past and may do so again in the future. This creates a sense of uneasiness among workers who fear for their future employment. These are only a couple of the challenges government employees face as they attempt to perform their duties.

Multiple Paragraphs (Keep it to fewer than five paragraphs)

- Introductory Paragraph
  - Position you are taking. This can be to agree or disagree with a statement, or to support both sides.
  - Briefly state arguments you will make (in one or two sentences).
- Paragraphs # 2, 3 and 4

- State your point.
- Provide your evidence.
- Comment on the point.

• Concluding Paragraph

- Restate the position you made in one or two sentences.

Example:

Government employees across Canada will face several challenges in the coming years which will require a great deal of personal sacrifice and commitment from members of the organization. These challenges range from a demand for more government accountability, to budget cuts and uncertainty about the future. In order to solve these problems, government employees will need to work more effectively and creatively.

The Gomery Inquiry raised many issues concerning the spending decisions of politicians and government employees. Several people were found to be at fault, but the problems that existed with the sponsorship programs cast a cloud of suspicion over everybody working for the government. New rules for how decisions are made and who has the authority to make spending decisions have caused confusion and a sense of mistrust among government employees. Despite the fact that most employees are honest and hardworking, many feel threatened and targeted. Their ability to perform their jobs in the most efficient and effective manner will be undermined as they question their decisions and fear unjust persecution.

Paragraph #3 – Budget Cuts

Paragraph #4 – Uncertain Future

Intense scrutiny, budget cuts and uncertainty about the future are challenges that government employees will have to overcome. By hiring and keeping dedicated people, and by working with integrity in the new system, government employees will succeed in meeting these challenges.

Summary Tips

- Time yourself appropriately. Spend a couple of minutes writing your main ideas out in point form before beginning.

- Don't write too much. You are under a time limit. Make your points simple and give yourself enough time to print legibly.

- Keep your words simple. Don't use words if you don't know how to spell them or use them properly.

- If you are writing multiple paragraphs, each paragraph should contain one idea. If you are only writing one paragraph, separate your ideas by sentence.

- Don't attempt to include too much information. Keep your points clear and simple.

- BE ORGANIZED! Follow the formats shown above for your essays and paragraphs.

Teaching Material General

Observation and Memory

Memory

Developing your memory is a skill like any other, and will improve the more you practice. There are several methods to go about doing this.

1) Practice as many of the practice tests as possible to become familiar with the methods used during the real exam.
2) Practice reading passages and pictures in newspapers and magazines. Focus on names, and test yourself 30 minutes later to see how you did.

Observation

The goal of this exercise is to test your observation capabilities. When answering block design questions, count the number of blocks in a systematic manner (right to left / top to bottom). This way you will not accidentally count blocks twice.

Tips to improve your observation skills include:

1) Take the practice exams in this book (or on the website) to become familiar with the testing process.

2) Purchase "spot the difference" puzzles.

3) Do word find puzzles in local papers.

Pattern Solving

When you are attempting to solve patterns, be very observant and look for consistent changes and developments. These changes can include, but are not exclusive to:

1) Number of objects
2) Size of objects
3) Colour of objects
4) Shape of objects
5) Rotation / Flip of objects
6) Number of unique identifying marks

There are a number of different clues you must look for. The only way to improve your skills for this stage of the exam is to practice the puzzles in this book, on the website or puzzle books you may find in bookstores.

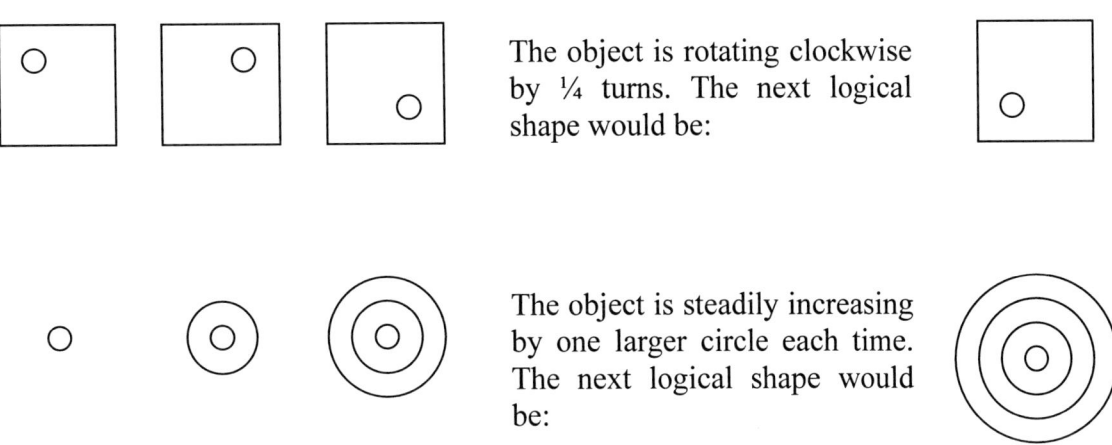

The object is rotating clockwise by ¼ turns. The next logical shape would be:

The object is steadily increasing by one larger circle each time. The next logical shape would be:

Sometimes you have to ignore information to detect the pattern.

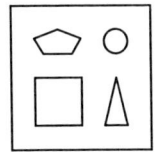 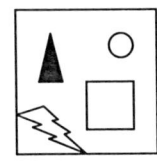 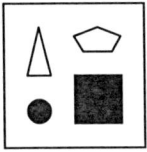

You must ignore the shapes in this case. The image is increasing the number of highlighted objects one at a time (0, 1, 2, 3). The next logical shape would be:

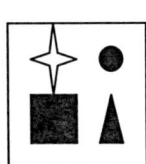

Spelling Section

The following is a list of words that you should be able to spell.

ability	abundance	absence	absolute
acceleration	acceptable	accessory	accident
accidentally	accuracy	accused	achieved
achievement	acknowledge	acknowledgement	acquaintance
acquired	acquittal	activity	actual
addition	addressed	adequate	administration
admissible	adolescent	advancement	advice
advise	agency	agreement	aggressive
alcohol	alight	align	alleged
allegedly	allergy	alliance	allocate
allowed	alternative	amateur	ambitious
ambulance	analyse	anniversary	announcement
annual	anonymous	answered	anticipated
antique	anxieties	anxious	apologise
apology	appalling	apparent	appeal
appearance	appliance	applicant	argument
artificial	assistance	attachment	authorities
authority	awkward	backwards	balance
bandage	bankrupt	barrister	basis
beautiful	before	behaviour	beneficial
bicycle	blanket	blatant	blockage
blurred	boredom	borrowed	boundaries
breach	broken	breathing	broaden
building	buoyant	bureau	burglaries
calculated	calendar	camera	campaign
candidate	capability	capital	cardboard
career	careful	carriage	casualty
caught	cause	centre	certificate
changing	chaos	character	chemical
circumstances	citizen	civil	claimed
clause	clearance	climate	coincide
colleague	collection	collision	column
combination	comment	commencement	commercial
commission	commissioner	commitment	committee
communication	community	compatible	competent
composure	comprehend	condemned	condition
consequence	consideration	consistent	constant
controversial	controversy	convenient	corpse
corroborate	corruption	coughing	courage
courageous	courteous	cultural	credible
criminal	critical	criticism	crucial
daughter	debris	decentralise	decisive
defendant	demonstrate	denial	deposit

depth	descendant	description	despite
detailed	determined	detour	development
diagnose	diameter	diesel	difference
direction	disability	disappointing	disappointment
disappearance	discipline	discount	discretion
discussion	disguise	dishonest	disillusionment
dismissed	disqualified	distance	distinction
distinguish	distressed	distribute	disturbance
diversity	division	document	domestic
dominant	double	doubtful	draught
duplicate	durable	duration	effective
efficient	electricity	element	eligible
eliminate	embarrass	emergency	eminent
emphasis	employment	empty	encounter
endeavour	energetic	enforce	engagement
enjoyable	enormous	enough	enthusiasm
environment	equality	equation	equipment
equity	eruption	essential	ethnic
evasion	exaggerate	examination	exceed
excess	exception	exceptional	executive
expenses	facilities	fatigue	favourite
feature	February	festival	fictitious
fierce	financial	fixture	floating
flowing	fluorescent	focussed	foreign
foreseeable	forgiveness	formal	fortnight
foundation	fraudulent	frightened	front
fulfilment	function	furniture	gauge
generate	genuine	government	gracious
gradually	grasping	grateful	grievance
grievous	growth	guarantee	guard
guest	guidance	handkerchief	handle
harbour	harden	haste	hazard
headquarters	health	height	heroin
highway	history	holiday	homicide
honesty	honorary	humour	hypnotize
ideal	identification	identify	ignore
illegal	illegible	illusion	illustrate
imagination	imitate	immature	immediately
immensely	immigration	impact	impartial
implement	implication	important	improvement
improvise	impulsive	inaccurate	incapable
incident	inclination	inclusion	income
incorporate	incredible	incriminate	inconsiderate
independent	indicate	indigenous	indirect
individual	industrial	inferior	inflammable

inflation	influence	influential	information
informative	inheritance	initial	initiative
injection	injuries	innocent	inspector
inspiration	instalment	instance	instead
institution	instrument	insulate	insurance
intangible	integrate	integrity	intellectual
intelligent	intend	intensity	intent
intercept	interference	interim	intermittent
internal	interpret	interrupt	view
intrigue	introduction	intrusion	invasion
investigation	invitation	irrational	irreconcilable
irresponsible	irritate	jealous	jeopardy
journalist	joyous	judgement	junior
juror	justice	justification	juvenile
keyboard	kilometre	kitchen	kneel
knocking	knowledge	knowledgeable	known
labourer	lacquer	laminate	language
laundry	lawful	leaflet	league
legality	legible	legislation	legitimate
leisure	length	leverage	liberty
library	licence	licensing	lighten
likelihood	limb	limited	linear
lining	liquidate	liquor	literally
literate	litigation	litre	location
logical	loose	lose	lunged
luxurious	machinery	magazine	magnificent
maintenance	malicious	management	manipulate
mannerism	manslaughter	marijuana	marketing
marriage	masculine	massacre	massive
material	maturity	maximum	mayor
measurement	mechanical	mediate	mediation
medicine	mediocre	memory	merchandise
merge	merit	metropolitan	microscope
middle	military	miniature	minimum
minister	mischievous	misconduct	miserable
missile	mission	mobile	modern
module	momentary	monitored	monopoly
monotonous	monument	motion	mould
mourning	movement	multiply	municipal
murmur	muscle	narcotic	narrative
narrow	nationality	naïve	natural
navigate	nearby	necessary	necessitate
negotiable	negotiation	neighbour	neighbourhood
nervous	neutral	niche	noisy
nominate	normally	nothing	novelty
nudged	nuisance	nurseries	nurture
nutrition	objective	obligation	obscenity
obscure	observation	obstacle	obsolete

obtain	obviously	occasion	occupation
occurred	occurrence	offence	offender
offensive	official	omitted	onus
opening	operation	opinion	opponent
opportunity	opposite	opposition	optimistic
option	ordeal	ordered	ordinary
organisation	orientation	original	otherwise
ought	outcome	outlining	overall
overturn	pacify	paddle	painting
palm	panic	parade	paragraph
parallel	parliament	participate	particle
particularly	particular	partition	partner
passage	patient	patrol	pattern
pause	pavement	payment	peculiar
pedestrian	penalty	pensioner	perceive
percentage	perception	perfect	performance
period	perish	permanent	permissible
permission	persevere	personal	personnel
persuade	pessimistic	petition	petrol
pharmacy	phase	phrase	physical
physique	picture	piece	pivot
placement	plaque	plastic	platform
plead	plenty	plight	plunge
poisonous	policing	policy	political
population	portable	portfolio	portion
position	positive	possession	possibility
postpone	posture	potential	practice
practising	practitioner	praise	precaution
precious	precise	predecessor	prediction
predominantly	preference	preferred	prejudice
preliminary	premature	premium	preparation
prescription	presence	presentation	preserve
pretence	preview	primary	priority
prison	private	privilege	probably
procedure	process	produce	professional
progression	prominent	promise	property
proprietor	prosecution	prospect	protection
protest	proved	provide	provoke
psychological	psychologist	publicity	publish
pulse	puncture	punishment	purchase
purpose	pursue	pursuit	quaint
qualification	qualify	quality	quantify
quantity	quarrelsome	quarter	quash
quell	questionable	queue	quickly
quiet	quite	quotation	racing
radiant	radical	radio	railing
random	range	rapid	rational
rationale	reaching	reactive	reading

realisation	reality	reasonable	reassurance
recalled	recede	receive	reception
recession	recipient	reckless	recognised
recommendation	reconciliation	reconstruct	recovery
recreation	recruit	rectify	recuperate
recurrence	reduction	redundancy	redundant
reference	reflecting	reflex	reformed
refreshment	refrigerator	refusal	registration
rehabilitation	reinforce	rejection	relapse
related	relationship	release	relief
relinquish	remaining	remember	remittance
remote	renowned	repair	repeated
repercussion	repetition	replica	reported
representation	reprisal	research	reservation
residential	resigned	resources	respectable
responsibility	responsible	restaurant	restitution
restriction	resuscitate	retention	retirement
retrenchment	reunited	review	reward
rival	robberies	rogue	rough
ruling	sacrifice	safety	salary
salvage	sample	satellite	savage
savoury	scald	scandal	scarce
schedule	scheme	scholar	scientist
scratched	search	secondary	secretaries
section	security	segment	seized
seizure	selection	sensible	sensitive
sentence	separate	sequence	sergeant
service	session	settlement	several
severe	shrewd	shriek	sign
signal	signature	significant	silence
simultaneous	situation	sizeable	skilful
smear	sociable	society	solemn
solicitor	solution	sophisticated	souvenir
specialize	specific	specifically	specimen
speculate	squander	square	stable
standard	staple	static	stationary
stationery	statistics	statue	strength
subject	submerged	subsequent	subscription
substance	substitute	succeed	sufficient
suggest	superintendent	superior	superstition
supplement	suppose	suppressed	surge
surrendered	survey	susceptible	suspend
suspicion	swallow	sympathy	tactic
technical	telephone	telephonist	syringe
tangled	technological	temperament	tenant
system	target	technology	temperature
tentative	temporary	terminated	termination
terminal	territory	tertiary	terrible

thirsty	thorough	theory	tissue
tobacco	thought	tongue	towards
tomorrow	traffic	tragedy	tradition
transfer	transparent	travelling	transport
triumph	trauma	truthful	turnover
trustworthy	ultimately	unaware	typical
unbelievable	unconscious	unbearable	undertaken
underrate	underground	uniform	union
unforeseen	unnecessary	unreliable	university
vacant	vacation	utilise	valuable
vandalism	vague	vehicle	venture
variation	version	vertical	verge
violence	visible	vigour	vocal
volume	vital	wager	warehouse
volunteer	wastage	waterproof	warrant
western	whereabouts	weapon	wilful
windcheater	whisper	withdrawal	worthy
window	wrong	wrongdoing	writing

Sorting Information

Alphabetic Ordering

Placing names in alphabetic order requires sorting names according to the conventional order of letters in the alphabet. Each nth letter is compared with the nth letter of other words in a list starting at the first letter of each word and advancing to the second, third, etc.

The words dovetail, manager, apple, dragon, animal and music would be placed in the following order:

animal, apple, dovetail, dragon, manager and music

This is done because **A** comes before **D** which comes before **M**. After the first letter of each word is sorted out, the second letter is looked at. **N** comes before **P**, **O** comes before **R** and **A** comes before **R**.

Names

With names, alphabetic ordering is done based on the last name, or surname, of an individual. The following people are placed in the correct alphabetic order:

Sean Bean, Michael Fox, Jeffery Michaels and Andrew Yang.

The last names determine the order of the list (Bean, Fox, Michaels, and Yang).

When two people share the same last name, the order is then based upon the first name. Jeff Stevens, Steven McCaffery and Trevor Stevens would be placed in the following order:

Steven McCaffery, Jeff Stevens, Trevor Stevens.

The order of the two "Stevens" last names is based on the first names Jeff and Trevor.

Titles

Titles are not considered in sorting until after the names have been sorted. For example:

Richard Allan III would come before Victor Allan II and
John Michael Jr. would come before Sean Michael.

Shorter Words

When attempting to alphebatize names which start with the same configuration of letters yet finish differently, the shorter word is place first in the order.

John Smithers, Michael Smith and Andrew Smitherson would be placed in the following order:

Michael Smith, John Smithers and Andrew Smitherson.

Dates

Dates are sorted by year, followed by month, and finally by day. The following dates are placed in order from earliest to latest:

Sample 1:
2001, June 12
2004, April 16
2005, December 8

It is usually safe to assume that the order is day/month/year:

Sample 2:
03/03/1975
13/10/1977
01/11/1977

However, sometimes there is a signal that month is placed first, as in the following sample. There cannot be a 15th month so the order of day and month must be reversed in this example:

Sample 3:
05/15/1981
07/08/1981
09/09/1983

Numbers

When sorting numbers, it is important to understand the proper place value of digits. Review the teaching material in the math section if necessary:

100 > 10 > 1 > 0.1 > 0.01 > 0.001

Only compare digits that share the same place value as the other digits. For example:

32 > 9 (compare 3 and 0)
0.1 > 0.0999 (compare 1 and 0)
3.2 > 3.1 (because 3 and 3 are equal, compare 2 and 1)
6.3 > 6.09 (because 6 and 6 are equal compare 3 and 0)

Coding & Decoding

Coding

Dealing with coding tables requires replacing information with numbers and letters. Below is an example of a coding table:

CODING TABLE
<u>Province Code</u>
British Columbia 3
Manitoba 4

<u>Age (years) Code</u>
18-24 C
25-34 D

<u>Sex Code</u>
Male 15
Female 16

<u>Years of Education Code</u>
Less than 8 H
9-12 J

The code for a 22 year old man from British Columbia with 7 years of education would be:

3 – C – 15 – H

3 replaces British Columbia
C replaces 22-year-old
15 replaces male and
H replaces 7 years of education

Decoding

For decoding, replace the existing code with the appropriate information from the table.

From the above example, the code 4 – D – 16 – H refers to a woman from Manitoba between 25 and 34 years of age who has less than 8 years of education.

Analogies and Sequences

Analogies and sequences are designed to measure a person's ability to reason. They are important components of general ability tests. Analogies tend to take the following format:

Telephone is to **numbers** just as **keyboard** is to:

- Letters
- Monitor
- Mouse
- Computer

Hat is to **uniform** just as **engine** is to:

- Steel
- Car
- Fast
- Movement

Dagger is to **sheath** just as **pistol** is to:

- Rifle
- Bullet
- Gun
- Holster

These questions test a person's ability to find a relationship between two words or symbols and to apply this relationship to another set of words or symbols. What you have to do is determine a linking word between the first two words, then apply that word to the second two words. From the above examples (the linking words are highlighted below):

Telephone **uses** numbers to dial just as keyboard **uses** letters to type.

Hat **is part of** a uniform, just as engine **is part of** a car.

Dagger **is stored** in a sheath, just as a pistol **is stored** in a holster.

Sample Questions

Attempt to solve the following questions using the above methodology. Answers are posted below.

1) Roads are to asphalt just as windows are to:

a) sun
c) glass
b) curtains
d) wall

2) Waves are to shore just as knife is to:

a) butter
c) cut
b) sheath
d) blood

3) Oxygen is to fire just as water is to:

a) land
c) earth
b) fish
d) human

4) Read is to book just as ride is to:

a) cat
c) television
b) stove
d) horse

5) Doctor is to medicine just as sun is to:

a) leaves
c) warmth
b) ocean
d) dark

Answers

1) Glass

Roads are made of asphalt just as windows are made with glass.

2) Butter

Waves cut into the shore just as a knife cuts into the butter.

3) Fish

Oxygen is required for fire to live just as water is required for fish to live.

4) Horse

Read is what you do to a book just as ride is what you do to a horse.

5) Warmth

Doctor distributes medicine just as sun distributes warmth.

OST

The Office Skills Test (OST) assesses an individual's ability to perform essential clerical tasks quickly and accurately. The test consists of five separately-timed sub-tests, each with 15 multiple-choice questions. The categories are:

· Filing
· Arithmetic
· Checking
· Vocabulary
· Following Directions

The test takes 1 1/2 hours to write and the minimum pass mark is 35/75. If you are unsuccessful you must wait 180 days before you can rewrite the test.

Only paper, pencils and erasers are allowed - no books, dictionaries, notes, writing paper, calculators, calculator watches or other aids are permitted in the room.

Detach the answer key to take the test.

OST ANSWER KEY

	A B C D E			A B C D E			A B C D E	
1)	○ ○ ○ ○ ○	___	16)	○ ○ ○ ○ ○	___	31)	○ ○ ○ ○ ○	___
2)	○ ○ ○ ○ ○	___	17)	○ ○ ○ ○ ○	___	32)	○ ○ ○ ○ ○	___
3)	○ ○ ○ ○ ○	___	18)	○ ○ ○ ○ ○	___	33)	○ ○ ○ ○ ○	___
4)	○ ○ ○ ○ ○	___	19)	○ ○ ○ ○ ○	___	34)	○ ○ ○ ○ ○	___
5)	○ ○ ○ ○ ○	___	20)	○ ○ ○ ○ ○	___	35)	○ ○ ○ ○ ○	___
6)	○ ○ ○ ○ ○	___	21)	○ ○ ○ ○ ○	___	36)	○ ○ ○ ○ ○	___
7)	○ ○ ○ ○ ○	___	22)	○ ○ ○ ○ ○	___	37)	○ ○ ○ ○ ○	___
8)	○ ○ ○ ○ ○	___	23)	○ ○ ○ ○ ○	___	38)	○ ○ ○ ○ ○	___
9)	○ ○ ○ ○ ○	___	24)	○ ○ ○ ○ ○	___	39)	○ ○ ○ ○ ○	___
10)	○ ○ ○ ○ ○	___	25)	○ ○ ○ ○ ○	___	40)	○ ○ ○ ○ ○	___
11)	○ ○ ○ ○ ○	___	26)	○ ○ ○ ○ ○	___	41)	○ ○ ○ ○ ○	___
12)	○ ○ ○ ○ ○	___	27)	○ ○ ○ ○ ○	___	42)	○ ○ ○ ○ ○	___
13)	○ ○ ○ ○ ○	___	28)	○ ○ ○ ○ ○	___	43)	○ ○ ○ ○ ○	___
14)	○ ○ ○ ○ ○	___	29)	○ ○ ○ ○ ○	___	44)	○ ○ ○ ○ ○	___
15)	○ ○ ○ ○ ○	___	30)	○ ○ ○ ○ ○	___	45)	○ ○ ○ ○ ○	___

	A B C D E			A B C D E	
46)	○ ○ ○ ○ ○	___	61)	○ ○ ○ ○ ○	___
47)	○ ○ ○ ○ ○	___	62)	○ ○ ○ ○ ○	___
48)	○ ○ ○ ○ ○	___	63)	○ ○ ○ ○ ○	___
49)	○ ○ ○ ○ ○	___	64)	○ ○ ○ ○ ○	___
50)	○ ○ ○ ○ ○	___	65)	○ ○ ○ ○ ○	___
51)	○ ○ ○ ○ ○	___	66)	○ ○ ○ ○ ○	___
52)	○ ○ ○ ○ ○	___	67)	○ ○ ○ ○ ○	___
53)	○ ○ ○ ○ ○	___	68)	○ ○ ○ ○ ○	___
54)	○ ○ ○ ○ ○	___	69)	○ ○ ○ ○ ○	___
55)	○ ○ ○ ○ ○	___	70)	○ ○ ○ ○ ○	___
56)	○ ○ ○ ○ ○	___	71)	○ ○ ○ ○ ○	___
57)	○ ○ ○ ○ ○	___	72)	○ ○ ○ ○ ○	___
58)	○ ○ ○ ○ ○	___	73)	○ ○ ○ ○ ○	___
59)	○ ○ ○ ○ ○	___	74)	○ ○ ○ ○ ○	___
60)	○ ○ ○ ○ ○	___	75)	○ ○ ○ ○ ○	___

Question 1
Place the following numbers in ascending order:
1) 357 2) 432 3) 271
4) 922 5) 1326

a) 3,2,1,4,5   b) 1,2,3,4,5
c) 2,5,4,3,1   d) 2,5,1,4,3
e) 3,1,2,4,5

Question 2
1) 20123 2) 20237 3) 20422
4) 20336 5) 20507

a) 1,2,4,5,3   b) 2,1,5,4,3
c) 3,1,4,5,2   d) 1,4,3,2,5
e) 1,2,4,3,5

Question 3
1) 10,321 2) 27,271 3) 18,491
4) 22,181 5) 29,231

a) 1,3,4,2,5   b) 5,2,4,3,1
c) 2,3,4,1,5   d) 3,5,1,4,2
e) 4,2,1,5,3

Question 4
Place the following names in alphabetical order:
1) Lisa Haff   2) Jack Miller   3) Victor Valentine
4) Robert Roby   5) Wendy Godwin

a) 5,2,1,4,3   b) 2,3,5,1,4
c) 3,4,2,1,5   d) 5,1,2,4,3
e) 1,5,2,3,4

Question 5
1) Richard Landon   2) Landon, Brandon 3) Michelle Landon
4) Landon, Caden   5) Mary Landon

a) 2,4,5,3,1   b) 1,3,5,4,2
c) 2,5,4,1,3   d) 5,2,4,1,3
e) 3,2,5,1,4

Question 6
Place the following dates in chronological order from earliest to most recent:

1) June 2, 1937 2) July 1, 1937 3) 3 June, 1937
4) 8/5/1937 5) February 20, 1937

a) 5,4,3,2,1 b) 2,5,1,3,4
c) 5,1,3,2,4 d) 3,5,1,2,4
e) 5,1,2,3,4

Question 7
1) 8/1/62 2) 10/2/63 3) 9/4/64
4) 8/7/62 5) 9/2/62

a) 1,4,3,2,5 b) 3,2,5,4,1
c) 4,1,5,2,3 d) 1,4,5,2,3
e) 1,5,3,2,4

Question 8
1) 5/8/1982 2) 9/27/82 3) 18/7/82
4) 15/5/1982 5) 10/12/82

a) 1,4,3,2,5 b) 4,5,1,2,3
c) 3,5,4,1,2 d) 5,2,3,4,1
e) 2,1,3,4,5

Question 9
Place the following numbers in ascending order:

1) 100,371 2) 100,221 3) 100,131
4) 100,522 5) 100,863

a) 2,3,4,5,1 b) 3,2,1,4,5
c) 1,4,2,5,3 d) 3,1,2,5,4
e) 4,5,3,1,2

Question 10
1) 20.07 2) 20.09 3) 20.11
4) 20.23 5) 20.04

a) 5,2,1,3,4 b) 5,1,2,4,3
c) 5,2,3,4,1 d) 5,1,2,3,4
e) 4,3,1,2,5

Question 11

1) 3 3/4	2) 5 3/4	3) 2 1/4
4) 6 2/3	5) 7 1/8	

a) 5,4,2,1,3   b) 3,1,2,4,5
c) 4,2,1,5,3   d) 2,1,5,4,3
e) 1,5,2,4,3

Question 12

Place the following names in alphabetical order:

1) Goody, Jacob   2) Isaac Goody   3) Linda Goody
4) Gliston Jr, Brady 5) Marcus Gliston III

a) 3,1,2,5,4   b) 4,5,1,3,2
c) 2,3,4,5,1   d) 2,5,4,1,3
e) 4,5,2,1,3

Question 13

1) Ruth Xavier   2) Ruth Yager   3) Ruth Yaeger
4) Ruth Xavvier   5) Ruth Yegar

a) 4,5,2,1,3   b) 1,4,3,2,5
c) 5,2,3,4,1   d) 2,5,1,4,3
e) 3,2,1,5,4

Question 14

Place the following dates in chronological order from earliest to most recent:

1) 22 March, 1992   2) 18 September, 1992 3) May 27, 1992
4) 8/21/1992   5) April 18, 1992

a) 1,5,2,3,4   b) 2,1,5,3,4
c) 3,1,4,5,2   d) 1,5,3,4,2
e) 5,2,3,1,4

Question 15

1) 1/9/1958   2) 9/25/1959   3) 7/19/1987
4) 11/28/1962   5) 10/2/1963

a) 3,5,4,2,1   b) 1,2,4,5,3
c) 3,1,2,4,5   d) 1,4,2,3,5
d) 3,2,1,4,5

Question 16
424 242 / 6 =
a) 70 605   b) 60 606
c) 70 607   d) none of these

Question 17
23.5 + 10 / 2 =
a) 16.75   b) 28.50
c) 13.25   d) 23.50

Question 18
Solve for "y":   3y + 7 = 28
a) 3   b) 9
c) 5   d) 7

Question 19
(42 + 7) / 7 =
a) 42   b) 27
c) 14   d) 7

Question 20
Which number is the smallest?
a) 11/32   b) 15/32
c) 1/4   d) 1/16

Question 21
3(4+12) + (5+7) =
a) 60   b) 72
c) 84   d) 93

Question 22
4{3 + (4x7) + (2x3)} =
a) 148   b) 46
c) 186   d) 59

Question 23
(4x5) + (3x6) + 12 =
a) 47   b) 61
c) 32   d) 50

Question 24
{(3+5) x (2+5)} + {(1+3) x (7+4)} =
a) 124 b) 100
c) 140 d) 222

Question 25
10(5+2) / 14=
a) 7 b) 11
c) 9 d) 5

Question 26
18/10 + 2.57 =
a) 4.2 b) 4.37
c) 3.79 d) None of the above

Question 27
2479.184 + 8739.838 + 6915.185 + 1845.493 + 3177.627 =
a) 22157.327 b) 2315.7327
c) 23157.237 d) None of the above

Question 28
Solve for y: 23 + 4 x y - 2 + 18 = 59
a) 3 b) 4
c) 5 d) None of the above

Question 29
25978 - 7975 =
a) 17993 b) 17893
c) 18003 d) None of the above

Question 30
807 x 138 =
a) 111366 b) 131166
c) 161366 d) None of the above

For the next 15 questions, identify how many columns from the original list match perfectly with the corresponding columns in the table.

Question 31

Original list
George Williams
463-987-123
Clarence Creek, Ont.
$45,672

Name:	P I Number	Address	Annual Salary
George Willaims	463-987-123	Clarence Creek, Ont.	$45,672
Peter Griffin	345-521-685	Marieville, Que	$56,839
Louise Harnell	746-831-930	Edmonton, Alberta	$31,298
Richard Pendegrast	431-287-623	Angasville, Man.	$25,310
Domnique Garcia	834-724-983	Kinkoro, P.E.I.	$83,245

a) One column is incorrect.

b) Two columns are incorrect.

c) Three columns are incorrect.

d) Four columns are incorrect.

e) No column is incorrect.

Question 32

Original list
Dominique Garcia
834-724-983
Kinkoro, P.E.I.
$82,345

Name:	P I Number	Address	Annual Salary
George Willaims	463-987-123	Clarence Creek, Ont.	$45,672
Peter Griffin	345-521-685	Marieville, Que	$56,839
Louise Harnell	746-831-930	Edmonton, Alberta	$31,298
Richard Pendegrast	431-287-623	Angasville, Man.	$25,310
Domnique Garcia	834-724-983	Kinkoro, P.E.I.	$83,245

a) One column is incorrect.

b) Two columns are incorrect.

c) Three columns are incorrect.

d) Four columns are incorrect.

e) No column is incorrect.

Question 33

Original list
Louise Harnell
746-831-930
Edmonton, Alberta
$31,298

Name:	P I Number	Address	Annual Salary
George Willaims	463-987-123	Clarence Creek, Ont.	$45,672
Peter Griffin	345-521-685	Marieville, Que	$56,839
Louise Harnell	746-831-930	Edmonton, Alberta	$31,298
Richard Pendegrast	431-287-623	Angasville, Man.	$25,310
Domnique Garcia	834-724-983	Kinkoro, P.E.I.	$83,245

a) One column is incorrect.

b) Two columns are incorrect.

c) Three columns are incorrect.

d) Four columns are incorrect.

e) No column is incorrect.

Question 34

Original list
Peter Grifinn
345-521-685
Mareville, Que.
$56,838

Name:	P I Number	Address	Annual Salary
George Willaims	463-987-123	Clarence Creek, Ont.	$45,672
Peter Griffin	345-521-685	Marieville, Que	$56,839
Louise Harnell	746-831-930	Edmonton, Alberta	$31,298
Richard Pendegrast	431-287-623	Angasville, Man.	$25,310
Domnique Garcia	834-724-983	Kinkoro, P.E.I.	$83,245

a) One column is incorrect.

b) Two columns are incorrect.

c) Three columns are incorrect.

d) Four columns are incorrect.

e) No column is incorrect.

Question 35

Original list
Richard Pendgrast
413-287-623
Angusville, Man.
$25,130

Name:	P I Number	Address	Annual Salary
George Willaims	463-987-123	Clarence Creek, Ont.	$45,672
Peter Griffin	345-521-685	Marieville, Que	$56,839
Louise Harnell	746-831-930	Edmonton, Alberta	$31,298
Richard Pendegrast	431-287-623	Angasville, Man.	$25,310
Domnique Garcia	834-724-983	Kinkoro, P.E.I.	$83,245

a) One column is incorrect.

b) Two columns are incorrect.

c) Three columns are incorrect.

d) Four columns are incorrect.

e) No column is incorrect.

Question 36

Original list
David Whitcomb
756-382-338
Winnipeg, MB
$67,435

Name:	P I Number	Address	Annual Salary
David Whitcolmb	756-382-383	Winnepeg, MO	$67,435
Ceasar Chavez	829-903-293	Bear River, Ont.	$72,134
Jack McCoy	987-284-654	Lewisville, Alberta	$89,546
Ryan Lockhardt	454-458-135	Hornepayne, Ont.	$22,345
Julia Childs	564-845-315	Chapais, Que.	$56,721

a) One column is incorrect.

b) Two columns are incorrect.

c) Three columns are incorrect.

d) Four columns are incorrect.

e) No column is incorrect.

Question 37
Original list
Jack McCoy
987-284-654
Lewisville, Alberta
$895.46

Name:	P I Number	Address	Annual Salary
David Whitcolmb	756-382-383	Winnepeg, MO	$67,435
Ceasar Chavez	829-903-293	Bear River, Ont.	$72,134
Jack McCoy	987-284-654	Lewisville, Alberta	$89,546
Ryan Lockhardt	454-458-135	Hornepayne, Ont.	$22,345
Julia Childs	564-845-315	Chapais, Que.	$56,721

a) One column is incorrect.

b) Two columns are incorrect.

c) Three columns are incorrect.

d) Four columns are incorrect.

e) No column is incorrect.

Question 38
Original list
Ryan Lockhart
454-485-135
Hornpayne, Ont.
$22,435

Name:	P I Number	Address	Annual Salary
David Whitcolmb	756-382-383	Winnepeg, MO	$67,435
Ceasar Chavez	829-903-293	Bear River, Ont.	$72,134
Jack McCoy	987-284-654	Lewisville, Alberta	$89,546
Ryan Lockhardt	454-458-135	Hornepayne, Ont.	$22,345
Julia Childs	564-845-315	Chapais, Que.	$56,721

a) One column is incorrect.

b) Two columns are incorrect.

c) Three columns are incorrect.

d) Four columns are incorrect.

e) No column is incorrect.

Question 39

Original list
Caesar Chavez
829-903-293
Beer River, Ont.
$72,143

Name:	P I Number	Address	Annual Salary
David Whitcolmb	756-382-383	Winnepeg, MO	$67,435
Ceasar Chavez	829-903-293	Bear River, Ont.	$72,134
Jack McCoy	987-284-654	Lewisville, Alberta	$89,546
Ryan Lockhardt	454-458-135	Hornepayne, Ont.	$22,345
Julia Childs	564-845-315	Chapais, Que.	$56,721

a) One column is incorrect.

b) Two columns are incorrect.

c) Three columns are incorrect.

d) Four columns are incorrect.

e) No column is incorrect.

Question 40

Original list
Julia Childs
564-845-315
Chapais, Que.
$56,721

Name:	P I Number	Address	Annual Salary
David Whitcolmb	756-382-383	Winnepeg, MO	$67,435
Ceasar Chavez	829-903-293	Bear River, Ont.	$72,134
Jack McCoy	987-284-654	Lewisville, Alberta	$89,546
Ryan Lockhardt	454-458-135	Hornepayne, Ont.	$22,345
Julia Childs	564-845-315	Chapais, Que.	$56,721

a) One column is incorrect.

b) Two columns are incorrect.

c) Three columns are incorrect.

d) Four columns are incorrect.

e) No column is incorrect.

Question 41
Original list
Lisa Barna
154-198-859
Thompson, Manitoba
$73,084

Name:	P I Number	Address	Annual Salary
Joseph Trabuco	156-458-456	Gagnon, Que.	$89,373
Emily Lawrence	231-451-854	Manitouwadge, Ont.	$90,738
Rebecca Lincoln	125-784-161	Sioux Lookout, Ont.	$28,385
Jonathan Fritz	871-569-158	Barrhead, Alberta	$58,493
Lisa Barna	154-198-859	Thompson, Manitoba	$73,084

a) One column is incorrect.

b) Two columns are incorrect.

c) Three columns are incorrect.

d) Four columns are incorrect.

e) No column is incorrect.

Question 42
Original list
Jonathan Frits
125-784-161
Barrhead, Alberta
$58,493

Name:	P I Number	Address	Annual Salary
Joseph Trabuco	156-458-456	Gagnon, Que.	$89,373
Emily Lawrence	231-451-854	Manitouwadge, Ont.	$90,738
Rebecca Lincoln	125-784-161	Sioux Lookout, Ont.	$28,385
Jonathan Fritz	871-569-158	Barrhead, Alberta	$58,493
Lisa Barna	154-198-859	Thompson, Manitoba	$73,084

a) One column is incorrect.

b) Two columns are incorrect.

c) Three columns are incorrect.

d) Four columns are incorrect.

e) No column is incorrect.

Question 43
Original list
Emily Lawrence
231-451-854
Manitouwadge, Ont.
$90,733

Name:	P I Number	Address	Annual Salary
Joseph Trabuco	156-458-456	Gagnon, Que.	$89,373
Emily Lawrence	231-451-854	Manitouwadge, Ont.	$90,738
Rebecca Lincoln	125-784-161	Sioux Lookout, Ont.	$28,385
Jonathan Fritz	871-569-158	Barrhead, Alberta	$58,493
Lisa Barna	154-198-859	Thompson, Manitoba	$73,084

a) One column is incorrect.

b) Two columns are incorrect.

c) Three columns are incorrect.

d) Four columns are incorrect.

e) No column is incorrect.

Question 44
Original list
Joseph Trabucco
156-458-465
Gagnon, Que.
$89,737

Name:	P I Number	Address	Annual Salary
Joseph Trabuco	156-458-456	Gagnon, Que.	$89,373
Emily Lawrence	231-451-854	Manitouwadge, Ont.	$90,738
Rebecca Lincoln	125-784-161	Sioux Lookout, Ont.	$20,385
Jonathan Fritz	871-569-158	Barrhead, Alberta	$58,493
Lisa Barna	154-198-859	Thompson, Manitoba	$73,084

a) One column is incorrect.

b) Two columns are incorrect.

c) Three columns are incorrect.

d) Four columns are incorrect.

e) No column is incorrect.

Question 45
Original list
Rebecca Lincoln
125-784-161
Sioux Look Out, Ont.
$28,358

Name:	P I Number	Address	Annual Salary
Joseph Trabuco	156-458-456	Gagnon, Que.	$89,373
Emily Lawrence	231-451-854	Manitouwadge, Ont.	$90,738
Rebecca Lincoln	125-784-161	Sioux Lookout, Ont.	$28,385
Jonathan Fritz	871-569-158	Barrhead, Alberta	$58,493
Lisa Barna	154-198-859	Thompson, Manitoba	$73,084

a) One column is incorrect.

b) Two columns are incorrect.

c) Three columns are incorrect.

d) Four columns are incorrect.

e) No column is incorrect.

Question 46
Expendable means:

a) Able to Grow   b) Disposable

c) Careful   d) Watchful

Question 47
Abominable means:

a) Hateful   b) Snowman

c) Violent   d) A bomb

Question 48
Mystique means:

a) Foggy   b) Air of Mystery

c) Failed   d) Began

Question 49
Commenced means:

a) Finished   b) Graduation

c) Failed   d) Began

Question 50
Daunting means:

a) Extensive   b) Developed

c) Charming   d) Discouraging

Question 51
Pigment means:
a) Colouring Agent b) Young Pig
c) Stupid d) Stubborn

Question 52
Forlorn means:
a) Worn Out b) Joyful
c) Dejected d) Grassy Quadrangle

Question 53
Vicious means:
a) Sticky b) Ferocious
c) Short d) Fast

Question 54
Malice means:
a) A Curse b) Hammer
c) Ill-will d) A Fever

Question 55
Sibling means:
a) Family b) Quarrel
c) Aunt d) Brother

Question 56
Larceny means:
a) Prostitution b) Robbery
c) Arrest d) Evasion

Question 57
Foreign means:
a) Unfamiliar b) Illegal Immigrant
c) Far Away d) Untrustworthy

Question 58
Atrocious means:
a) Attack b) Angry
c) Horrible d) Challenging

Question 59
Ethics means:

a) Tribal
b) Principles
c) Cultures
d) Corrections

Question 60
Adherent means:

a) Obeying
b) Disciple
c) Struggle
d) Angle

Answer the following 15 questions based on the information contained in the corresponding calendars

Question 61
<u>Information List</u>
Holidays are in bold.
Saturdays and Sundays are weekend days.
All days except holidays and weekends are working days.

S	M	T	W	T	F	S
	1	2	**3**	4	5	6
7	8	9	10	11	**12**	13
14	15	16	17	18	19	20
21	22	23	24	25	26	27
28	**29**	30				

What is the 10th day before the last weekend?

a) 17th
b) 16th
c) 15th
d) 14th
e) 13th

Question 62
What is the 3rd working day after the second holiday?

a) 22nd
b) 17th
c) 4th
d) 26th
e) 28th

Question 63
What is the 5th day before the second holiday?

a) 10th
b) 23rd
c) 7th
d) 18th
e) 2nd

Question 64
Information List
Holidays are in bold.
Saturdays and Sundays are weekend days.
All days except holidays and weekends are working days.

S	M	T	W	T	F	S
	1	2	**3**	4	5	6
7	8	9	10	11	**12**	13
14	15	16	17	18	19	20
21	22	23	24	25	26	27
28	**29**	30				

What is the last working day of this month?

a) 27th b) 19th

c) 22nd d) 30th

e) 12th

Question 65

What day of the week is the last holiday of this month?

a) Tuesday   b) Thursday

c) Friday   d) Sunday

e) Monday

Question 66
Information List
Holidays are in bold.
Saturdays and Sundays are weekend days.
All days except holidays and weekends are working days.

S	M	T	W	T	F	S
		1	2	3	4	5
6	**7**	8	9	10	11	12
13	14	15	16	17	18	19
20	21	22	**23**	24	25	26
27	28	29	30	31		

What is the last working day before the last weekend in the month?

a) 25th b) 26th

c) 28th d) 29th

e) 31st

Question 67

Information List
Holidays are in bold.
Saturdays and Sundays are weekend days.
All days except holidays and weekends are working days.

S	M	T	W	T	F	S
		1	2	3	4	5
6	**7**	8	9	10	11	12
13	14	15	16	17	18	19
20	21	22	**23**	24	25	26
27	28	29	30	31		

What is the fifth working day after the first holiday?

a) 10th b) 14th

c) 15th d) 8th

e) 3rd

Question 68

What date should an employee schedule an appointment if he does not want to use time off?

a) 18th b) 22nd

c) 7th d) 11th

e) 30th

Question 69

What is the last working day before the second holiday?

a) 27th b) 9th

c) 24th d) 22nd

e) 18th

Question 70

How many days are holidays this month?

a) 7 days b) 19 days

c) 6 days d) 5 days

e) 2 days

Question 71

Information List
Holidays are in bold.
Saturdays and Sundays are weekend days.
All days except holidays and weekends are working days.

S	M	T	W	T	F	S
			1	2	3	4
5	6	7	8	9	10	11
12	13	14	**15**	**16**	17	18
19	20	21	22	23	24	25
26	27	28	29	**30**	31	

How many working days lapse between the second and third holidays?

a) 9 days b) 13 days

c) 10 days d) 11 days

e) 15 days

Question 72

How many days are holidays this month?

a) 5 days b) 3 days

c) 12 days d) 7 days

e) 9 days

Question 73

How many days lapse between the first day of the month and the first holiday?

a) 12 days b) 8 days

c) 13 days d) 10 days

e) 16 days

Question 74

What is the 6th day immediately before the last holiday?

a) 15th b) 19th

c) 21st d) 24th

e) 26th

Question 75

What is the last working day this month?

a) 1st b) 24th

c) 18th d) 15th

e) 31st

OST Answer Key

1) E	26) B	51) A
2) E	27) D	52) C
3) A	28) C	53) B
4) D	29) C	54) C
5) A	30) A	55) D
6) C	31) A	56) B
7) D	32) B	57) A
8) A	33) E	58) C
9) B	34) C	59) B
10) D	35) D	60) B
11) B	36) C	61) A
12) E	37) A	62) B
13) B	38) D	63) C
14) D	39) C	64) D
15) B	40) E	65) E
16) D	41) E	66) A
17) B	42) B	67) B
18) D	43) A	68) C
19) D	44) C	69) D
20) D	45) B	70) E
21) A	46) B	71) A
22) A	47) A	72) B
23) D	48) B	73) C
24) B	49) D	74) D
25) D	50) D	75) E

GCT Level 1

The General Competency Test: Level 1 (GCT1) measures an individual's general cognitive ability. There are 50 multiple-choice questions covering the following three areas:

· Understanding Written Material
· Solving Numerical Problems
· Drawing Logical Conclusions

The test takes 45 minutes to write and the minimum pass mark is 18/50. If you are unsuccessful you must wait 180 days before you can rewrite the test.

Only paper, pencils and erasers are allowed - no books, dictionaries, notes, writing paper, calculators, calculator watches or other aids are permitted in the room.

Detach the answer key to take the test.

GCT1 ANSWER KEY

	A	B	C	D			A	B	C	D			A	B	C	D	E	
1)	○	○	○	○	___	11)	○	○	○	○	___	21)	○	○	○	○	○	___
2)	○	○	○	○	___	12)	○	○	○	○	___	22)	○	○	○	○	○	___
3)	○	○	○	○	___	13)	○	○	○	○	___	23)	○	○	○	○	○	___
4)	○	○	○	○	___	14)	○	○	○	○	___	24)	○	○	○	○	○	___
5)	○	○	○	○	___	15)	○	○	○	○	___	25)	○	○	○	○	○	___
6)	○	○	○	○	___	16)	○	○	○	○	___	26)	○	○	○	○	○	___
7)	○	○	○	○	___	17)	○	○	○	○	___	27)	○	○	○	○	○	___
8)	○	○	○	○	___	18)	○	○	○	○	___	28)	○	○	○	○	○	___
9)	○	○	○	○	___	19)	○	○	○	○	___	29)	○	○	○	○	○	___
10)	○	○	○	○	___	20)	○	○	○	○	___	30)	○	○	○	○	○	___

	A	B	C	D			A	B	C	D	
31)	○	○	○	○	___	41)	○	○	○	○	___
32)	○	○	○	○	___	42)	○	○	○	○	___
33)	○	○	○	○	___	43)	○	○	○	○	___
34)	○	○	○	○	___	44)	○	○	○	○	___
35)	○	○	○	○	___	45)	○	○	○	○	___
36)	○	○	○	○	___	46)	○	○	○	○	___
37)	○	○	○	○	___	47)	○	○	○	○	___
38)	○	○	○	○	___	48)	○	○	○	○	___
39)	○	○	○	○	___	49)	○	○	○	○	___
40)	○	○	○	○	___	50)	○	○	○	○	___

Question 1

There are 4 fathers and their children at the local mall. The children are ages 1, 2, 3 and 4. It was John's child's birthday. Brian is not the oldest child. Billy welcomed Anne just over a year ago. Ryan's child will be 3 next birthday. Daniel is older than Charlie. Jay's child is the oldest. Charlie is older than Ryan's child. How old is John's child?

a) 1 year old.   b) 2 years old.
c) 3 years old.   d) 4 years old.

Question 2

There are 4 fathers and their children at the local mall. The children are ages 1,2,3 and 4. It was John's child's birthday. Brian is not the oldest child. Billy welcomed Anne just over a year ago. Ryan's child will be 3 next birthday. Daniel is older than Charlie. Jay's child is the oldest. Charlie is older than Ryan's child. How old is Ryan's child?

a) 1 year old.   b) 2 years old.
c) 3 years old.   d) 4 years old.

Question 3

You are in charge of giving time off for the employees in your department. At Christmas time you must consider seniority for time off requests. Junior staff members get two weeks off, regular staff members get three weeks off, and senior level members get 4 weeks off. Team 1 has three regular staff member, one junior staff member and two senior staff members. Team 2 has four regular staff members, two junior staff members and three senior staff members. Which team has more than 20 weeks of time off available?

a) Team 2   b) Team 1.
c) Both Team 1 and 2   d) Neither team.

Question 4

Four types of plants grow in the garden, all during different seasons of the year. Lilies bloom in a season after roses. Ferns bloom before daffodils. Just as roses are dying off for the year, ferns are beginning to grow. All plants have a life span of two seasons. What is the order that the plants grow?

a) Lilies - Daffodils - Roses – Ferns   b) Daffodils – Ferns - Roses – Lilies
c) Roses - Daffodils – Lilies – Ferns   d) Daffodils – Roses – Lilies - Ferns

Question 5

There is a head of cabbage, a sheep and a wolf that need to be moved across a river. You can only move one at a time. The sheep will eat the head of cabbage and the wolf will eat the sheep if left alone together. What is the shortest number of river crossings it takes to transport everything across the river without having anything eaten?

a) 3   b) 5
c) 7   d) 9

Question 6

Your office has limited space to keep old files. Financial records are kept for 7 years. Medical insurance information is kept for 1 year. Job applications are kept for 3 years. Which of the following boxes of files can be discarded?

    A. A box containing 10-year-old financial records and 6-month-old medical insurance information.

    B. A box containing 2-year-old job applications and 7-year-old financial records.

a) A only

b) B only

c) Neither box A or B

d) Boxes A & B

Question 7

The police force has had five different police dogs over the past 10 years. They were named Sniffy, Dopey, Butch, Princess and Puff. Princess was not the first. Puff was the last dog used. Butch was on the force before Sniffy and after Princess. Who was the first dog the force used?

a) Butch

b) Dopey

c) Princess

d) Puff

Question 8

We are thinking of a letter between A and H. The letter is after C and before F. The letter is not E. Which letter are we thinking of?

a) D

b) C

c) F

d) E

Question 9

There are five video games to choose from. They are Carworld, The Zilla, Kong, Arctic Rush and Starfix. You have a Johnson gaming system. Only two of the games are compatible with your gaming system. Kong involves beat up a monkey. The Zilla is a fighting game. You do not like to play games that are violent. Starfix and Arctic Rush are made only for the Stanley gaming system. Which game will you play?

a) The Zilla

b) Kong

c) Carworld

d) Starfix

Question 10

There are a few guidelines to help screen job applications. All applications with no experience are discarded. Applications with job experience are forwarded to human resources and applications with management experience are only forwarded to department heads. You have received 15 applications. There are 3 with no experience and 4 with management experience. How many will be forwarded to human resources?

a) 7

b) 11

c) 5

d) 8

Question 11

Constable Smith issued 16 speeding tickets and 5 driving under the influence charges last month. The Police department had a total of 64 speeding tickets and 20 DUI charges last month. What percentage of speeding tickets last month were issued by Constable Smith?

a) 12%
b) 29%
c) 10%
d) 25%

Question 12

Constable Smith issued 16 speeding tickets and 5 driving under influence charges last month. The Police department had a total 64 speeding tickets and 20 DUI charges last month. What percentage of DUI chargers made last month was issued by Constable Smith?

a) 20%
b) 25%
c) 45%
d) 50%

Question 13

Every year, donations are made to the Rancher's Fund. The donations this year were $65,000, $28,000, and $800. What was the average donation made this year?

a) $28,000.67
b) $31,266.67
c) $32,900.67
d) $35,645.67

Question 14

The deceleration rate is 2 mph per second. If a car is traveling at 50 mph, how long will it take it to come to a complete stop?

a) 50 seconds
b) 100 seconds
c) 25 seconds
d) 75 seconds

Question 15

A chemical spill at a laboratory is moving at 20 gallons per minute. If the upended container holds 3,000 gallons, how long will it take for the container to empty half way?

a) 75 minutes
b) 150 minutes
c) 300 minutes
d) 50 minutes

Question 16

The total population of Baltimore State Prison is 350,000 inmates. 150,000 inmates white. The number of Hispanics is twice the number of African Americans. There are only whites, Hispanics and African Americans in the prison. How many Hispanics are in the prison?

a) 144,444
b) 66,667
c) 75,555
d) 133,334

Question 17

The dimensions of a storage building are 20' x 15' x 10'. What is the total available storage space if there is a mandatory 2' space required on top for ventilation?

a) 3400 cubic feet
b) 3000 cubic feet
c) 2400 cubic feet
d) 2000 cubic feet

Question 18

The annual salary of a manager is $65,000. If taxes and other benefits amount to 12% of the salary, what would be the total monthly take home pay?

a) $3572
b) $4767
c) $5417
d) $6532

Question 19

There are 60 stacks of money with 10 bills in each stack. The stacks are in denominations of $20, $5 and $1. There are 24 stacks of $1 bills and there are three times as many stacks of $5 bills as $20 bills. What is the dollar value of the $5 bills?

a) $2450
b) $240
c) $1800
d) $1350

Question 20

There are 24 stacks of money. Each stack of $20 bills contains 50 bills. Each stack of $5 bills contains 23 bills. Each stack of $1 bills contains 50 bills. There are twice as many stacks of $1 bills as $20 bills and three times as many $5 bills as $20 bills. What is the total amount of money?

a) $5780
b) $5620
c) $4750
d) $4375

Question 21

Government of Canada MEMORANDUM
To: All employees
From: Manager

Please note that effective April 2, 2005, the Federal Operations building will be closed. The offices will be moved to a new location on 1st Street. The old building needs to have some health-related renovations performed. Please route any calls for Federal Operations workers to the front office receptionist at the 1st Street location until further notice.

What is the general purpose of this memorandum?

a) Provide notification of what needs to be done with Federal Operation calls.

b) Discuss the health-related problems of fellow employees.

c) Provide notification of the receptionist's role.

d) Provide notification that a building will close for repairs.

e) Inform employees that the building is not safe for their health.

Question 22

When is the change effective?

a) 06/07/2004 b) 04/02/2005 c) 03/05/2001

d) 05/01/2003 e) 02/03/2005

Question 23

What location will the workers be moved to?

a) Main Street b) Fannin Street c) 1st Street

d) Louisiana Street e) 11th Street

Question 24

Which workers are affected by the change?

a) Purchasing b) Federal Operations c) Technical Support

d) Data Management e) Vendor Relations

Question 25

What should be done with phone calls to those people who have been moved?

a) Send them to voice mail.

b) Transfer them to the new location.

c) Send them to the person they are asking for.

d) Handle the call yourself.

e) Send them to the front office receptionist.

Question 26

Government of Canada MEMORANDUM
To: All employees
From: Manager

Review time has come and gone again. There have been some new promotions within our department and others. Let's congratulate John Wilcox on his promotion to Sr. Manager. Also, Susan Whitaker has received the honour of Vice President of Operations. In the Human Resource department, you will now need to request vacation time via Joshua McSpadden.

What is the general purpose of this memorandum?

a) Inform employees of recent promotions.

b) Inform employees that reviews are over.

c) Inform employees of staff member names.

d) Inform employees of staff member duties.

e) Inform employees that they did not receive a raise.

Question 27

Where have promotions taken place?

a) Inside of the department.
b) Inside and outside of the company.
c) Outside of the department.
d) Inside and outside of the department.
e) Outside of the company.

Question 28

Who was promoted to Sr. Manager?

a) John Wilcox
b) Susan Whitaker
c) Joshua McSpadden
d) Tim Turner
e) William Matthews

Question 29

Who was promoted to Vice President of Operations?

a) Joshua McSpadden
b) John Wilcox
c) Tim Turner
d) Susan Whitaker
e) William Matthews

Question 30

Who should vacation requests be directed at?

a) Susan Whitaker
b) John Wilcox
c) Tim Turner
d) Joshua McSpadden
e) Willam Matthews

Question 31

There are four cubicles in an office space where Jane, Kevin, Sean and Naomi work. The cubicles were placed in different positions as if they were points of a clock face. All of the workers face into the centre when they are working in the cubicles. Jane's cubicle was located at the start of every full hour. Sean was opposite Jane. When Kevin looked to his left he saw Jane's cubicle. Which of the following statements is true?

a) Kevin's cubicle is opposite Sean's.

b) Naomi's cubicle is located at 3 o'clock.

c) When Naomi looks to her right she sees Kevin.

d) Naomi's cubicle is between Kevin's and Sean's.

Question 32

Paintballs at Splatter Games come in red, blue, yellow and green. Bill, Ted, Marie, and Lisa are wearing shirts the same colours as the paintballs being used. Bill wears a red shirt, the same colour as Marie's paintballs. Lisa uses blue paintballs, the same colour as Ted's shirt. Ted's paintballs are the same colour as Lisa's shirt and vice versa. Bill and Marie also had alternated shirt and paintball colourations. Bill uses green paintballs. What colour is Lisa's shirt?

a) Blue.
b) Green.
c) Red.
d) Yellow.

Question 33

Can you tell what colour Ted's paintballs are?

a) Green.
b) Yellow.
c) Blue.
d) Red.

Question 34

Can you tell what colour Bill's paintballs are?

a) Red.
b) Blue.
c) Green.
d) Yellow.

Question 35

Can you tell what colour Marie's shirt is?

a) Yellow.
b) Green.
c) Red.
d) Blue.

Question 36

The population decrease in North Dakota occurs at an average rate of 3% per year. If the population were 300,000 in 2002, what would the population be in 2004?

a) 282,000
b) 318,270
c) 318,000
d) 282,270

Question 37

The homicide rate in 2000 was 543 murders. The murder rate increased by 2% each year between 2000 and 2004. The murder rate then dropped in 2005 by 5%. What is the murder rate in 2005?

a) 558
b) 587
c) 557
d) 561

Question 38

The total cost of a uniform is $255. The employee is allowed 6 weeks to pay for the uniform. If the employee pays $42.50 towards the total for the 6 weeks, what is the percentage paid each time?

a) 14%
b) 16%
c) 15%
d) 17%

Question 39

A field test for an unknown substance takes 15 seconds to come back on cocaine. Marijuana takes twice as long as cocaine to test for while LSD takes three times as long as marijuana to test for. How long does it take for an LSD test to come back?

a) 30 seconds
b) 90 seconds
c) 60 seconds
d) 45 seconds

Question 40

Two laptops and a stereo were stolen from a car. Together these items were sold to a pawnshop for $2000. The stereo was sold for $450 and the laptops for 30% of their original worth. The laptops were valued equally. How much was each laptop originally worth?

a) $ 1865
b) $ 2583
c) $ 2210
d) $ 2172

Question 41

Two printers and a computer were stolen. The thief got $550 for the three items. The thief sold the printers to relatives for $80 each. The computer was sold to a pawnshop for 62% of its original worth. How much was the computer sold for?

a) $270
b) $630
c) $390
d) $430

Question 42

The firehouse covers 5 distinct areas of the city; North, South, East, West, and Central. The North district of covered by 15 firefighters. South is covered by 10 firefighters. East is covered by twice as many as South, and Central is covered by three times as many as East. West is covered by one half as many as Central. How many firefighters cover the West district?

a) 30
b) 60
c) 20
d) 15

Question 43

It takes 3 minutes to drive from one stop-light to the next. To reach a client an employee must travel through three stop-lights. There is construction on two of the corners, which add an additional 4 minutes each. How long does it take the employee to get to the client?

a) 6 minutes
b) 12 minutes
c) 17 minutes
d) 9 minutes

Question 44

An employee injured at work will receive 60% of their normal pay while on medical leave. If the employee normally makes $36,500 gross each year, what will be the gross pay each month while on medical leave?

a) $3041
b) $1825
c) $1217
d) $1490

Question 45

At retirement, an employee receives 85% of the average of their last three annual salary amounts. If the three salaries used were $45,000, $52,000, and $65,000, what amount would the employee receive yearly after retirement?

a) $45,900

b) $44,200

c) $55,250

d) $54,970

Question 46

Answer the following questions based on what is stated or implied in the preceding passage.

Ontario outpaced the rest of the country during the strong economic boom of the 90's because it is the most integrated into the US economy of all the provinces. This integration has also led to the current economic slow down. The US has been sliding into a recession and the Canadian job market has lost 10,000 jobs since June. Recessions are cyclical events and Ontario will have to make it through some tough times ahead. While some provinces have gained, Ontario has lost 29,000 jobs. It is against that harsh reality - and forecasts of worse to come - that Finance Minister Jim Flaherty delivers his economic statement tomorrow. Up until now, Flaherty has been emphasizing that the long-term outlook for Ontario is positive. The immediate economic forecast is a problem. Since the only tune the Mike Harris government seems to know is 99 tax cuts and it's off to the mall, Flaherty is probably disposed to add another refrain. Tax cuts are not necessarily the most effective form of stimulus for an economy that is suffering due to a global recession. But tax cuts won't do much for Ontarians who lose their jobs to recession. These are usually the most vulnerable workers - the workers with the fewest skills, the lowest incomes and the most meagre savings to fall back on.

What is the meaning of the word "emphasizing" in this paragraph?

a) denying, falsifying

b) guessing, hypothesizing

c) stressing, accentuating

d) crediting, acknowledging

Question 47

Vulnerable in this paragraph means:

a) flexible

b) open

c) uneducated

d) susceptible

Question 48

One general theme that the author is suggesting is:

a) Tax cuts will help fight the economic downturns.

b) Governments are not in complete control of the economy.

c) Ontario has a stronger economy than the US.

d) The previous government had better management packages.

Question 49

Which of the following actions would the author probably like the government to take?

a) Reduced reliance on the American economy.

b) Downsizing government to improve efficiency.

c) Further corporate tax cuts to encourage growth.

d) Increased spending on job training.

Question 50

Which of the following statements is true according to the above article?

a) America is to blame for the economic downturn.

b) Recessions occur about once every seven years.

c) Ontario's economy is more integrated with the American economy than Alberta.

d) Ontario has lost 39,000 jobs in the last year.

GCT1 Answer Key

1) C	26) A
2) B	27) D
3) A	28) A
4) D	29) D
5) C	30) D
6) C	31) B
7) B	32) D
8) A	33) B
9) C	34) C
10) D	35) B
11) D	36) D
12) B	37) A
13) B	38) D
14) C	39) B
15) A	40) B
16) D	41) C
17) C	42) A
18) B	43) C
19) D	44) B
20) A	45) A
21) E	46) C
22) B	47) D
23) C	48) B
24) B	49) D
25) E	50) C

Question 1

The clue about Billy lets you know that Anne is the 1 year old. The clue about Ryan lets you know that his child is 2 years old. The clue about Jay lets you know his child is the 4 year old. This leaves John's child to be the 3 year old.

Question 2

The clue about Billy lets you know that Anne is the 1 year old. The clue about Ryan lets you know that his child is 2 years old. The clue about Jay lets you know his child is the 4 year old. This leaves John's child to be the 3 year old.

Question 3

Team 1 calculations: (3 X 3) + (1 X 2) + (2 X 4) = 19 weeks

Team 2 calculations : (4 X 3) + (2 X 2) + (3 X 4) = 28 weeks.

Question 4

As roses are dying off, ferns are beginning to grow, so there is a season between roses and ferns.　　　　　　　　...Ferns - ? - Roses - ? - Ferns...

Lilies bloom after roses, and because every plant blooms during a different season, the final order has to be:　　　　...Ferns - Daffodils - Roses - Lilies...

Question 5

Cross 1 – Sheep
Cross 2 – Return
Cross 3 – Cabbage
Cross 4 – Return with sheep
Cross 5 – Wolf
Cross 6 – Return
Cross 7 - Sheep

Question 6

Box A cannot be kept since the medical insurance information is less than a year old. Box B cannot be kept since the job applications are less than 3 years old.

Question 7

The clue about Puff places that dog as the last one. Princess was not the first one and Butch and Sniffy both come after Princess. This makes Dopey the first dog.

Question 8

The letter must be either D or E and the last clue lets you know that it isn't E.

Question 9

The clue about the type of games that Kong and The Zilla lets you know the person would not play them since they are violent. The games Starfix and Arctic Rush are not compatible with your system. This leaves Carworld.

Question 10

The 3 applications with no experience and the 4 with management experience will not be forwarded to human resources. 15 - 7 = 8. This leaves 8 applications to be forwarded to human resources.

Question 11

D - Total speeding tickets issued = 64. Speeding tickets issued by Constable = 16.
Thus percentage = 16/64 = 0.25 or 25%.

Question 12

B - Total DUI charges = 20. DUI charges issued by Constable = 5.
Thus percentage = 5/20 x 0.25 or 25%.

Question 13

$65,000 + $28,000 + $800= $93,800. $93,800 / 3= $31,266.67.

Question 14

50/2=25.

Question 15

First, determine how much 1/2 of the container holds.

    3000/2 = 1500 gallons.

Then, determine how long it will take to drain 1500 gallons.

    1500 / 20 = 75 minutes.

Question 16

x = African American population
2x = Hispanic population
150,000 + x + 2x = 350,000
3x = 200,000
x = 66,667
2x = 133,334

Question 17

Length x width x (height-2) = 20 x 15 x 8 = 2400 cubic feet.

Question 18

$65,000 x 0.88 = $4767

Question 19

There are a total of 60 stacks of bills, so the algebraic equation would look like this:
24 + y + 3y = 60 ("y" represents the number of $20 bills).
4y = 36
y = 9 (there are 9 stacks of $20 bills, therefore there are 27 stacks of $5 bills).
$5 x 10 x 27 = $1,350 in $5 bills.

Question 20

There are a total of 24 stacks of bills, so the algebraic equation would look like this:
y + 2y + 3y = 24
6y = 24
y = 4 (there are 4 stacks of $20 bills)
The next step is to sum the total value of all bills.
($20 x 4 x 50) + ($1 x 8 x 50) + ($5 x 12 x 23) = $5,780

Refer to the Answer Key for answers to Questions 21-30

Question 31

Jane's cubicle is at 12 o'clock.
Naomi's cubicle is at 3 o'clock.
Sean's cubicle is at 6 o'clock.
Kevin's cubicle is at 9 o'clock.

Question 32

The first clue lets you know that Marie's paintballs are red and Bill's shirt is red. You know Lisa had blue paintballs and Ted's shirt is blue as well. You are told that Bill had green paintballs. This leaves yellow as the only other colour.

Question 33

The first clue lets you know that Marie's paintballs are red and Bill's shirt is red. You know Lisa had blue paintballs and Ted's shirt is blue as well. You are told that Bill had green paintballs. This leaves yellow as the only other colour.

Question 34

The first clue lets you know that Bill's shirt was red which is the same colour as Marie's shirt. Lisa has blue paintballs, which is the same colour as Ted's shirt. Since Lisa has a yellow shirt you know that Ted is using blue paintballs. This leaves green for the other team.

Question 35

The first clue lets you know that Bill's shirt was red, which is the same colour as Marie's shirt. Lisa has blue paintballs, which is the same colour as Ted's shirt. Since Lisa has a yellow shirt you know that Ted is using blue paintballs. This leaves green for the other team.

Question 36

300,000 x 0.03=9,000
300,000 - 9,000=291,000 in 2003
291,000 x 0.03 = 8,730
291,000 - 8,730=282,270 in 2004

Question 37

2000 = 543
2001 = 543 x 1.02 = 553.86
2002 = 553.86 x 1.02 = 564.9372
2003 = 564.9372 x 1.02 = 576.2359
2004 = 576.2359 x 1.02 = 587.7607
2005 = 587.7607 x 0.95 = 558.372 which rounds to 558

Question 38

$42.50/ $255 = 0.166666 or 16.6% which rounds to 17%.

Question 39

Cocaine = 15 seconds, Marijuana = 15 x 2=30 seconds.
LSD = 30 x 3 = 90 seconds.

Question 40

The laptops brought in $2000 - 450 = $1550 dollars or $775 each.
The original value of the laptops is determined by setting up an algebraic equation.
Laptops = 775 x 100 / 30 = $ 2583.33.

Question 41

All three units were sold for $550. The two printers represent $160 (80 x 2). This means that the computer was sold for $550 – $160 = $390. There is unnecessary information in the question that must be discarded.

Question 42

North = 15 firefighters.

South = 10 firefighters.

East = 10 x 2 = 20 firefighters.

Central = 20 x 3 = 60 firefighters.

West = 60 / 2 = 30 firefighters.

Question 43

(3 x 3) + 8 = 17

Question 44

(36,500/12) x 0.6 = $1,825

Question 45

($45,000 + $52,000 + $65,000) / 3 = $ 54,000
$54,000 x 0.85 = $ 45,900

Refer to the Answer Key for answers to questions 46-50

GCT Level 2

The General Competency Test: Level 2 (GCT2) measures an individual's general cognitive ability. There are 90 multiple-choice questions. The categories of the exam include:

· Vocabulary
· Figural Relations
· Number and Letter Series
· Numerical Problems
· Analytical Reasoning

The test takes 2 1/4 hours to write and the minimum pass mark is 51/90. If you are unsuccessful you must wait 180 days before you can rewrite the test.

Only paper, pencils, erasers and calculators are allowed - no books, dictionaries, notes, or other aids are permitted in the room.

Detach the answer key to take the test.

GCT2 ANSWER KEY

Question 1

The neighbourhood children are waiting for the bus. They are in kindergarten, grade 2, 3, 6, 7 and 9. Lisa is in a lower grade than Bonnie, but in a higher grade than Jimmy. Michael is in the lowest grade. Robert is in a grade lower than Jimmy. Bonnie is two grades lower than Rachael. Robert is older than Michael but younger than Jimmy. Rachael is oldest of all. Jimmy is three grades higher than Michael. What grade is Bonnie in?

a) 7th
b) 6th
c) 3rd
d) 9th

Question 2

The horse race is underway. The solid brown horse is ahead of the solid black horse, who is ahead of the white horse with brown spots. The black horse with brown spots is trailing the white horse with brown spots. Which horse is in second place?

a) White with brown spots.
b) Solid brown.
c) Black with brown spots.
d) Solid black.

Question 3

Three girls on the gymnastics team recently completed a competition. Their events were beam, bars and floor. Amber placed second in beam, ahead of Elaine. Sarah was last on the bars, immediately behind Elaine. The team member who placed 2nd and 3rd in the other two events placed 1st in floor. What place did Sarah get on the beam?

a) 3rd
b) 2nd
c) 1st
d) 4th

Question 4

There are more employees working at noon than overnight. There are fewer employees working in the morning than in the evening. Morning and evening times require more employees than noon and overnight. Which shift uses the most employees?

a) Morning.
b) Evening.
c) Noon.
d) Overnight.

Question 5

Four women are talking about their favourite flower. They agree on Indian paintbrush, bluebonnet, daisy and rose. Each chooses a different favourite. Roberta likes the flower whose colour starts with the letter of her first name. Nancy's favourite colour is blue and so is her flower. Veronica does not like the Indian paintbrush. What is Tina's favourite flower?

a) Daisy.
b) Rose.
c) Indian paintbrush.
d) Bluebonnet.

Question 6

Students trying out for the swim team are tested to see how far they can swim. Gina has an asthma attack while in the water and has to stop swimming. Tina swims 10 metres less than Nina and 45 metres less than Christa. Who was able to swim the farthest?

a) Christa.   b) Tina.
c) Gina.   d) Nina.

Question 7

The men in an office decided to measure how much water they were drinking in a day. Ryan was drinking more than Tom. Jim was drinking less than Tom and Bob was drinking less than Jim. Who was drinking the second least amount of water each day?

a) Ryan.   b) Jim.
c) Bob.   d) Tom.

Question 8

The women in an office compared the different lengths of their hair. Britney has longer hair than Veronica, but shorter hair than Courtney. Lisa and Veronica have the same length of hair. Suzanne has longer hair than Julie. Julie has the same length of hair as Britney. Who in the office has medium-length hair?

a) Courtney and Lisa.   b) Julie and Lisa.
c) Veronica and Suzanne.   d) Britney and Julie.

Question 9

Some friends go to adopt a cat at the local pet store. There is an orange tabby, a white, long haired Persian, a tan Siamese with blue eyes and a calico mix. Julie does not like the colour white and is allergic to long fur. Charlie only likes long-haired cats and does not like cats with blue eyes. Leslie only likes blue-eyed cats and Danny does not mind a mixed cat. Julie's favourite color is orange. What cat does Charlie pick?

a) White Persian.   b) Tan Siamese.
c) Orange tabby.   d) Calico mix.

Question 10

The rehabilitation clinic sees more knee than neck problems. They see more shoulder problems than back problems. They see fewer shoulder problems than neck problems, but more knee than neck problems. What is the problem most often seen at the rehabilitation clinic?

a) Shoulder.   b) Neck.
c) Knee.   d) Back.

Question 11

Which is the missing image in the following patterns?

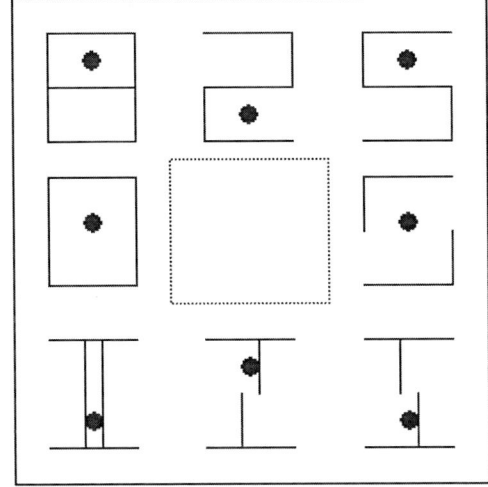

a) b) c) d)

e) f) g) h)

Question 12

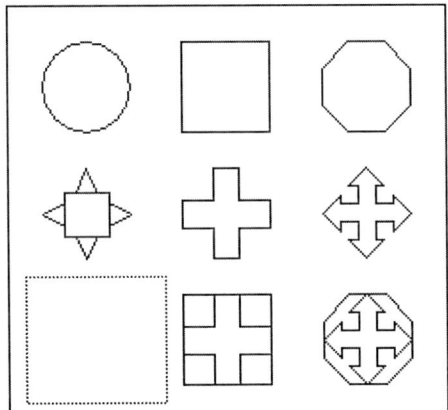

a) b) c) d)

e) f) g) h)

Question 13

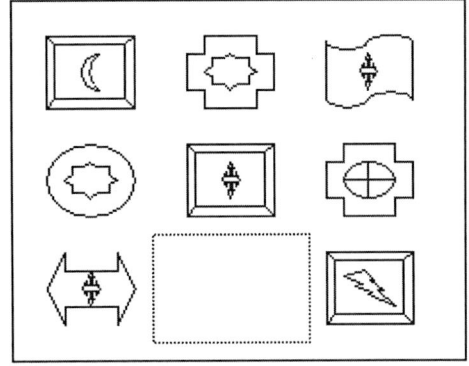

a) b) c) d)

e) f) g) h)

Question 14

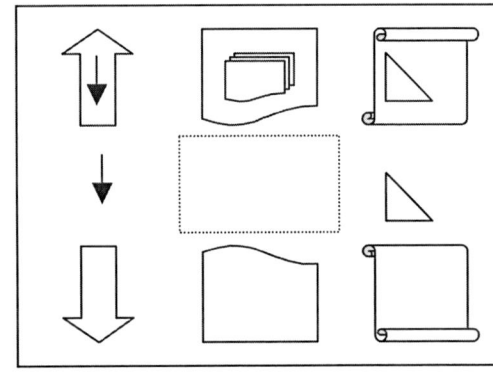

a) b) c) d)

e) f) g) h)

Question 15

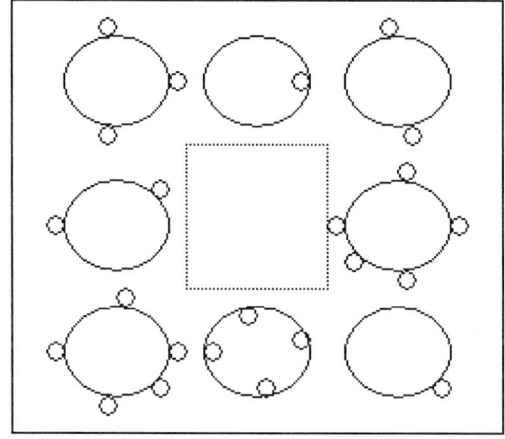

 a)
 b)
 c)
 d)

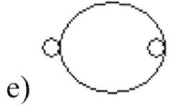 e)
 f)
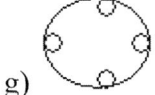 g)
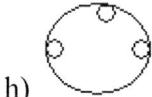 h)

Question 16

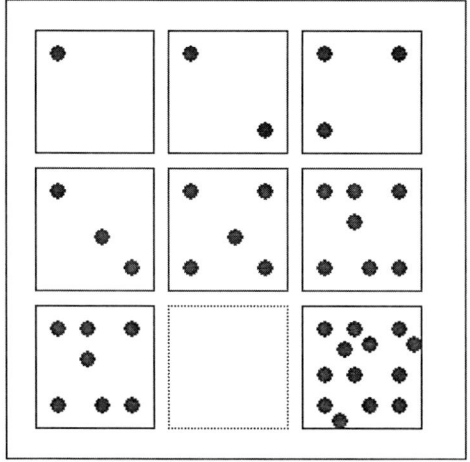

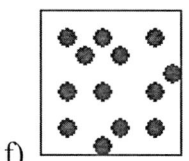
a)   b)   c)   d)

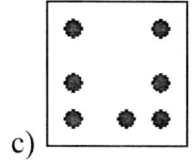
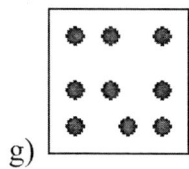
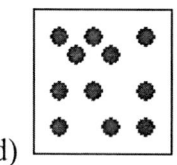
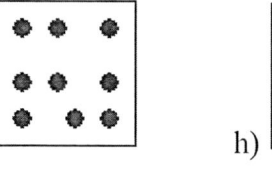
e)   f)   g)   h)

Question 17

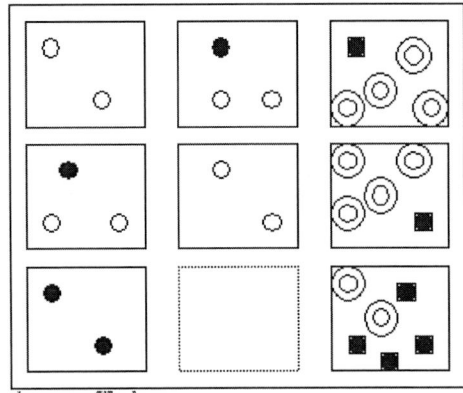

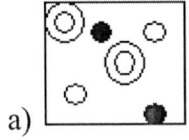 a)
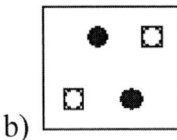 b)
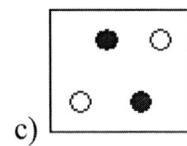 c)
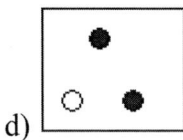 d)

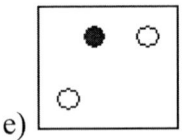 e)
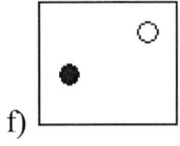 f)
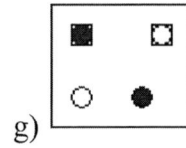 g)
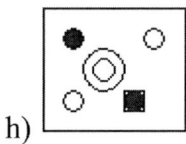 h)

Question 18

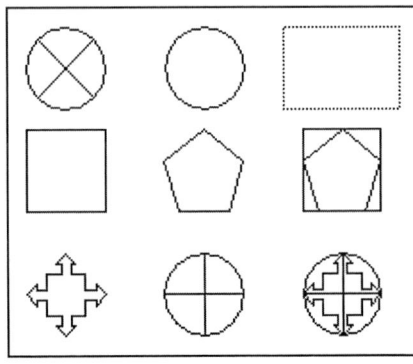

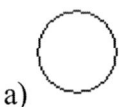 a)
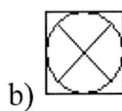 b)
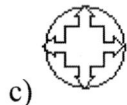 c)
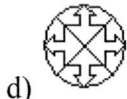 d)

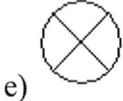 e)
 f)
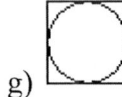 g)

Question 19

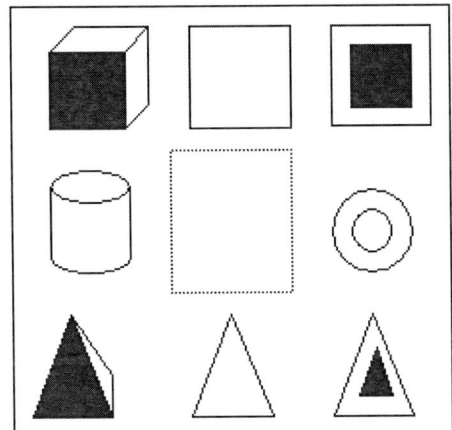

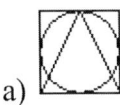
a)

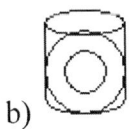
b)

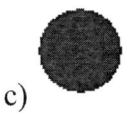
c)

d)

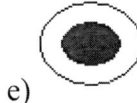
e)

f)

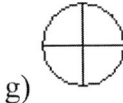
g)

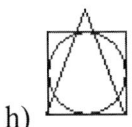
h)

Question 20

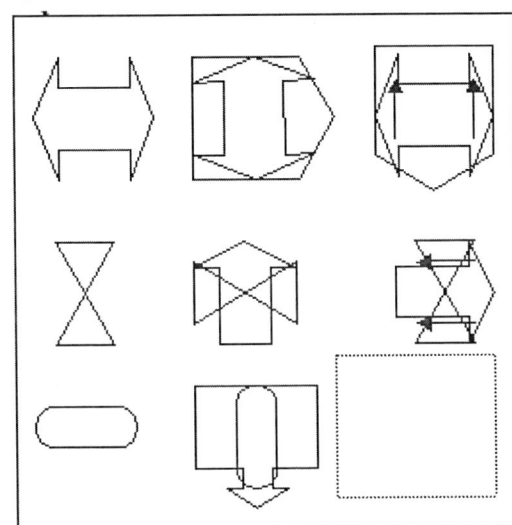

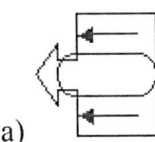
a)

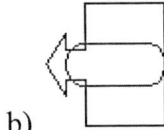
b)

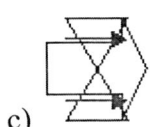
c)

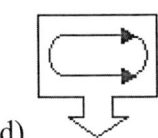
d)

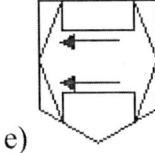
e)

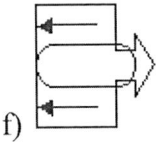
f)

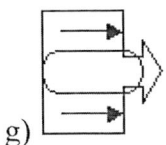
g)

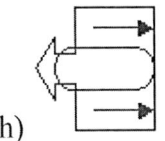
h)

Question 21

75 people came to the single's dance. If there were five more women than men, how many men were there?

a) 25   b) 30

c) 35   d) none of these

Question 22

Paulina is painting a picture on a canvas measuring 2 m by 3 m. She has painted 35% of the area. How much area is left to be painted?

a) 2.7 meters squared   b) 3.5 meters squared

c) 3.9 meters squared   d) 4.3 meters squared

Question 23

Natasha Kaya works 8 hours a day, 38 hours a week. She earns $6 an hour. How much will she earn in 3 weeks?

a) $226   b) $228

c) $660   d) $684

Question 24

A car stereo was stolen from a car outside of the pawn shop. It was originally purchased for $600. Street value is only 15% of the original purchase price. How much can the criminal resell the stereo for?

a) $15   b) $65

c) $70   d) $90

Question 25

140 pounds of drugs are confiscated during an arrest. There is marijuana, cocaine and crystal meth. If 20% of the drugs are cocaine and the remainder was made up of equal parts of marijuana and crystal meth, how many pounds of marijuana were confiscated?

a) 42 pounds   b) 50 pounds

c) 56 pounds   d) 62 pounds

Question 26

In phys. Ed class, Stephen Chan completed the 4 km run in 24 minutes. What is this speed in kilometres per hour?

a) 10   b) 11

c) 12   d) 13

Question 27

Solve for "x": $(7 - x) / 4 = x - 10$

a) 11.3   b) 9.4

c) 7.4   d) 5.3

Question 28

A sink holds 12 L of water. Water drains from it at a rate of 44 L a minute. How long would it take to empty the sink?

a) 1.2 minutes	b) 16 seconds
c) 12 seconds	d) 20 seconds

Question 29

Water flows through a pipe at 20,000 cm cubed per second. How many minutes does it take to fill a rectangular tank 3m x 4m x 5m?

a) 20 minutes	b) 35 minutes
c) 50 minutes	d) none of these

Question 30

There are 240 people at a picnic. People have a choice of cola or lemonade. For every two people that had a cola, one had a lemonade. How many people had cola?

a) 100	b) 160
c) 190	d) none of these

Question 31

If, when driving, you see a ball bounce into the road you should look for a _____ to come next.

a) bat	b) car
c) child	d) bicycle

Question 32

The young prince was so _____ , he laid his coat over a puddle for the princess to step over.

a) gallant	b) inhibited
c) passive	d) timid

Question 33

In the Middle Ages _____ were used to throw large stones over fortified walls.

a) pistols	b) catapults
c) shotguns	d) slingshots

Question 34

A country which does not take sides during a war or international crises is considered to be _____ .

a) neutral	b) aggressive
c) threatening	d) chicken

Question 35
When an aquatic rescue is being made, Coast Guard officers need to avoid placing too much _____ on the rescue lines. This can cause the lines to snap.

a) laxity　　　　　　　　　　　　b) strain

c) water　　　　　　　　　　　　d) lubricant

Question 36
Identify the synonym for the following words.

Prototype

a) Archetype　　　　　　　　　　b) Typewriter Ribbon

c) Standard　　　　　　　　　　 d) Oblique

Question 37
Arbitration

a) Severance　　　　　　　　　　b) Mediation

c) Aggression　　　　　　　　　 d) Channel

Question 38
Council

a) Advice　　　　　　　　　　　　b) Judgment

c) Ruling Body　　　　　　　　　d) Encourage

Question 39
Revere

a) Turn Around　　　　　　　　　b) Despise

c) Respect　　　　　　　　　　　d) Coat Lapel

Question 40
Route

a) Intercourse　　　　　　　　　b) Direction

c) Challenge　　　　　　　　　　d) Encourage

Question 41
Identify which number should replace the asterisk in the following questions.

	135	486
36	45	162
*	15	27

a) 6　　　　　　　　　　　　　　b) 8

c) 10　　　　　　　　　　　　　 d) None of the above.

Question 42

	203	207
195	197	199
189	191	*

a) 196

b) 193

c) 197

d) None of the above.

Question 43

12	48	*
6		96
3	12	48

a) 154

b) 176

c) 192

d) None of the above.

Question 44

4	12	72
2	6	*
1		18

a) 30

b) 36

c) 22

d) None of the above.

Question 45

103	354	*
225	476	727
	351	602

a) 601

b) 724

c) 607

d) None of the above.

Question 46

What are the missing numbers in the following patterns?
?, 16, 32, 64, 128, 256, ?...

a) 10, 524

b) 8, 512

c) 6, 412

d) None of the above.

Question 47

-14, ?, ?, 7, 14, 21...

a) -7, -1

b) -6, -1

c) -7, 0

d) None of the above.

Question 48
100, 97, 91, 82, 70, ?...
a) 61
b) 65
c) 67
d) None of the above.

Question 49
2, 8, 26, 80, ?...
a) 240
b) 232
c) 252
d) None of the above.

Question 50
?, 15, 27, 51, ?, 195...
a) 9, 93
b) 7, 97
c) 9, 99
d) None of the above.

Question 51
You are expecting an important shipment of auto parts. You placed the order three weeks ago, but the suppliers advised it would be running late. Four days ago you were advised that the parts were arriving in six days, and would immediately be shipped to you. You typically expect shipping to take two days. When should you expect the delivery?

a) 4 days
b) 2 weeks
c) 8 days
d) 10 days

Question 52
The ladies in the office wear different styles of pants and skirts. There are fewer long skirts than short skirts. There are fewer shorts than long skirts. There are more shorts than pants. Which type of clothing is the least prevalent in the office?

a) Short skirts.
b) Pants.
c) Long skirts.
d) Shorts.

Question 53
Four teams are playing in a tournament. Half way through the day, Team 4 is ahead of Team 1, but behind Team 2. Team 3 is ahead of Team 2 at this point in the day. Which team is in the same place as their team number?

a) Team 1.
b) Team 2.
c) Team 3.
d) Team 4.

Question 54

The family has decided to paint four rooms in the house: the kitchen, the dining room, the master bedroom and the guest bathroom. The kitchen is larger than the guest bathroom, but smaller than the dining room. The master bedroom is not smaller than any of the rooms. Which room will take the least amount of paint?

a) Dining room.
b) Master bedroom.
c) Kitchen.
d) Guest bathroom.

Question 55

The customer service department determines bonuses paid based on the number of calls an employee completes each day. Kristina handles twice as many calls as Frank. Frank handles more calls than Natalie. Angela handles as many as Natalie and Frank combined. Which operator handles the most calls?

a) Frank.
b) Angela.
c) Natalie.
d) Kristina.

Question 56
What are the next items in the patterns below?

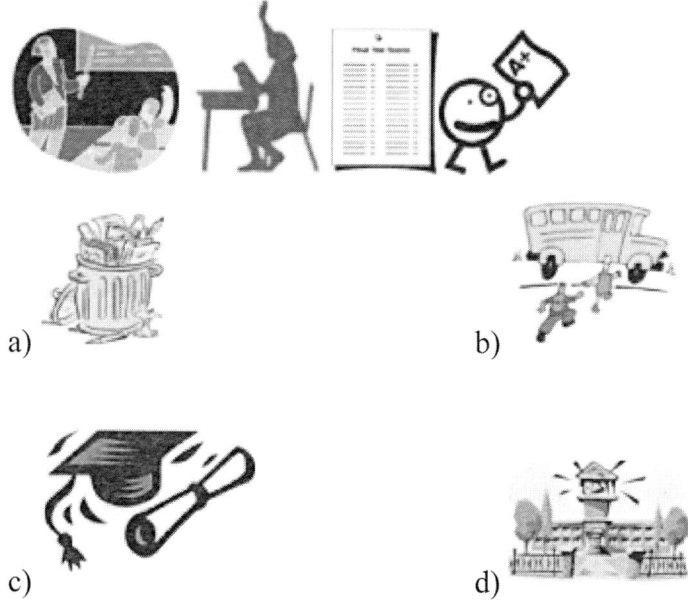

Question 57

Apple, cat, enigma, giraffe…

a) Ostrich, umbrella, guinea
b) Insane, kitten, monkey
c) Stop, under, yak
d) Cantaloupe, quill, wombat

Question 58

Apple, car, bat, dingo, cover, engine…

a) Oat, nickel, simple, rhinoceros
b) Elephant, jungle, tipped, car
c) Dent, fox, elbow, goose
d) Quail, walrus, x-ray, zebra

Question 59

a) 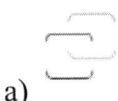
b) 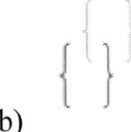
c) 
d)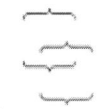

Question 60

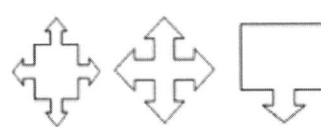

a) 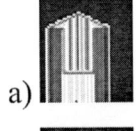
b) 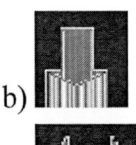
c) 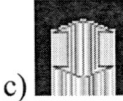
d)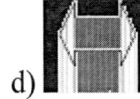

Question 61

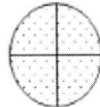  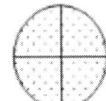

a)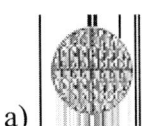

b)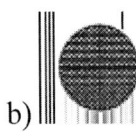

c)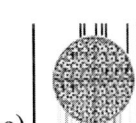

d)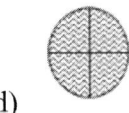

Question 62

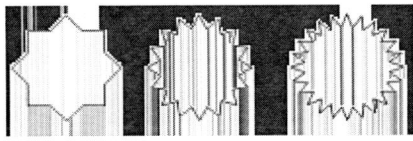

a)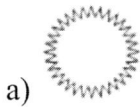

b)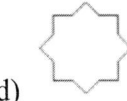

c)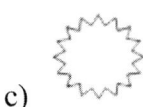

d)

Question 63

AB YZ CD WX EF ...
a) OP GH KL ST
c) UV GH OP IJ

b) UV JK NO AB
d) QR KL MN ST

Question 64

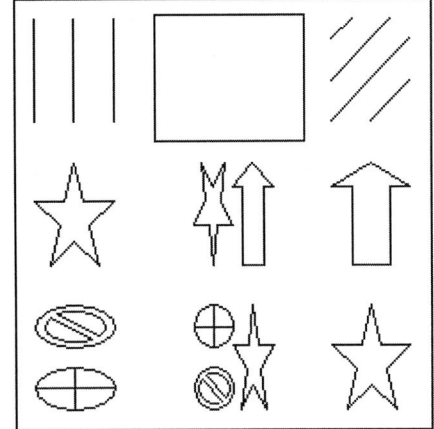

Question 65

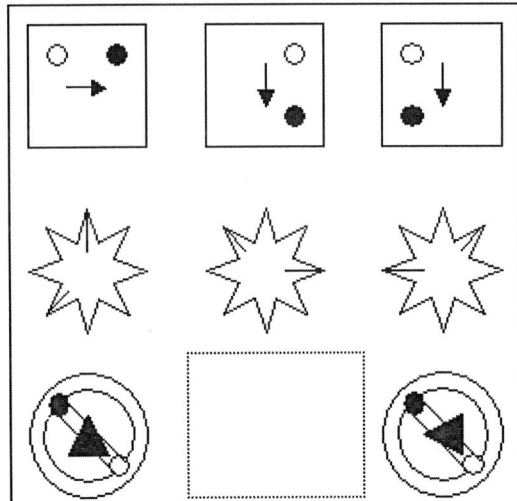

Question 66

Rita is able to read 30 pages an hour. For an assignment she has two books to read. The first book has 1,350 pages and the second book has 2,010 pages. How many hours will it take Rita to finish both books?

a) 75   b) 110

c) 112   d) 121

Question 67

A car can accelerate at 5 kph per second. How much time will it take the car to reach 75 kph?

a) 15 seconds   b) 22 seconds

c) 25 seconds   d) 27 seconds

Question 68

John travels 75 KM to work each way. If he averages 120 kph, how many minutes does he spend driving to and from work each day?

a) 1.25   b) 75

c) 50   d) 60

Question 69

An officer's quota for speeding tickets each month is 0.5% of the average traffic flow on Highway 401. Each month the average flow is 13 million cars. If the officer has issued 50,000 tickets at mid-month, how many more tickets are needed to reach the quota?

a) 25,000   b) 15,000

c) 20,000   d) 30,000

Question 70

Students want to convert a spare room into a lab. The room space is 10' x 10'. A lab needs to have 120 square feet minimum for ventilation. How many more square feet are needed for this lab to be a "safe" environment to enter?

a) 30   b) 50

c) 40   d) 20

Question 71

A truck trailer is filled with explosives. The dimensions of the trailer are 25' x 10' x 15'. The explosives are in crates measuring 5' x 5' x 5'. How many crates of explosives can fit in the truck?

a) 27   b) 30

c) 42   d) 51

Question 72

There are 10 Caucasian, 14 African American and 12 Hispanic people in the office. If there are an equal number of men and women of each race, how many African American women are in the office?

a) 6
b) 7
c) 5
d) 18

Question 73

The average amount of snowfall in Maine increases by 6% each year. If the snowfall amount was 23 inches in 2001, what will the snowfall amount be in 2006?

a) 25.8 inches
b) 27.4 inches
c) 29.0 inches
d) 30.8 inches

Question 74

A park is planned and will be 3 city blocks by 3 city blocks in size. Each city block is 20 metres in length. What is the total area covered by the new park?

a) 1600 square metres
b) 2400 square metres
c) 3600 square metres
d) 4200 square metres

Question 75

A new, entry level employee makes $23,000 per year. If the salary level increases by 2% after every 3 years of service, what will her salary be after 8 years of work?

a) $23,460
b) $23,929
c) $24,408
d) $24,168

Question 76

Identify the synonym for the following words.

Irksome

a) Annoying
b) Irrational
c) Sour
d) Diseased

Question 77

Arraign

a) Sue
b) Confess
c) Exonerate
d) Prosecute

Question 78

Arduous

a) Clever
b) Emotional
c) Difficult
d) Thoughtful

Question 79
Perjury

a) Lying Under Oath
b) Testimony
c) Evidence
d) Selecting a Jury

Question 80
Pedestrians

a) Motorists
b) Toys
c) Athletes
d) Citizens on Foot

Question 81
What number should replace the asterisk in the following questions?

	32	18
154	23	9
145	14	*

a) 1
b) 3
c) 6
d) None of the above.

Question 82

21	63	*
3	9	27
	48	144

a) 81
b) 189
c) 154
d) None of the above.

Question 83

4	100	500
12	300	1500
	900	*

a) 3000
b) 3500
c) 4500
d) None of the above.

Question 84

3	12	48
	24	96
12	48	*

a) 192
b) 208
c) 480
d) None of the above.

Question 85

	3	18
2	6	*
4	12	72

a) 32

b) 36

c) 42

d) None of the above.

Question 86

What are the missing numbers in the following patterns?

1, ?, ?, 27, 81, 243, 729...

a) 3, 12

b) 4, 9

c) 3, 9

d) None of the above.

Question 87

2, ?, 4, 9, 6, 11, 8...

a) 6

b) 7

c) 8

d) None of the above.

Question 88

50, 0, 0, -40, -40, -70, -70, -90, -90, ?, ?...

a) -95, -100

b) -95, -95

c) -100, -100

d) None of the above.

Question 89

6, 16, 36, 76, 156, ?...

a) 316

b) 286

c) 356

d) None of the above.

Question 90

2, 4, ?, 256...

a) 12

b) 16

c) 20

d) None of the above.

GCT2 Answer Key

1) A	26) A	51) A	76) A
2) D	27) B	52) B	77) D
3) C	28) B	53) B	78) C
4) B	29) C	54) D	79) A
5) C	30) B	55) D	80) D
6) A	31) C	56) C	81) D
7) B	32) A	57) B	82) B
8) D	33) B	58) C	83) C
9) A	34) A	59) D	84) A
10) C	35) B	60) B	85) B
11) C	36) A	61) D	86) C
12) E	37) B	62) A	87) B
13) A	38) C	63) C	88) C
14) E	39) C	64) B	89) A
15) B	40) B	65) G	90) B
16) H	41) D	66) C	
17) C	42) B	67) A	
18) E	43) C	68) B	
19) C	44) B	69) B	
20) H	45) D	70) D	
21) C	46) B	71) B	
22) C	47) C	72) B	
23) D	48) D	73) D	
24) D	49) D	74) C	
25) C	50) C	75) B	

Question 1

The children from the lowest to highest grade are: Michael, Robert, Jimmy, Lisa, Bonnie and then Rachael.

Question 2

The order of the horses from first to last is: solid brown, solid black, white with brown spots and then black with brown spots.

Question 3

The places of the girls on the beam from first to last are: Sarah, Amber and then Elaine.

Question 4

The order of employees, working from most to least, is: evening, morning, noon and then overnight.

Question 5

The women and their best-liked flower are as follows: Tina-Indian Paintbrush, Roberta-Rose, Veronica-daisy, Nancy-bluebonnets.

Question 6

The order that the girls could swim, from farthest to least, is: Christa, Nina, Tina, and then Gina.

Question 7

The order of water consumption from highest to lowest is: Ryan, Tom, Jim and then Bob.

Question 8

The girls with short hair are Veronica and Lisa, with medium hair are Britney and Julie, and with long hair are Courtney and Suzanne.

Question 9

Julie picks the orange tabby, Charlie picks the white Persian, Leslie picks the tan Siamese, and Danny picks the calico mix.

Question 10

The order of problems seen, from most to least, is: knee, neck, shoulder and then back.

Question 11

From left to right, the top left and bottom right line are lost. Then the top right and bottom left line are lost. Dots alternate from top to bottom to top on the top line, straight across on the middle line and bottom top bottom on the bottom line.

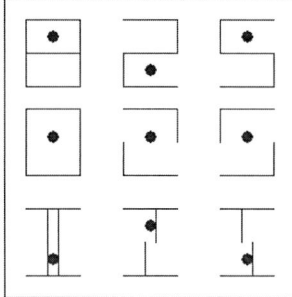

Question 12

An object from first row is superimposed on an object from the second row to create an object in the third row.

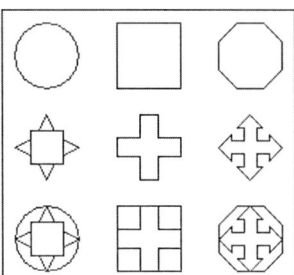

Question 13

Outside shapes remain consistent as you travel diagonally from top left to bottom right. Inside shapes remain consistent as you travel diagonally from top right to bottom left.

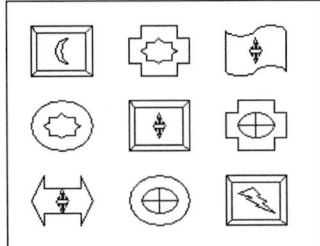

Question 14

The row consists of superimposing the middle row on the mirror image of the bottom row.

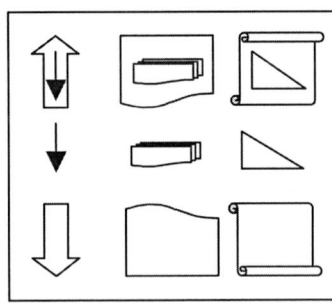

Question 15

Circles on outside represent positive integers; circles on the inside represent negative intergers.

Row one is added to row two resulting in row three. (3 – 1 = 2, 2 + 3 = 5, 5 – 4 = 1)

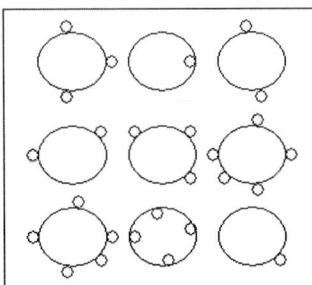

Question 16

The number of dots in the first row increase by one from left to right. The number of dots in the second row increase by two from left to right and by three in the third row.

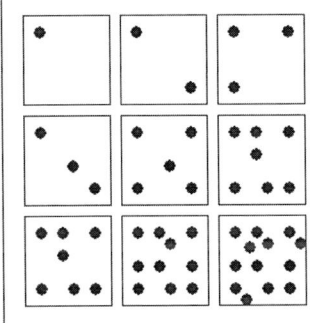

Question 17

To determine the third column, the shapes in the first column are added to the shapes in the second column. The black circles are covered by a black square in the third column, and the white circles are surrounded by another circle.

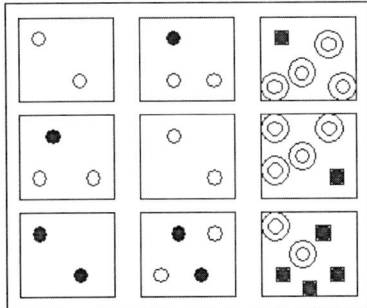

Question 18

The shapes from column one are superimposed on the shapes from column two which results in column three.

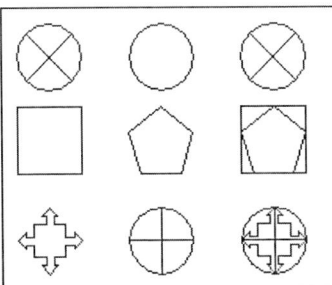

Question 19
A three-dimensional object in column one is followed by a two-dimensional object in column two, which is followed by a double image. Solid black shapes cross diagonally.

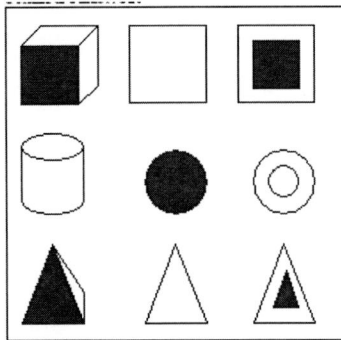

Question 20
The object in column one rotates 90 degrees clockwise in column two and a further 90 degrees in column three. The object that first appears in column two rotates 90 degrees clockwise in column three. The arrows that first appear in column three point in the opposite direction of the object that first appears in column two.

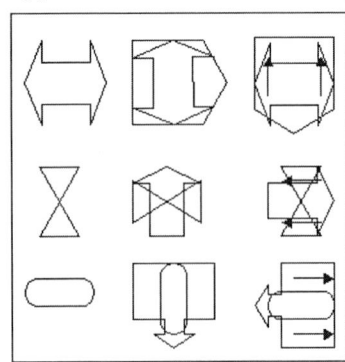

Question 21
To solve this problem, set up an algebraic equation. "Y" will represent the number of men and the number of women will equal y + 5. When you add the women to the men, the total is 75.

$$y + y + 5 = 75$$
$$2y + 5 = 75$$
$$2y = 70$$
$$y = 35$$

Therefore, there are 35 men at the dance.

Question 22
First, determine the total area of the canvas. 2m x 3m = 6 square metres.
Second, determine how much has been painted. 6 x 35% = 2.1 metres.
Finally, determine how much is left to be painted 6 – 2.1 = 3.9 square metres.

Question 23
Determine how much money is made in one week (38 x $6 = $228), and then multiply that total by the number of weeks ($228 x 3 = $684).

Question 24
600 x 15% = 90

Question 25
140 x 0.2 = 28 lbs. of cocaine. 140–28 = 112 lbs. remaining. 112/2 = 56 lbs. of marijuana.

Question 26
An algebraic equation will be required for this question.

$\dfrac{4 \text{ km}}{y \text{ km}} = \dfrac{24 \text{ minutes}}{60 \text{ minutes}}$ Multiply both sides by "y". $4 = \dfrac{24 y}{60}$

Multiply both sides by 60.   240 = 24 y   then divide both sides by 24.   10 = y

Stephen Chan was running at 10 km per hour.

Question 27
An algebraic equation will be required for this question.

$\dfrac{(7 - x)}{4} = x - 10$ Multiply both sides by 4.   7 – x = 4x – 40

Add 40 to each side.   47 – x = 4x   Add y to both sides.   47 = 5x

Finally divide both sides by 5.   47/5 = x = 9.4.

Question 28
First, determine how many litres are drained each second. 44 litres / 60 seconds = 0.73. Therefore, 0.73 litres are drained from the sink each second.

Second, divide 0.73 litres into the 12 litre capacity of the sink. 0.73 / 12 = 16.4 seconds.

Question 29
First, calculate the total volume of the tank. 300 x 400 x 500 = 60,000,000 cubic cm. Second, determine the number of seconds that it will take to fill the tank. Divide the volume by the rate the water is flowing.
    6,000,000 / 20,000 = 3,000 minutes to fill the tank.
Finally, convert 3,000 seconds to minutes. 3,000 / 60 = 50 minutes to fill the tank.

Question 30
First, set up an algebraic equation where "y" represents the number of people who had a cola. ½ y would be the number of people who had lemonade.
    y + ½ y = 240 or 1.5 y = 240
To isolate "y" divide both sides by 1.5.
    y = 240/1.5 = 160 people were drinking cola.

Question 31
"Child" would be the most logical answer, as they would be most likely to chase the ball.

Question 32
"Gallant" is the correct answer, meaning courteous or chivalrous.

Question 33
A "catapult" is an older weapon that flung large rocks like missiles.

Question 34
"Neutral" means refusing to take sides.

Question 35
"Strain" is the most likely cause of a rope snapping.

Refer to the Answer Key for answers to questions 36-40

Question 41
Multiplying

	108	135	486
3	36	45	162
	12	15	27

Question 42
Adding → 2

	201	203	207
6	195	197	199
	189	191	193

Question 43
Multiplying → 4

	12	48	192
2	6	24	96
	3	12	48

Question 44
Multiplying → 3   6

	4	12	72
2	2	6	36
	1	3	18

Question 45

Adding 251 →

103	354	605
225	476	727
100	351	602

Question 46

The numbers are increasing by multiples of 2. (8, 16, 32, 64, 128, 256, 512...).

Question 47

The numbers are being added by 7. (-7. 0, 7, 14, 21, 28...).

Question 48

The numbers are declining by multiples of 3 in the following pattern: -3, -6, -9, -12 etc. (100, 97, 91, 82, 70, 55, ...)

Question 49

The numbers are being multiplied by 3 and then added by 2 (2, 8, 26, 80, 242...).

Question 50

The numbers are being multiplied by 2 and subtracted by 3 (9, 15, 27, 51, 99, 195...).

Question 51

If you spoke with the supplier four days ago and they advised the parts would be shipped in 6 days that means the parts will be shipped in 2 days. Add another 2 days for shipping and the answer is 4 days.

Question 52

The order of items, from most to least worn, is: short skirts, long skirts, shorts and then pants.

Question 53

The teams are in the following places, from first to last: Team 3, Team 2, Team 4, and then Team 1.

Question 54

The amount of paint needed by room, from most to least is: bedroom, dining room, kitchen, and then bathroom.

Question 55

Natalie handles fewer calls than Frank, so their combined total would not be as high as doubling Frank's production. Kristina, therefore, takes the most calls.

Question 56

If you go to school, ask questions, take the test and get A's, you will graduate next.

Question 57

The first letter of each word skips every second letter of the alphabet (A, C, E, G...)

Question 58

The first letter of each word skips a letter, then goes back one, then skips one, etc.

Question 59
Round brackets convert to curved brackets vertically. The same process is repeated horizontally.

Question 60
The block is in the centre of arrows, then the block is gone. The block is at the top of the arrow, then the block is gone.

Question 61
The pattern goes from small dots to wavy lines and repeats.

Question 62
The first star has 8 points. These points increase by 8 so that the final star has 32 points.

Question 63
First two letters of the alphabet are followed by the last two. The next letters are the third and fourth letters of the alphabet followed by the third and fourth last letters of the alphabet. The next would be fifth and sixth letters of the alphabet, followed by the fifth and sixth last letters of the alphabet and so on…

Question 64
The middle column is a compressed merger of the first and second columns. The image from the first column is also rotated 180 degrees.

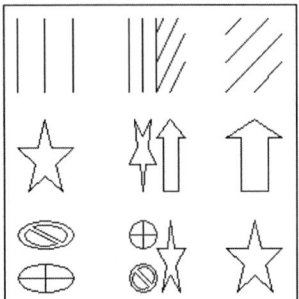

Question 65
The mages rotates 90 degrees between columns 1 and 2. Column 3 is a mirror image of column 2.

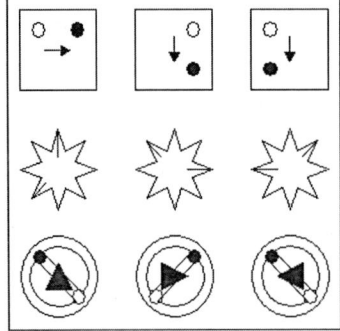

Question 66
First, calculate the total number of pages Rita must read [1,350 + 2,010 = 3,360]. Then, divide the total number pages by her reading speed [3,360/30 = 112 minutes].

Question 67
75/5=15   It will take 15 seconds to accelerate to 75 kph.

Question 68
Calculate John's total return trip driving distance [75 + 75 = 150KM]. Then divide total distance by his average driving speed [150/120=1.25hr]. Then convert 1.25 hours to minutes by multiplying by 60, to arrive at 75 minutes.

Question 69
13,000,000 x 0.005=65,000

65,000 - 50,000 = 15,000 tickets

Question 70
10 x 10 = 100 square feet

120 – 100 = 20 square feet

Question 71
25 x 10 x 15 = 3750 cubic feet

5 x 5 x 5 = 125 cubic feet

3750 / 125 = 30 boxes

Question 72
14 / 2 = 7

Question 73
2002: 23 x 1.06 = 24.38   2003: 24.38 x 1.06 = 25.84   2004: 25.84 x 1.06 = 27.39

2005: 27.39 x 1.06 = 29.036 2006: 29.036 x 1.06 = 30.8

Question 74
The perimeter would be 60 metres by 60 metres (20 x 3 = 60). The area would be 60 x 60 = 3600 square metres.

Question 75
Eight years of employment would provide 2 pay increases.

23,000 x 1.02 = $23,460   23,460 x 1.02 = $23,939

Refer to the Answer Key for answers to questions 76-80

Question 81

Adding

163	32	18
154	23	9
145	14	0

9 ↑

Question 82

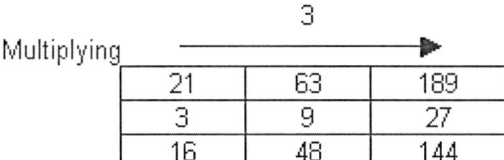

Question 83

Multiplying

3 ↓	4	100	500
	12	300	1500
	36	900	4500

Question 84

Multiplying → 4

2 ↓	3	12	48
	6	24	96
	12	48	192

Question 85

Multiplying 3 → 6

2 ↓	1	3	18
	2	6	36
	4	12	72

Question 86

The numbers are increasing by multiples of 3 (1, 3, 9, 27, 81, 243, 729...)

Question 87

The numbers grow by 5 then decrease by 3 (2, 7, 4, 9, 6, 11, 8...).

Question 88

The pattern is subtracting a declining multiple of 10 (50 then 40 then 30 etc.), followed by subtracting 0. -50, -0, -40, -0, -30, -0, -20, -0, etc. (50, 0, 0, -40, -40, -70, -70, -90, -90, -100, -100...).

Question 89

The numbers are being added by 2 and then multiplied by 2 (6, 16, 36, 76, 156, 316,...).

Question 90

The numbers are being squared (2, 4, 16, 256, 65536...).

GRT

The Graduate Recruitment Test (GRT) consists of four subjects, with a total of 55 multiple-choice questions. The subjects are:

· Word Similarities
· Arithmetic
· Figure Analogies
· Number Sequences

The test takes 1 1/2 hours to write.

Only paper, pencils and erasers are allowed - no books, dictionaries, notes, writing paper, calculators, calculator watches or other aids are not permitted in the room.

Detach the answer key to take the test.

GRT ANSWER KEY

```
     A B C D E                A B C D E
 1)  ○ ○ ○ ○ ○  ____      11) ○ ○ ○ ○ ○  ____
 2)  ○ ○ ○ ○    ____      12) ○ ○ ○ ○ ○  ____
 3)  ○ ○ ○ ○    ____      13) ○ ○ ○ ○    ____
 4)  ○ ○ ○ ○    ____      14) ○ ○ ○ ○    ____
 5)  ○ ○ ○ ○    ____      15) ○ ○ ○ ○    ____
 6)  ○ ○ ○ ○    ____      16) ○ ○ ○ ○    ____
 7)  ○ ○ ○ ○    ____      17) ○ ○ ○ ○    ____
 8)  ○ ○ ○ ○    ____      18) ○ ○ ○ ○    ____
 9)  ○ ○ ○ ○ ○  ____      19) ○ ○ ○ ○ ○  ____
10)  ○ ○ ○ ○    ____      20) ○ ○ ○ ○ ○  ____

     A B C D E                A B C D E
21)  ○ ○ ○ ○ ○  ____      31) ○ ○ ○ ○ ○  ____
22)  ○ ○ ○ ○    ____      32) ○ ○ ○ ○ ○  ____
23)  ○ ○ ○ ○    ____      33) ○ ○ ○ ○ ○  ____
24)  ○ ○ ○ ○    ____      34) ○ ○ ○ ○    ____
25)  ○ ○ ○ ○    ____      35) ○ ○ ○ ○    ____
26)  ○ ○ ○ ○    ____      36) ○ ○ ○ ○    ____
27)  ○ ○ ○ ○    ____      37) ○ ○ ○ ○    ____
28)  ○ ○ ○ ○    ____      38) ○ ○ ○ ○    ____
29)  ○ ○ ○ ○    ____      39) ○ ○ ○ ○    ____
30)  ○ ○ ○ ○ ○  ____      40) ○ ○ ○ ○    ____

     A B C D E                A B C D E
41)  ○ ○ ○ ○ ○  ____      51) ○ ○ ○ ○    ____
42)  ○ ○ ○ ○ ○  ____      52) ○ ○ ○ ○    ____
43)  ○ ○ ○ ○ ○  ____      53) ○ ○ ○ ○ ○  ____
44)  ○ ○ ○ ○ ○  ____      54) ○ ○ ○ ○ ○  ____
45)  ○ ○ ○ ○    ____      55) ○ ○ ○ ○ ○  ____
46)  ○ ○ ○ ○ ○  ____
47)  ○ ○ ○ ○    ____
48)  ○ ○ ○ ○    ____
49)  ○ ○ ○ ○    ____
50)  ○ ○ ○ ○    ____
```

In the following questions, choose the pair that refers most directly to a single concept:

Question 1

a) Car - People
b) Motor - Boat
c) Hook - Hanger
d) Loose - Unravel
e) Garbage - Roof

Question 2

a) Boy – Girl
b) Adult - Boy
c) Male – Girl
d) Female - Boy
e) Adult - Girl

Question 3

a) Compute – Consider
b) Think - Begin
c) Covet - Choice
d) Mind - Think
e) Exercise - Health

Question 4

What are the missing numbers in the following patterns?
?, ?, 28, 25, 21, 16, 10.

a) 31, 29
b) 32, 30
c) 32, 31
d) None of the above.

Question 5

5, 13, ?, 61, 125, ?...

a) 27, 243
b) 29, 253
c) 29, 243
d) None of the above.

Question 6

7, 6, 4, ?, -3, -8...

a) 0
b) 1
c) 2
d) None of the above.

Question 7

A chemical plant has had an accident. One of the main supply pipelines has been fractured. Liquid nitrogen is spilling out at a rate of 12 gallons every 30 seconds. If the flow continues for 15 minutes before it is stopped, how much would have spilled?

a) (12 + 12) x 15 =
b) 12 + 12 x 15 =
c) 15 x 12 x 12 =
d) 15 + 12 x 12 =

Question 8

The total cost of a uniform is $255. You have 6 weeks to pay for the uniform. If you pay $42.50 towards the total for the 6 weeks, what is the percentage paid each time?

a) 6 x 42.50 / 255 =   b) 42.50 x 6 / 255 =
c) 42.50 / 255 x 6 =   d) 42.50 / 255 =

Question 9

Which is the missing image in the pattern below?

 is to 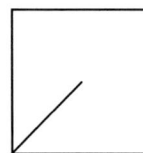 just as 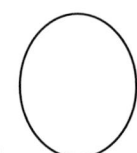 is to

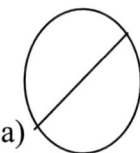
a)   b)   c)   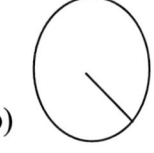   d)    e)

Select the pair that refers most directly to a single concept in the following questions

Question 10

a) Lid - Handle   b) Knob - Door
c) Container – Pot   d) Handle – Knob
e) Bell – Sound

Question 11

a) Planet - Moon   b) Comet - Earth
c) Star – Sun   d) Sun – Earth
e) Earth – Moon

Question 12

a) Ruby – Sapphire   b) Gold - Diamond
c) Emerald – Silver   d) Platinum - Sapphire
e) Copper - Cloth

What are the missing numbers in the following patterns?

Question 13
4, 6, ?, 18, 34, 66...

a) 12   b) 14
c) 11   d) None of the above.

Question 14

45, 47, 51, ?, 65, 75...

a) 57
b) 59
c) 55
d) None of the above.

Question 15

-3, ?, ?, 9, 17, 27, 39...

a) -1, 3
b) 0, 4
c) -1, 4
d) None of the above.

Question 16

The homicide rate in 2000 was 543 murders. The murder rate increased by 2% each year between 2000 and 2004. The murder rate then dropped in 2005 by 5%. What is the murder rate in 2005?

a) 543 x 1.02 x 4 x 0.95 =
b) 543 x 102% x 102% x 102% x 102% x 95% =
c) (543 x 1.02 * 0.95) x 4 =
d) 543 x 0.95 x 1.02 x 1.02 x 1.02 =

Question 17

The population decrease in North Dakota occurs at an average rate of 3% per year. If the population was 300,000 in 2002, what would the population be in 2004?

a) 300,000 x 3% - 300,000 =
b) 300,000 - (300,000 x 94%) =
c) 300,000 - 300,000 x 0.94 =
d) 300,000 x 0.97 x 0.97 =

Which are the missing images in the patterns below?

Question 18

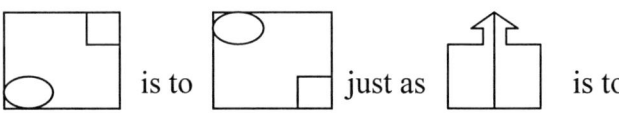

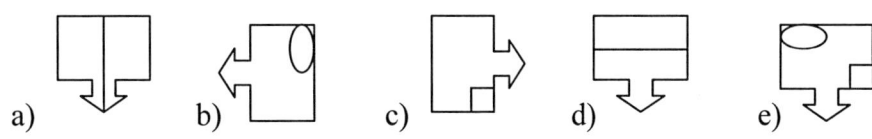

Question 19

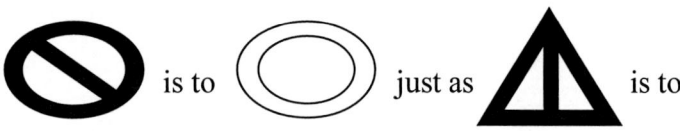

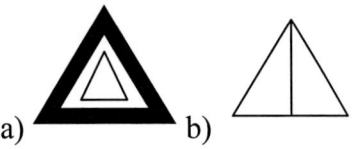 a)   b)   c)   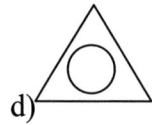 d)   e)

In the following questions, select the pair that refers most directly to a single concept.

Question 20
a) Hair – Bun
b) Sincerity – Hypocrite
c) Sibling – Brother
d) Courage - Hero
e) Tools – Tradesmen

Question 21
a) Diocese – Venomous
b) Pill – Solve
c) Vitamin - Venture
d) Disease – Cure
e) Leader – Chaos

Question 22
a) Clever – Quaintness
b) Conceit - Arrogance
c) Neglectful – Skittish
d) Courageous – Intelligent
e) Hopeful – Negligent

Question 23
a) Nail – Claw
b) Nose – Sensation
c) Digit – Subtraction
d) Nail – Hammer
e) Claw – Hammer

What are the missing numbers in the following patterns?

Question 24
1, 4, 9, 16, ?, ?...
a) 20, 30
b) 24, 38
c) 25, 36
d) None of the above.

Question 25
?, 198, 63, 126, 43, 86.
a) 63
b) 84
c) 99
d) None of the above.

Question 26
3, 4, 2, 3, 1, 2, 0, 1, ?, ?...
a) -1, 0
b) -2, -1
c) 0, -1
d) None of the above.

Question 27
?, 1, 2, 6, 24, 120, 720, 5040.
a) –2
b) -1
c) 0
d) None of the above.

Question 28

There are a total of 60 stacks of money. There are 10 bills in each stack. The stacks are in denominations of $20, $5 and $1. There are 24 stacks of $1 bills and there are three times as many stacks of $5 bills as $20 bills. What is the total amount of money from the $5 bills?

a) 60 x 10 x 3/4 - 24 x 5 =
b) (60 - 24) x 10 x 3/4 x 5 =
c) (60 -24) x 2/3 x 5 =
d) (60 - 24) x 5 x 2/3 x 10 =

Question 29

Doug was responsible for filling out insurance requisitions at his office. In May, he was able to process 1,322 requests. In June his number of requests completed fell by 15%. In July he was able to improve on his June numbers by 17%. How many requisitions did Doug complete in July?

a) (1,322 x 0.95) x 1.17 =
b) (1,322 - (1,322 x 0.15)) x 1.17 =
c) (1,322 - 0.15) x 1.17 =
d) (1,322 - (1,322 x 0.15)) x 1,322 x 1.17 =

In the following questions, select the pair that refers most directly to a single concept.

Question 30
a) Stick – Pipe
b) Cage – Animal
c) Oar – Pedal
d) Towel – Rack
e) Quiver – Bow

Question 31
a) Justice – Blindness
b) Honesty – Truth
c) Careful – Creative
d) Colourful – Hypnotizing
e) Sheltered – Guided

Question 32
a) Artillery – Weapon
b) Vein – Artery
c) Canker – Cure
d) Conundrum – Antic
e) Cover – Mail

Question 33

a) Boy – Scout
b) Sex – Act
c) Sex – Gender
d) Animal – Plant
e) Mouth – Body

What are the missing numbers in the following patterns?

Question 34

4, 11, 25, ?, 109, 221.

a) 47
b) 51
c) 55
d) None of the above.

Question 35

?, 5, 7, 11, 19, 35.

a) 2
b) 3
c) 4
d) None of the above.

Question 36

-13, -11, -7, -1, ?, 17.

a) 7
b) 9
c) 5
d) None of the above.

Question 37

?, 22, 32, ?, 52, ?...

a) 10, 42, 64
b) 12, 44, 64
c) 14, 44, 64
d) None of the above.

Question 38

The capacity of a women's shelter is 130. On the coldest night of the year a police officer comes across 6 homeless women. While speaking to the shelter, police are informed that they are at 96.2% occupancy. What will their new occupancy rate be if they accept the six women?

a) 130 x 96.2% + 6 / 130 =
b) (130 x 0.962) + 6 / 130 =
c) (96.2% x 130 + 6) / 130 =
d) (96.2% x 130) / (130 + 6) =

Question 39

There are 4 offspring in the Yang family. They live in 6 different houses. Each offspring is married and has 3 babies. We must give 4 stuffed animals to each baby. How many stuffed animals do we need to buy?

a) 2 (4) + 2(3) =
b) 4 x 3 x 4 =
c) 2 (3 x 4) =
d) 2 (4 x 4 x 3) =

Question 40

Customs Agent Arquet was involved in a major drug bust at the airport. She arrested three suspects. Each of the suspects had two suitcases, each containing 5 kilograms of cocaine. Which of the following formulas would Arquet use to calculate the total number of kilograms seized during the arrest?

a) 3 (2) (5) =
b) 5 x 3 x 2 =
c) 5 + 5 + 5 + 5 + 5 + 5 =
d) Any of the above.

Question 41

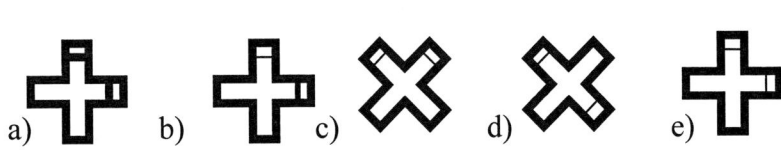

Question 42

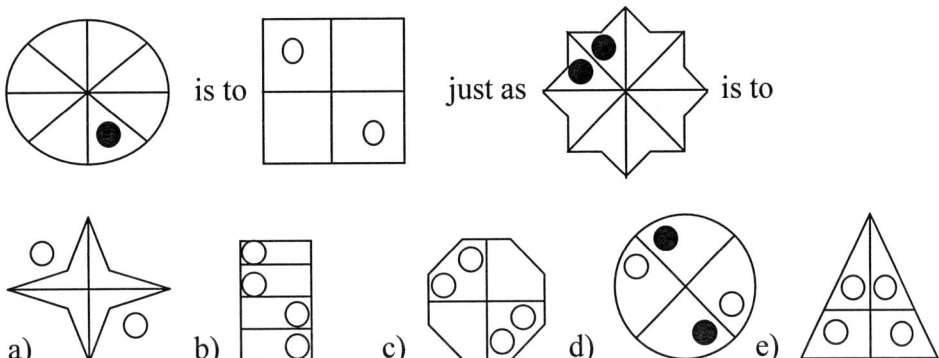

In the following questions, select the pair that refers most directly to a single concept.

Question 43

a) Democracy – Capitalism
b) Dictatorship – Economics
c) Ergonomics – Economics
d) Dictatorship – Ergonomics
e) Communism – Socialism

Question 44

a) Thought – Dream
b) Creativity – Arrogance
c) Mind – Foot
d) Interior – Decorating
e) Think – Existence

Question 45

a) Shyness – Painful
b) Captivity – Undermining
c) Insecurity – Confidence
d) Hero – Stoic
e) Cool – Kitchen

Question 46

a) Army – Dictator
b) Fascism – Enthusiasm
c) Ethnocentric – Society
d) Democracy – Dictatorship
e) Democracy – Choice

Question 47

What are the missing numbers in the following patterns?
0, -2, ?, -12, -20, ?, -42

a) -4, -28
b) -6, -32
c) -8, -34
d) None of the above.

What number should replace the asterisk in the following questions?

Question 48

1	2	8
3	6	*
9		72

a) 18
b) 24
c) 32
d) None of the above

Question 49

15	45	135
120	*	1080
	2880	8640

a) 480
b) 360
c) 280
d) None of the above

Question 50

Illio put change in a bottle. He put in 2 pennies, 5 quarters, 3 dimes and 1 nickel. What is the probability of picking out a penny?

a) 2 / (2 + 1 + 3 + 5) =
b) 2 / (5 + 3 + 1) =
c) 2 / 2 + 5 + 3 + 1 =
d) (1 + 5 + 3) / 2 =

Question 51

Kal Green bought 4 tapes at $8 each. He then found $17 on the street corner. He now has $40. How much money did Kal have before he bought the tapes?

a) 40 - 17 + (8 x 4) =   b) 40 + 17 + (8 x 4) =
c) 17 - 40 + (8 x 4) =   d) (8 x 4) + 17 - 40 =

Question 52

The cash fund for a small office is being added up. There are six $20 bills, two $5 bills, 12 quarters and 15 nickels. How much money is there in coins?

a) (6 x 20) + (2 x 5) + 12 + 15 =   b) (12 x 0.25) + (15 x 0.05) =
c) 12 x 0.25 + 15 x 0.05 - 6 x 20 + 2 x 5 =   d) 12 x 0.05 + 15 x 0.25 =

Question 53

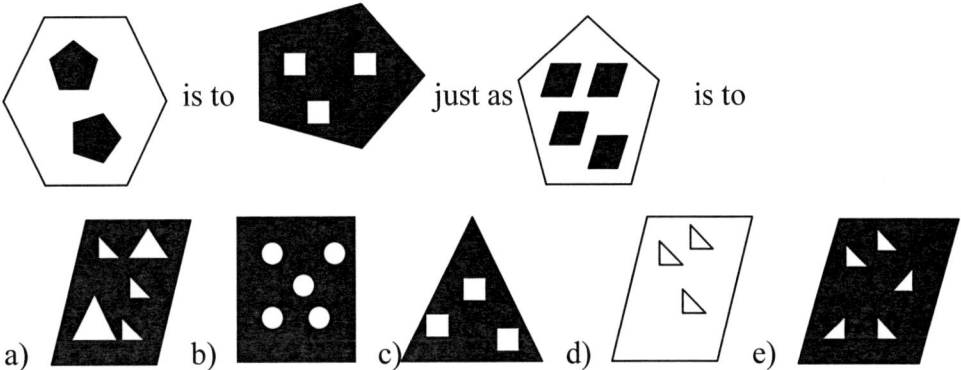

Question 54

In the following questions, select the pair that refers most directly to a single concept.

a) Chest – Shout   b) Lungs – Breathe
c) Heart – Stop   d) Feet – Signal
e) Arm – Wave

Question 55

a) Angle – Obtuse   b) Shape – Multiply
c) Addition – Mathematics   d) Study – Education
e) Obtuse – Acute

GRT Answer Key

1) C	12) A	23) A	34) D	45) C
2) A	13) D	24) C	35) C	46) D
3) A	14) A	25) C	36) A	47) D
4) D	15) A	26) A	37) D	48) B
5) B	16) B	27) D	38) C	49) B
6) B	17) D	28) B	39) B	50) A
7) A	18) A	29) B	40) D	51) A
8) D	19) E	30) C	41) B	52) B
9) D	20) C	31) B	42) C	53) E
10) D	21) D	32) B	43) E	54) B
11) C	22) B	33) C	44) A	55) E

Question 1
A hook and a hanger are both used to hold up clothing and refer most to a single concept. The other options contain words that may be used together, or may cause each other to occur, but they do not refer to as single a concept as hook and hanger.

Question 2
Boy and girl both refer to young male and female children. The other options do not refer a single concept as closely as boy and girl do as they refer to different age groups and different genders, or generic categories such as adult or male.

Question 3
Compute and consider are both forms of thinking and refer most to a single concept. The other options include word pairs where one may lead to the other, or one may require the other, but none refer to as single a concept.

Question 4
The numbers are decreasing by factors of 1, then 2, 3, 4 etc (31, 30, 28, 25, 21, 16, 10...).

Question 5
The numbers are being multiplied by 2 and added by 3 (5, 13, 29, 61, 125, 253...).

Question 6
The numbers are declining by -1, -2, -3, -4 etc. (7, 6, 4, 1, -3, -8...)

Question 7
12 x 2 = 24 gallons per minute   24 x 15 = 360 gallons in 15 minutes

Question 8
42.5 / 255 = 0.166 or 16.7%

Question 9

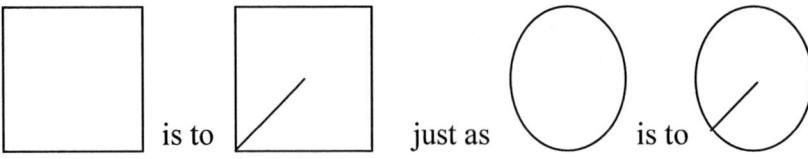

The image has added a new line from the bottom left corner to the centre from A to B.

Question 10
A knob and a handle are both used as levers or grips to open objects, or handle them. Knob and handle most refer to a single concept. The other options contain words that are part of one another or may have similar shape, but different purposes.

Question 11
The sun is a star and this pair refers most to a single concept. Planets, moons, and comets are all objects found in space but are not as closely related as sun and star.

Question 12
Ruby and sapphire are both precious stones, whereas the other options are a mix of metals, stones and cloth.

Question 13
The numbers are being multiplied by 2 and subtracted by 2 (4, 6, 10, 18, 34, 66...).

Question 14
The numbers are being added by 2 then 4, 6, 8 etc. (45, 47, 51, 57, 65, 75...).

Question 15
The numbers are increasing by a factor of 2, then 4, 6, 8 etc. (-3, -1, 3, 9, 17, 27, 39...)

Question 16
In 2000 there were 543 murders.
2001   543 x 1.02 = 553.86   2002   553.86 x 1.02 = 564.9372
2003   564.9372 x 1.02 = 576.2359   2004   576.2359 x 1.02 = 587.7607
2005   587.7607 x 0.95 = 558.372

Question 17
2002   300,000 x 0.97 = 291,000   2003   291,000 x 0.97 = 282,270

Question 18
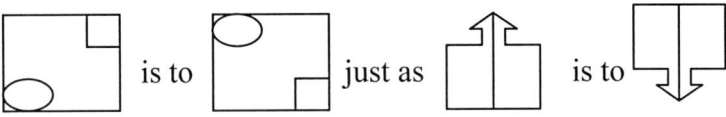

The image is a mirror image horizontally.

Question 19
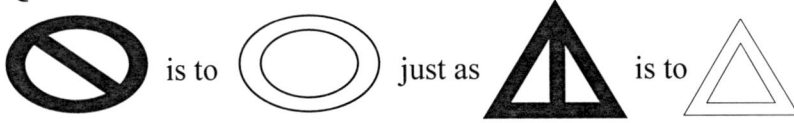

The image becomes unfilled, and the interior line disappears.

Question 20
Sibling and brother are synonyms and refer most to a single concept. The other options may be used together, or may be people that act in the same manner as the other, but do not refer as closely to a single concept.

Question 21
Disease and cure are both factors that affect a person's health, one damages health, and the other fixes it. This pair refers most to a single concept. The other options have very little in common with each other.

Question 22
Conceit and arrogance are both feelings of pride or vanity and refer most to a single concept. The other options involve other feelings and states of mind that are not as closely connected.

Question 23
Nail and claw are both parts of digits on humans and animals (fingernails, and animal claws). The other options are used together, or part of one another, but fail to refer to a single concept.

Question 24
The numbers reflect the squares of 1, then 2, 3, 4, 5 etc. (1, 4, 9, 16, 25, 36, 49...)

Question 25
The numbers are being multiplied by two and then divided by 3 (99, 198, 63, 126, 43, 86...).

Question 26
The numbers are adding 1, then subtracted by 2 (3, 4, 2, 3, 1, 2, 0, 1, -1, 0...).

Question 27
The numbers are being multiplied by 1, then 2, 3, 4, 5 etc (1, 1, 2, 6, 24, 120, 720, 5040...).

Question 28
60 – 24 = 36 stacks of bills ($20 and $5)   36 x 3/4 = 27 stacks of $5 bills
27 x 10 x $5 = $1,350

Question 29
May = 1,322 requests   June = 1,322 x 0 85 = 1,124 requests
July = 1,124 x 1.17 = 1,315 requests

Question 30
An oar and a pedal are both used to move vehicles through muscular force, one a canoe and the other a bicycle. This pair of words refers most to a single concept. The other options may share similar properties such as shape, or may be used together, but they do not refer as closely to a single concept.

Question 31
Honesty and truth are synonyms and most refer to a single concept of all the word pairs. The other word pairs may be part of common expressions, or share some properties, but they do not refer as closely to a single concept as honesty and truth.

Question 32
Veins and arteries are both used to transport blood throughout the body and refer most to a single concept. Weapon would be the name of a group of things of which artillery is an example (as are guns, knives, etc). The other options share commonalities, but do not refer as closely to a single concept.

Question 33
Sex and gender are synonyms and refer most to a single concept of all word pairs. The other options may be used together in common language, but they refer to different concepts individually. Animal and plant are both living creatures, but are not as closely tied to a single concept as sex and gender.

Question 34
The numbers are being multiplied by 2 and then added by 3 (4, 11, 25, 53, 109, 221...).

Question 35
The numbers are being multiplied by 2 and subtracted by 3 (4, 5, 7, 11, 19, 35...).

Question 36
The numbers are increasing at rates in the following pattern: +2, +4, +6, etc (-13, -11, -7, -1, 7, 17...).

Question 37

The numbers are increasing by 10 (12, 22, 32, 42, 52, 62...).

Question 38

130 x 96.2% = 125 current occupancy   125 + 6 = 131   131 / 130 = 101%

Question 39

4 x 3 = 12 babies   12 x 4 = 48 toys

Question 40

3 x 2 x 5 = 30 kg

Question 41

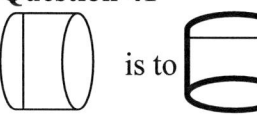 is to 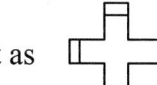 just as  is to

The image rotates 90 degrees. The outside lines and one internal line become thicker.

Question 42

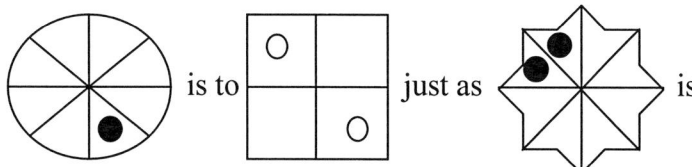

The image changes from 8 slices to four slices. The number of small circles inside doubles, and are displayed in opposite corners. The internal circles also change from back to white.

Question 43

Communism and socialism are both descriptive terms of economic systems and refer most to a single concept. Democracy and dictatorship are political systems (who is in charge), while capitalism, communism and socialism are economic systems (how economy works). Economics is a term for an entire subject and ergonomics refers to human engineering.

Question 44

Thought and dream are both activities of the mind and refer most to a single concept. Creativity would be a skill while arrogance would be personality trait. Mind and foot are two very different human parts (one physical, one a concept). The other options may be used together in common language, but individually are different concepts.

Question 45

Insecurity and confidence are both feelings expressing ideas of self-worth and refer most to a single concept. The other options may be used together, or result from one another, but do not refer as much to a single concept as insecurity and confidence.

Question 46

Democracy and dictatorship are both forms of political systems and refer most to a single concept. The other options may require one another, or describe one another, but fail to refer as closely to a single concept.

Question 47

The numbers are decreasing by a factor of 2, then 4, 6, 8 etc (0, -2, -6, -12, -20, -30,...).

Question 48

Multiplying	2	4
1	2	8
3	6	24
9	18	72

(3 ↓)

Question 49

Multiplying	3	
15	45	135
120	360	1080
960	2880	8640

(8 ↓)

Question 50

Total coins = 2 + 5 + 3 + 1 = 11   2 pennies / 11 coins = 0.181 or 18.1 %

Question 51

Current money = $40   Money found on corner = $17
Money spent on tapes = 8 x 4 = $32 $40 – 17 + 32 = $55

Question 52

12 x 0.25 = $ 3 in quarters   15 x 0.05 = $ 0.75 in nickels
Total = $ 3.75 in change

Question 53

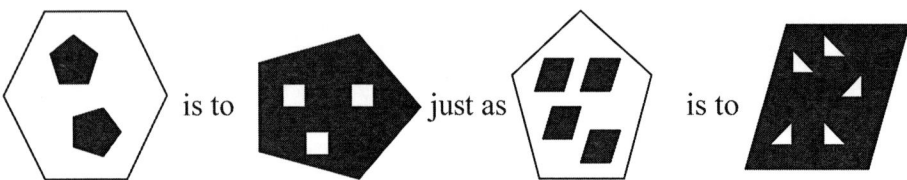

The large and small shapes are switching colours. The number of sides for both the large and small shapes is decreasing by 1. The number of small shapes is increasing by 1 and the shapes are equally sized.

Question 54

All of the different body parts are linked with an action, but only lungs is paired with its primary role (to breathe) and this pair therefore refers most to a single concept.

Question 55

Obtuse and acute are both types of angles and refer most to a single concept. The other options include examples of one another (obtuse - angle, addition - mathematics) or similar categories.

SJT

The Situational Judgement Test (SJT) assesses judgement required for solving problems in work-related situations. There are 50 short descriptions of problem situations followed by two questions (most and least effective response to the situation). The problem situations include work-related encounters, dealing with teams and other workplace scenarios.

The test takes 90 minutes to complete. If you are unsuccessful you must wait 180 days before you can rewrite the test.

Only paper, pencils and erasers are allowed - no books, dictionaries, notes, writing paper, calculators, calculator watches or other aids are permitted in the room.

Detach the answer key to take the test.

SJT ANSWER KEY

	A	B	C	D	E	
1)	○	○	○	○	○	____
2)	○	○	○	○	○	____
3)	○	○	○	○	○	____
4)	○	○	○	○	○	____
5)	○	○	○	○	○	____
6)	○	○	○	○	○	____
7)	○	○	○	○	○	____
8)	○	○	○	○	○	____
9)	○	○	○	○	○	____
10)	○	○	○	○	○	____

	A	B	C	D	E	
11)	○	○	○	○	○	____
12)	○	○	○	○	○	____
13)	○	○	○	○	○	____
14)	○	○	○	○	○	____
15)	○	○	○	○	○	____
16)	○	○	○	○	○	____
17)	○	○	○	○	○	____
18)	○	○	○	○	○	____
19)	○	○	○	○	○	____
20)	○	○	○	○	○	____

	A	B	C	D	E	
21)	○	○	○	○	○	____
22)	○	○	○	○	○	____
23)	○	○	○	○	○	____
24)	○	○	○	○	○	____
25)	○	○	○	○	○	____
26)	○	○	○	○	○	____
27)	○	○	○	○	○	____
28)	○	○	○	○	○	____
29)	○	○	○	○	○	____
30)	○	○	○	○	○	____

	A	B	C	D	E	
31)	○	○	○	○	○	____
32)	○	○	○	○	○	____
33)	○	○	○	○	○	____
34)	○	○	○	○	○	____
35)	○	○	○	○	○	____
36)	○	○	○	○	○	____
37)	○	○	○	○	○	____
38)	○	○	○	○	○	____
39)	○	○	○	○	○	____
40)	○	○	○	○	○	____

	A	B	C	D	E	
41)	○	○	○	○	○	____
42)	○	○	○	○	○	____
43)	○	○	○	○	○	____
44)	○	○	○	○	○	____
45)	○	○	○	○	○	____
46)	○	○	○	○	○	____
47)	○	○	○	○	○	____
48)	○	○	○	○	○	____
49)	○	○	○	○	○	____
50)	○	○	○	○	○	____

	A	B	C	D	E	
51)	○	○	○	○	○	____
52)	○	○	○	○	○	____
53)	○	○	○	○	○	____
54)	○	○	○	○	○	____
55)	○	○	○	○	○	____
56)	○	○	○	○	○	____
57)	○	○	○	○	○	____
58)	○	○	○	○	○	____
59)	○	○	○	○	○	____
60)	○	○	○	○	○	____

	A	B	C	D	E	
61)	○	○	○	○	○	____
62)	○	○	○	○	○	____
63)	○	○	○	○	○	____
64)	○	○	○	○	○	____
65)	○	○	○	○	○	____
66)	○	○	○	○	○	____
67)	○	○	○	○	○	____
68)	○	○	○	○	○	____
69)	○	○	○	○	○	____
70)	○	○	○	○	○	____

	A	B	C	D	E	
71)	○	○	○	○	○	____
72)	○	○	○	○	○	____
73)	○	○	○	○	○	____
74)	○	○	○	○	○	____
75)	○	○	○	○	○	____
76)	○	○	○	○	○	____
77)	○	○	○	○	○	____
78)	○	○	○	○	○	____
79)	○	○	○	○	○	____
80)	○	○	○	○	○	____

	A	B	C	D	E	
81)	○	○	○	○	○	____
82)	○	○	○	○	○	____
83)	○	○	○	○	○	____
84)	○	○	○	○	○	____
85)	○	○	○	○	○	____
86)	○	○	○	○	○	____
87)	○	○	○	○	○	____
88)	○	○	○	○	○	____
89)	○	○	○	○	○	____
90)	○	○	○	○	○	____

	A	B	C	D	E	
91)	○	○	○	○	○	____
92)	○	○	○	○	○	____
93)	○	○	○	○	○	____
94)	○	○	○	○	○	____

	A	B	C	D	E	
95)	○	○	○	○	○	____
96)	○	○	○	○	○	____
97)	○	○	○	○	○	____

	A	B	C	D	E	
98)	○	○	○	○	○	____
99)	○	○	○	○	○	____
100)	○	○	○	○	○	____

Question 1

The assembly line requires that everyone work proficiently. On this particular line, there is one man who is inefficient and easily distracted. He is always holding up the line. **What is the most effective way to deal with this situation?**

a) Offer an incentive program for productivity.

b) Increase the number of personnel on the line.

c) Allow it to continue.

d) Go to management for help.

e) Talk to him about how his work is affecting others.

Question 2

What is the least effective way to deal with this situation?

a) Offer an incentive program for productivity.

b) Increase the number of personnel on the line.

c) Allow it to continue.

d) Go to management for help.

e) Talk to him about how his work is affecting others.

Question 3

While working a shift you witness one of your co-workers lose his temper. He pushes an employee against the wall and yells "you better not punch me again". You did not see anyone throw a punch. As a result of a complaint, this matter has gone to the internal review board. **What is the most effective way to deal with this situation?**

a) Discuss the incident with your co-worker.

b) Report the truth of the incident to the review board.

c) Go to upper management.

d) Tell the review board that he was defending himself from a punch.

e) Speak to your supervisor about the incident.

Question 4

What is the least effective way to deal with this situation?

a) Discuss the incident with your co-worker.

b) Report the truth of the incident.

c) Go to upper management.

d) Tell the review board that he was defending himself from a punch.

e) Speak to your supervisor about the incident.

Question 5

You work with another man at an air conditioner service shop. Your promise is to answer service calls within 6 hours. Your co-worker never makes it to a call within this timeframe. He always has excuses, such as bad traffic or unclear directions, ready. You do not have this problem and his being late is creating a heavier workload for you. **What is the most effective way to deal with this situation?**

a) Talk to him about its effect on you.

b) Cover for him since it will not get any better.

c) Help him map his routes.

d) Assign him to a familiar territory.

e) Ask him to come in early to ensure he will be on time.

Question 6

What is the least effective way to deal with this situation?

a) Talk to him about its effect on you.

b) Cover for him since it will not get any better.

c) Help him map his routes.

d) Assign him to a familiar territory.

e) Ask him to come in early to ensure he will be on time.

Question 7

You have been given suggestions on how to improve your work and that of others in your department. One co-worker tells you that there is no way she is going to change the way she does things. She says her way has been good enough for years and there is no need to fix what isn't broken. **What is the most effective way to deal with this situation?**

a) Offer to counsel her.

b) Go to the trainer about the problems.

c) Remind the employees that change can be good.

d) Ignore their behaviour.

e) Talk to management about the problems.

Question 8

What is the least effective way to deal with this situation?

a) Offer to counsel her.

b) Go to the trainer about the problems.

c) Remind the employees that change can be good.

d) Ignore their behaviour.

e) Talk to management about the problems.

Question 9

When you approach a co-worker with a problem he is sarcastic and does not offer any help with a solution. His sarcasm is becoming overbearing and you are growing annoyed with your co-worker. **What is the most effective way to deal with this situation?**

a) Be sarcastic back to him.

b) Talk to him about the level of sarcasm.

c) Seek the advice of the human resources department.

d) Talk to the manager first.

e) Speak to his co-workers about how they deal with him.

Question 10

What is the least effective way to deal with this situation?

a) Be sarcastic back to him.

b) Talk to him about the level of sarcasm.

c) Seek the advice of the human resources department.

d) Talk to the manager first.

e) Speak to co-workers about how they deal with him.

Question 11

Your manager has behavioural quirks that many find distracting. However, you do not have any problem with him. Your co-workers ask you to talk to him about his strange behaviour. **What is the most effective way to deal with this situation?**

a) Offer to speak to him.

b) Provide advice on how to talk to him.

c) Go to management.

d) Tell them to keep away from him.

e) Offer to be the go-between.

Question 12

What is the least effective way to deal with this situation?

a) Offer to speak to him.

b) Provide advice on how to talk to him.

c) Go to management.

d) Tell them to keep away from him.

e) Offer to be the go-between.

Question 13

You are a new hire. Many times when you ask your manager for assistance, he sends you to someone else or tells you to do your own research. Often you can't find the answer or the assistance you need. **What is the most effective way to deal with this situation?**

a) Speak to his fellow managers.

b) Brush up on your knowledge to be able to perform your job better.

c) Ask him about his passing you off on others.

d) Go to the human resources department.

e) Deal with it and say nothing.

Question 14

What is the least effective way to deal with this situation?

a) Speak to his fellow managers.

b) Brush up on your knowledge to be able to perform your job better.

c) Ask him about his passing you off on others.

d) Go to the human resources department.

e) Deal with it and say nothing.

Question 15

Teams have been created according to skill sets rather than personal compatibility. Two team members who have always disliked each other and cannot work together have been assigned to the same team. Within ten minutes they are arguing. **What is the most effective way to deal with this situation?**

a) Remind them of the difference between a personal and professional relationship.

b) Look into having one employee transferred to another team.

c) Force them to work together.

d) Bring in the management.

e) Bring in a third party to help mediate.

Question 16

What is the least effective way to deal with this situation?

a) Remind them of the difference between a personal and professional relationship.

b) Assign the two to separate duties when possible.

c) Force them to work together.

d) Bring in the management.

e) Bring in a third party to help mediate.

Question 17

One team member is not doing his fair share of the work. This is causing tension among the other members, who feel they are being overworked, and is creating a hostile work environment. **What is the most effective way to deal with this situation?**

a) Speak to him about the importance of doing his fair share.

b) Ignore this and pick up the slack yourself.

c) Have a group meeting about it.

d) Remind the team of the importance of everyone doing their own part (avoid speaking directly to him).

e) Go to upper management.

Question 18

What is the least effective way to deal with this situation?

a) Speak to him about the importance of doing his fair share.

b) Ignore this and pick up the slack yourself.

c) Have a group meeting about it.

d) Remind the team of the importance of everyone doing their own part (avoid speaking directly to him).

e) Go to upper management.

Question 19

Many of your co-workers are late or away on the days company meetings are held. Management is asking for suggestions about how to encourage people to attend meetings and participate. Your co-workers do not attend because they feel excluded from participation. **What is the most effective way to deal with this situation?**

a) Inform management that many workers feel excluded at meetings.

b) Ask co-workers for their suggestions.

c) Remind them of the importance of meetings.

d) Do not offer any suggestions to help management.

e) Tell management about the co-workers' refusals.

Question 20

What is the least effective way to deal with this situation?

a) Inform management that many workers feel excluded at meetings.

b) Ask co-workers for their suggestions.

c) Remind them of the importance of meetings.

d) Do not offer any suggestions to help management.

e) Tell management about the co-workers' refusals.

Question 21

As part of a rebellion against mandatory meetings, some of your colleagues plan to call in sick on meeting days. You know they are not sick and encourage them to attend. They refuse. **What is the most effective way to deal with this situation?**

a) Remind them again of the importance of the meetings.

b) Suggest offering incentives for attending.

c) Go to management.

d) Contact human resources.

e) Drop it, since it is not your problem.

Question 22

What is the least effective way to deal with this situation?

a) Remind them again of the importance of the meetings.

b) Suggest offering incentives for attending.

c) Go to management.

d) Contact human resources.

e) Drop it, since it is not your problem.

Question 23

One of your employees is a diabetic. When presentations run too long he needs to eat something. A co-worker sees this and begins to loudly eat large meals at the same presentations. **What is the most effective way to deal with this situation?**

a) Take a vote about breaks during the meetings.

b) Explain why the other employee is allowed to eat.

c) Allow him to leave to snack.

d) Ignore his behaviour.

e) Ask the diabetic employee to step out to eat.

Question 24

What is the least effective way to deal with this situation?

a) Take a vote about breaks during the meetings.

b) Explain why the other employee is allowed to eat.

c) Allow him to leave to snack.

d) Ignore his behaviour.

e) Ask the diabetic employee to step out to eat.

Question 25

Everyone takes phone calls off a queue system, which randomly routes calls to the next available operator. The woman beside you takes restroom breaks every 30 minutes. Because of this, everyone else is forced to take more calls than is normal. **What is the most effective way to deal with this situation?**

a) Take up her slack on the phones.

b) Go to management.

c) Ask her if there is a problem since you notice she has been up often.

d) Go to human resources.

e) Offer to schedule around her breaks.

Question 26

What is the least effective way to deal with this situation?

a) Take up her slack on the phones.

b) Go to management.

c) Ask her if there is a problem since you notice she has been up often.

d) Go to human resources.

e) Offer to schedule around her breaks.

Question 27

The company allows employees to take as much sick time as needed. This does not reduce the amount of vacation or personal time. One employee takes more sick time than anyone else, yet comes to work obviously sick. This is a problem for everyone working in the office. **What is the most effective way to deal with this situation?**

a) Go to management.

b) Remind the employee of company policy regarding sick time.

c) Keep away from him at all costs.

d) Offer to cover his work for him.

e) Ask if other coworkers have a problem with his behaviour.

Question 28

What is the least effective way to deal with this situation?

a) Go to management.

b) Remind the employee of company policy regarding sick time.

c) Keep away from him at all costs.

d) Offer to cover his work for him.

e) Ask if other coworkers have a problem with his behaviour.

Question 29

Company policy clearly states that only plants are allowed on desks at work. A co-worker brings a fish to the office. The fish does not bother you, nor have any other co-workers mentioned it to you. **What is the most effective way to deal with this situation?**

a) Make an anonymous tip.

b) Offer to help her take it home.

c) Push the issue with her.

d) Go to management.

e) Ignore the situation as someone else can deal with it if they want to.

Question 30

What is the least effective way to deal with this situation?

a) Make an anonymous tip.

b) Offer to help her take it home.

c) Push the issue with her.

d) Go to management.

e) Drop the issue.

Question 31

You keep a bowl of candy on your desk for everyone to enjoy. One co-worker eats more than anyone else in the office. You ask the co-worker to help replenish the supply for you and they promise to bring it in Monday. Monday passes without them making good on their promise. **What is the most effective way to deal with this situation?**

a) Refill it yourself.

b) Take it to management.

c) Ask him for the candy again.

d) Ask him to reimburse you the cost.

e) Take the bowl down.

Question 32

What is the least effective way to deal with this situation?

a) Refill it yourself.

b) Take it to management.

c) Ask him for the candy again.

d) Ask him to reimburse you the cost.

e) Take the bowl down.

Question 33

A front desk employee is giving customers angry looks without realizing it. You have spoken with him about the situation but they were very defensive about it. He has not stopped despite your bringing it to his attention. **What is the most effective way to deal with this situation?**

a) Take the issue to management.

b) Talk to the human resource department.

c) Offer to cover his position.

d) Film the behaviour and show it to her.

e) Drop the issue.

Question 34

What is the least effective way to deal with this situation?

a) Take the issue to management.

b) Talk to the human resource department.

c) Offer to cover her position.

d) Film the behaviour and show it to her.

e) Drop the issue.

Question 35

You are on a panel of judges of a musical contest. You overhear one of the judges tell another judge that the winner should be one of their friends. **What is the most effective way to deal with this situation?**

a) Encourage the judge to remain objective.

b) Let the competitor know the rules about judges.

c) Request the judge step down due to the conflict of interest.

d) Ignore this fact since you will vote for his friend as well.

e) Go to the head judge for advice.

Question 36

What is the least effective way to deal with this situation?

a) Encourage the judge to remain objective.

b) Let the competitor know the rules about judges.

c) Request the judge step down due to the conflict of interest.

d) Ignore this fact since you will vote for his friend as well.

e) Go to the head judge for advice.

Question 37

On your first day at a new job your manager is rude to you and ignores your questions. After 3 weeks he warms up to you and is more willing to help. Later, you see him treat another new hire this way. **What is the most effective way to deal with this situation?**

a) Do nothing.

b) Ask the manager about it.

c) Talk to other co-workers.

d) Speak to human resources.

e) Make an anonymous report.

Question 38

What is the least effective way to deal with this situation?

a) Do nothing.

b) Ask the manager about it.

c) Talk to other co-workers.

d) Speak to human resources.

e) Make an anonymous report.

Question 39

You are a male employee experiencing difficulty with your manager. You notice that other male employees have the same trouble with this manager, but females do not. Other employees have voiced similar concerns to you. **What is the most effective way to deal with this situation?**

a) Offer your advice on how to deal with the situation.

b) Talk to the manager.

c) Talk to the human resource department.

d) Go over his head to his manager.

e) Tell people to deal with it.

Question 40

What is the least effective way to deal with this situation?

a) Offer your advice on how to deal with the situation.

b) Talk to the manager.

c) Talk to the human resource department.

d) Talk to his manager.

e) Tell people to deal with it.

Question 41

You are having difficulty finding your manager in his office and must seek necessary answers from different managers. When you ask your manager about this, he tells you that you must make an appointment to see him. **What is the most effective way to deal with this situation?**

a) Go to his manager about him not being available.

b) Talk to human resources.

c) Argue your point with him about his needing to be readily available.

d) Make an appointment with him.

e) Ask to make his availability part of the policy manual.

Question 42

What is the least effective way to deal with this situation?

a) Go to his manager about him not being available.

b) Talk to human resources.

c) Argue your point with him about his needing to be readily available.

d) Make an appointment with him.

e) Ask to make his availability part of the policy manual.

Question 43

The R&D department has developed a toy that does not meet all of the safety requirements to be suitable for young children. Despite this fact, the head of the department wants to market the toys immediately. He thinks generating immediate revenue justifies risking a recall. **What is the most effective way to deal with this situation?**

a) Go along with the launch since it is not going to be your problem in the future.

b) Remind him of the problems with the toy and the negative impact this could have.

c) Contact management with your concerns about launching the toy.

d) Go to the approval department with your concerns about launching the toy.

e) Write a report about your concerns with launching the toy.

Question 44

What is the least effective way to deal with this situation?

a) Go along with the launch since it is not going to be your problem in the future.

b) Remind him of the problems with the toy and the negative impact this could have.

c) Contact management with your concerns about launching the toy.

d) Go to the approval department with your concerns about launching the toy.

e) Write a report about your concerns with launching the toy.

Question 45

Many telephone service customers have been receiving their bills after their due dates. When you contact the head of the billing department, she curses at you and tells you that the customers are stupid. **What is the most effective way to deal with this situation?**

a) Waive the late fees.

b) Ignore the problem.

c) Explain the error.

d) Go to her manager.

e) Notate the customer accounts.

Question 46

What is the least effective way to deal with this situation?

a) Waive the late fees.

b) Ignore the problem.

c) Explain the error.

d) Go to her manager.

e) Notate the customer accounts.

Question 47

A co-worker, known for violent threats against others outside of work, threatens his manager for not allowing him to take next week off. **What is the most effective way to deal with this situation?**

a) Offer to mediate for the two at a later time.

b) Suggest anger management classes.

c) Speak to the employee and manager immediately.

d) Call in human resources.

e) Walk away completely.

Question 48

What is the least effective way to deal with this situation?

a) Offer to mediate for the two at a later time.

b) Suggest anger management classes.

c) Speak to the employee and manager immediately while the incident is occurring.

d) Call in human resources.

e) Walk away completely.

Question 49

You work for a charity organization which designates funds to specific causes. A new employee asks if he can use funds where they are most needed despite their designation. You tell him that he cannot. Later that week you notice this same employee mixing up the donations. **What is the most effective way to deal with this situation?**

a) Go to management.

b) Ask him to leave.

c) Remind him again.

d) Work on your own and ignore him.

e) Take over his project for him.

Question 50

What is the least effective way to deal with this situation?

a) Go to management.

b) Ask him to leave.

c) Remind him again.

d) Work on your own and ignore him.

e) Take over his project for him.

Question 51

An industry pricing body dictates the price a company can charge for certain services. Your employer has been overcharging some customers for services. You bring this to her attention and she threatens your job if you say anything about her practices. **What is the most effective way to deal with this situation?**

a) Do not say anything.

b) Make a report to the pricing body.

c) Refund the overage to the customers.

d) Charge the correct prices.

e) Refuse to work there.

Question 52

What is the least effective way to deal with this situation?

a) Do not say anything.

b) Make a report to the pricing body.

c) Refund the overage to the customers.

d) Charge the correct prices.

e) Refuse to work there.

Question 53

Your employer, a pharmacist, has made a pile of expired medications to be destroyed. You see a co-worker load the medications into his locker. He tells you he has been changing the expiration dates and selling them to drug addicts. **What is the most effective way to deal with this situation?**

a) Go to the pharmacist with this information.

b) Tell him his behaviour is illegal.

c) Go in on it with him.

d) Speak to the human resource department.

e) Contact local authorities.

Question 54

What is the least effective way to deal with this situation?

a) Go to the pharmacist with this information.

b) Tell him his behaviour is illegal.

c) Go in on it with him.

d) Speak to the human resource department.

e) Contact local authorities.

Question 55

Your claims procedure is extremely complex. You overhear a co-worker oversimplifying the procedure and telling a customer things that are not entirely true. When you ask him about it he tells you it is funny to confuse the customer.
What is the most effective way to deal with this situation?

a) Offer to help him explain it.

b) Take over his calls while he listens.

c) Go to management.

d) Remind him of his duty.

e) Agree with him and go on with your own work.

Question 56

What is the least effective way to deal with this situation?

a) Offer to help him explain it.

b) Take over his calls while he listens.

c) Go to management.

d) Remind him of his duty.

e) Agree with him and go on with your own work.

Question 57

You have been told that a co-worker is making empty threats when collecting company debts. He tells you that he was told to do whatever it takes to collect these debts. You later overhear him making these threats when a customer irritates him. **What is the most effective way to deal with this situation?**

a) Talk to the trainer to change company policies.

b) Reprimand the co-worker for being threatening.

c) Ignore it, since he will not listen.

d) Go to management.

e) Offer to show him alternatives to his approach.

Question 58

What is the least effective way to deal with this situation?

a) Talk to the trainer to change company policies.

b) Reprimand the co-worker for being threatening.

c) Ignore it, since he will not listen.

d) Go to management.

e) Offer to show him alternatives to his approach.

Question 59

It is against company policy to contact customers at work about billing issues. However, the customer's work phone numbers are in your system. Complaints are coming in about a new employee who has been calling people at work. **What is the most effective way to deal with this situation?**

a) Ask him if he would like you to mentor him.

b) Listen to his calls for mistakes.

c) Go to management.

d) Speak to the employee.

e) Log the complaints but do not tell anyone.

Question 60

What is the least effective way to deal with this situation?

a) Ask him if he would like you to mentor him.

b) Listen to his calls for mistakes.

c) Go to management.

d) Speak to the employee.

e) Log the complaints but do not tell anyone.

Question 61

The telemarketers rely on the computer system to monitor time zone differences so they do not call after legal hours. When the callers get complaints about calling too late, they tell the manager. He decides to ignore the complaints and continue calling. **What is the most effective way to deal with this situation?**

a) Make as many phone calls as you can.

b) Refuse to make the calls.

c) Submit another report complaining about the illegal activity.

d) Take a break until the list is changed.

e) Pretend to be making calls.

Question 62

What is the least effective way to deal with this situation?

a) Make as many phone calls as you can.

b) Refuse to make the calls.

c) Submit another report complaining about the illegal activity.

d) Take a break until the list is changed.

e) Pretend to be making calls.

Question 63

One of your co-workers is always ahead of schedule on his projects. He likes to brag about this to the other employees and is doing this more often. **What is the most effective way to deal with this situation?**

a) Work harder to finish sooner.

b) Tell management.

c) Attack him back.

d) Tell him how harmful he is being.

e) Ignore his attacks.

Question 64

What is the least effective way to deal with this situation?

a) Work harder to finish sooner.

b) Tell management.

c) Attack him back.

d) Tell him the harm of this.

e) Ignore his attacks.

Question 65

When a co-worker has completed his assigned work he sits idle at his desk. However, the company wants employees to assist others when their own work is completed. You hear this co-worker on the phone bragging about his speed and his refusal to assist others. **What is the most effective way to deal with this situation?**

a) Go to management.

b) Remind him of company policy and threaten to go to the manager.

c) Ask him for help.

d) Refuse to help him at a later date.

e) Drop your work on his desk and demand he complete it.

Question 66

What is the least effective way to deal with this situation?

a) Go to management.

b) Remind him of company policy.

c) Ask him for help.

d) Refuse to help him at a later date.

e) Drop your work on his desk and demand he complete it.

Question 67

A co-worker needs time off for a doctor's appointment. She tells you she will be gone two hours. She does not return for the remainder of the day and never calls in to say why. **What is the most effective way to deal with this situation?**

a) Speak to human resources.

b) Ask her to cover your shift for the difference.

c) Ask her what happened the next day.

d) Stop taking her calls after the first two hours.

e) Complain to management.

Question 68

What is the least effective way to deal with this situation?

a) Speak to human resources.

b) Ask her to cover your shift for the difference.

c) Ask her what happened the next day.

d) Stop taking her calls after the first two hours.

e) Complain to management.

Question 69

While picking up your print job, you notice there are invitations printed on the colour copier. It is against company policy to use the printers for personal matters. **What is the most effective way to deal with this situation?**

a) Leave them on the printer and say nothing.

b) Remind the co-worker about company policy on printer use.

c) Place one in the supervisor's box.

d) Leave them on the co-worker's desk.

e) Let management know.

Question 70

What is the least effective way to deal with this situation?

a) Leave them on the printer and say nothing.

b) Remind the co-worker about company policy on printer use.

c) Place one in the supervisor's box.

d) Leave them on the co-worker's desk.

e) Let management know.

Question 71

You are the team leader of a work group. One member would rather work on a project alone. He takes on more responsibility so that he does not have to work with others, but this bothers the other team members. **What is the most effective way to deal with this situation?**

a) Speak to management.

b) Allow him to work alone; he gets better results that way.

c) Show him the benefits of cooperation.

d) Create more teamwork projects that everyone might enjoy.

e) Work with him yourself for the first few projects.

Question 72

What is the least effective way to deal with this situation?

a) Speak to management.

b) Allow him to work alone; he gets better results that way.

c) Show him the benefits of cooperation.

d) Create more teamwork projects that everyone might enjoy.

e) Work with him yourself for the first few projects.

Question 73

A more efficient method of performing key procedures has been introduced to the team members. A couple of workers have told you that they will not implement this new procedure. **What is the most effective way to deal with this situation?**

a) Offer to help them change the procedures so they will be able to keep up.

b) Tell management.

c) Allow them to get into trouble for not implementing the changes.

d) Sign them up for another training session on the new procedures.

e) Show how the changes can be used in their department.

Question 74

What is the least effective way to deal with this situation?

a) Offer to help them change the procedures so they will be able to keep up.

b) Tell management.

c) Allow them to get into trouble for not implementing the changes.

d) Sign them up for another training session on the new procedures.

e) Show how the changes can be used in their department.

Question 75

Major changes have been made to the way flex-time is applied at the company. This is causing problems for you because of daycare restrictions.
What is the most effective way to deal with this situation?

a) Rearrange your own schedule.

b) Speak to management.

c) Pay for after-hours care.

d) Say nothing and bring your children to work.

e) Request a raise to cover the added cost.

Question 76

What is the least effective way to deal with this situation?

a) Rearrange your own schedule.

b) Speak to management.

c) Pay for after-hours care.

d) Say nothing and bring your children to work.

e) Request a raise to cover the added cost.

Question 77

Management has asked if anyone is available to work nights. When not enough people volunteer, they force people to work nights on a rotating basis. You care for an aging parent at night, so you cannot work then. **What is the most effective way to deal with this situation?**

a) Say nothing, but do not show up when you need to take care of the parent.

b) Hire a live-in caregiver.

c) Ask to perform work from home.

d) Talk to co-workers about covering the shifts.

e) Explain your situation to management.

Question 78

What is the least effective way to deal with this situation?

a) Say nothing, but do not show up when you need to take care of the parent.

b) Hire a live-in caregiver.

c) Ask to perform work from home.

d) Talk to co-workers about covering the shifts.

e) Explain your situation to management.

Question 79

You have been training older employees on the computer. One employee cannot grasp the concept you are presenting. Numerous different approaches with this employee have failed. **What is the most effective way to deal with this situation?**

a) Ask someone else to try a fresh approach to teaching him.

b) Speak to management about the training problems.

c) Give up and get angry about things.

d) Offer some one-on-one sessions with the employee.

e) Allow them to sit with you as part of a mentor program.

Question 80

What is the least effective way to deal with this situation?

a) Ask someone else to try a fresh approach to teaching him.

b) Speak to management about the training problems.

c) Give up and get angry about things.

d) Offer some one-on-one sessions with the employee.

e) Allow them to sit with you as part of a mentor program.

Question 81

You have been trying to accommodate a disabled co-worker who has asked that others perform his basic function at work. There are laws about what must be done when a person is physically incapable of performing a job. **What is the most effective way to deal with this situation?**

a) Ask human resources for assistance.

b) Pass his work onto others.

c) Redefine his position.

d) Speak to him about the limits of the law.

e) Offer to transfer to another position.

Question 82

What is the least effective way to deal with this situation?

a) Ask human resources for assistance.

b) Pass his work onto others.

c) Redefine his position.

d) Speak to him about the limits of the law.

e) Offer to transfer to another position.

Question 83

A co-worker whom you work closely with often stays late and uses candles for lighting. He has left candles burning all night at times. **What is the most effective way to deal with this situation?**

a) Tell your supervisor.

b) Allow him to continue and hope he will eventually learn.

c) Request a new partner.

d) Ask for some refresher training.

e) Talk to him about how his behaviour is putting you both at risk.

Question 84

What is the least effective way to deal with this situation?

a) Tell your supervisor.

b) Allow him to continue and eventually he will learn.

c) Request a new partner.

d) Ask for some refresher training.

e) Talk to him about how his behaviour is putting you both at risk.

Question 85

In the emergency room you see many different types of people with a great variety of personal problems. A co-worker is quick to vocalize her judgment and opinion of these patients. **What is the most effective way to deal with this situation?**

a) Speak to the head nurse.

b) Apologize to the patients.

c) Ask her to keep them to herself.

d) Go along with what she says to keep the peace.

e) Request a sensitivity training class be mandatory.

Question 86

What is the least effective way to deal with this situation?

a) Speak to the head nurse.

b) Apologize to the patients.

c) Ask her to keep them to herself.

d) Go along with what she says to keep the peace.

e) Request a sensitivity training class be mandatory.

Question 87

A headstrong co-worker has difficulty with authority. You have made suggestions to him about how to better handle his assignments, but he tells you to mind your own business. **What is the most effective way to deal with this situation?**

a) Pursue it again.

b) Engage him in a discussion.

c) Ask human resources for assistance.

d) Allow him to perform his assignments as he sees fit.

e) Talk to management about the problems.

Question 88

What is the least effective way to deal with this situation?

a) Pursue it again.

b) Engage him in a discussion.

c) Ask human resources for assistance.

d) Allow him to perform his assignments as he sees fit.

e) Talk to management about the problems.

Question 89

A group of employees like to joke around at inappropriate times. They come across as harsh and unfeeling to others. Because they are your friends, you have been asked to speak to them about how they make others feel. **What is the most effective way to deal with this situation?**

a) Explain that the jokesters shouldn't be taken seriously.

b) Listen to their complaints but do nothing to help.

c) Tell the others to talk to the jokesters about how they make them feel.

d) Play a joke on the jokesters in the office.

e) Go to management with the dilemma.

Question 90

What is the least effective way to deal with this situation?

a) Explain that the jokesters shouldn't be taken seriously.

b) Listen to their complaints but do nothing to help.

c) Tell the others to talk to the jokesters about how they make them feel.

d) Play a joke on the jokesters in the office.

e) Go to management with the dilemma.

Question 91

Company policy does not allow employees to book off time for more than one holiday in a row. A co-worker has called in sick for herself or her children for every holiday in the past 6 months. This is resented by others who have wanted time off. **What is the most effective way to deal with this situation?**

a) Allow others to have their time off and work short-handed.

b) Reduce the woman's cheque for the extra time off.

c) Inform her how her absence is impacting the holidays of others.

d) Speak to management about it.

e) Fire her for violating policy.

Question 92

What is the least effective way to deal with this situation?

a) Allow others to have their time off and work short handed.

b) Reduce the woman's cheque for the extra time off.

c) Inform her how her absence is impacting the holidays of others.

d) Speak to management about it.

e) Fire her for violating policy.

Question 93

A co-worker who is displeased with her raise has been very vocal about it. She is telling others how much she makes, which is against policy and is creating a tense environment. **What is the most effective way to deal with this situation?**

a) Remind her of the policy.

b) Discuss your pay rate with her.

c) Inform management.

d) Call in human resources.

e) Encourage her to speak to management about her displeasure.

Question 94

What is the least effective way to deal with this situation?

a) Remind her of the policy.

b) Discuss your pay rate with her.

c) Inform management.

d) Call in human resources.

e) Encourage her to speak to management about her displeasure.

Question 95

You are the switchboard operator for your company. It is against policy to receive too many personal phone calls at work. One employee receives many personal calls each day. **What is the most effective way to deal with this situation?**

a) Go to management with the information.

b) Offer to take a message for her.

c) Remind her of the company policy on personal calls.

d) Refuse to transfer personal calls.

e) Inform the callers of the policy in place.

Question 96

What is the least effective way to deal with this situation?

a) Go to management with the information.

b) Offer to take a message for her.

c) Remind her of the company policy on personal calls.

d) Refuse to transfer personal calls.

e) Inform the callers of the policy in place.

Question 97

Your company has lately received a lot of media attention. A co-worker has told you that he has recently given a candid and revealing off-camera interview. This has caused a lot of trouble for the company. **What is the most effective way to deal with this situation?**

a) Continue as if you do not know who the source was.

b) Ask him to consider recanting the story and have him speak to management.

c) Go to management with the information.

d) Make a rebuttal statement to the media.

e) Make an anonymous statement about the source.

Question 98

What is the least effective way to deal with this situation?

a) Go along as if you do not know the source.

b) Ask him to consider recanting the story and have him speak to management.

c) Go to management with the information.

d) Make a rebuttal statement to the media.

e) Make an anonymous statement about the source.

Question 99

Decisions in your department are made by voting. One member of the department argues with every decision, even when the vote is unanimous. He likes to confide in you about his dissatisfaction. **What is the most effective way to deal with this situation?**

a) Encourage him to file an appeal on the circumstance.

b) Tell him to get over it and that you do not care about his problems.

c) Remind him it is a democratic system.

d) Ask him to evaluate the importance of the decision to him.

e) Inform management of his dissatisfaction.

Question 100

What is the least effective way to deal with this situation?

a) Encourage him to file an appeal on the circumstance.

b) Tell him to get over it and that you do not care about his problems.

c) Remind him it is a democratic system.

d) Ask him to evaluate the importance of the decision to him.

e) Inform management of his dissatisfaction.

SJT Answer Key

1) E	26) A	51) B	76) D
2) C	27) B	52) A	77) E
3) B	28) C	53) A	78) A
4) D	29) E	54) C	79) B
5) A	30) A	55) D	80) C
6) B	31) C	56) E	81) D
7) C	32) B	57) E	82) B
8) D	33) A	58) C	83) E
9) B	34) E	59) D	84) B
10) A	35) C	60) E	85) C
11) B	36) D	61) B	86) D
12) D	37) B	62) A	87) D
13) C	38) A	63) D	88) E
14) E	39) B	64) C	89) C
15) B	40) E	65) C	90) B
16) C	41) D	66) E	91) C
17) A	42) B	67) C	92) E
18) B	43) B	68) D	93) A
19) A	44) A	69) B	94) B
20) D	45) D	70) A	95) C
21) C	46) B	71) C	96) D
22) E	47) C	72) B	97) B
23) B	48) E	73) E	98) A
24) D	49) C	74) C	99) C
25) C	50) D	75) B	100) B

Question 1

Allow the employee to change his behaviour before bringing in management. The best way to do this is to show him that he is affecting the productivity of others.

Question 2

This will only cause the problem to worsen. The employee may not realize that he is causing problems and allowing it to continue will hurt employee morale.

Question 3

Telling the truth is always the best thing to do.

Question 4

It is never appropriate to lie about a situation. It will only cause problems for you later.

Question 5

Allow the employee to know how his actions affect others. Helping him map his routes would not be effective, as you are not convinced that his excuses are legitimate. He is already expected to be on time, so asking him to come in early would not be effective.

Question 6

This is not acceptable as it gives him the impression that he is performing his job well enough.

Question 7

This reminder can foster a more accepting attitude without having to bring in management. Suggest that change can make her work even more efficient.

Question 8

By ignoring their behaviour you are indirectly agreeing with them.

Question 9

If possible, it is best to first deal with a co-worker directly.

Question 10

This is confrontational and does not accomplish anything. It also condones continual unacceptable behaviour from him.

Question 11

This will allow the employees who are having trouble with him to deal with him directly. It is not your responsibility to do so.

Question 12

This action does not solve the problem. Also, it is not your responsibility to solve a problem you are not having.

Question 13

It is best to air your concerns rather than bottling them up. It is also the responsibility of your manager to deal with your queries.

Question 14

This action will not deal with the problem or provide the answers you seek. It will also undermine your relationship with your manager.

Question 15

Sometimes two people cannot work together. This is a long-term relationship issue, and keeping them separated makes the most sense.

Question 16

This is not a solution because it will impede the progress of the work teams.

Question 17

It is important to deal directly with the co-worker with whom you are having the problem. Also, failure to do so might encourage similar behaviour in others.

Question 18

By ignoring the problem you are condoning the behaviour. You also risk encouraging it in others.

Question 19

It is the responsibility of management to create an inclusive environment at the meetings. Providing the feedback requested is the best solution.

Question 20

This is not helpful to anyone. Management should be made aware of the reasons your co-workers are not coming to meetings.

Question 21

Because these employees are blatantly breaking company policy by calling in sick, this needs to be referred to their superiors. Otherwise, more workers might be coerced into joining in.

Question 22

This is a matter for management. Keeping this information from them will only allow the problem to grow.

Question 23

Providing the employee with the reasons why his co-worker is allowed to eat will help the employee to understand why he cannot.

Question 24

Ignoring his behaviour could be misconstrued as condoning it. Soon your meetings and presentations will become impractical because everyone will be distracted by noisy eating.

Question 25

This will open channels of communication about a medical condition that she has been reluctant to divulge, or any other problems she is having.

Question 26

This covers up rather than solves the problem.

Question 27

Give the co-worker a chance to deal with his situation before telling him what to do.

Question 28

You may avoid getting sick, but you will be avoiding the problem of the employee abusing company policy.

Question 29

If a co-worker is breaking a rule that is not affecting you or anyone else, and the behaviour is obvious to everyone, you should leave it to management to make a decision.

Question 30

In this situation, no one is bothered by the co-workers actions. If there were concerns you should take it up with the co-worker yourself, or speak to a manager, instead of dropping an anonymous tip. This could create a hostile work environment.

Question 31

This is the best way to deal with it since it deals with the employee directly.

Question 32

This is not important enough to take to management. Good employees should be able to work these things out between one another.

Question 33
This needs to be taken to management since the co-worker is not doing anything to correct their behaviour.

Question 34
By dropping the issue you are allowing the poor customer service to continue.

Question 35
The judge must be dismissed because of his demonstrated inability to remain objective.

Question 36
This is the worst option because it condones unfair behaviour on the part of the judge.

Question 37
It is best to deal directly with the person with whom you have a problem.

Question 38
Ignoring his treatment of others will perpetuate it. He might not be aware of how he is affecting people.

Question 39
It is best to speak directly to the manager with whom you are having the problem.

Question 40
This is not helpful because it will allow the manager to continue in his behaviour.

Question 41
This compromise will allow you to see your manager and allow him to keep his other scheduled appointments.

Question 42
Because your manager might be legitimately busy, going behind his back could create a hostile work environment. It is preferable to approach him directly, or speak with his peers (the other managers), before creating a human resources issue.

Question 43
Give the department head a chance to change his mind before taking it to his superiors.

Question 44
This attitude might create an unsafe situation. When the recall occurs it will result in a lack of trust with the public. You might also be risking the health and safety of others.

Question 45
Because she was not receptive to your notification of the problem, this needs to be referred to management.

Question 46
Ignoring the problem sends the message that her behaviour is acceptable.

Question 47
It is best to deal with the situation as it is occurring.

Question 48
This action sends the message that you condone the behaviour that you witnessed.

Question 49

This will give the employee a chance to correct his behaviour. Perhaps he didn't properly hear what you told him. You also cannot be certain whether he is making an honest mistake or not.

Question 50

This action does not solve the problem. Rather, it sends the message that company policies are not important.

Question 51

This is the best action since they have the authority to enforce the pricing guidelines.

Question 52

This action avoids the situation and allows the overcharging to continue.

Question 53

An employee is committing an illegal act, which could have major consequences for the company. He may also be endangering peoples' lives. You must notify a manager immediately.

Question 54

This does not solve the problem behaviour. In fact, it encourages it.

Question 55

It is important to reinforce the job duties and allow the co-worker to correct his behaviour.

Question 56

If you agree with incorrect behaviour you are condoning it.

Question 57

It is best to talk to your co-worker about his problems before bringing them to management. You may be able to show him a more effective way of handling customers.

Question 58

This action will only allow the problem to continue.

Question 59

If possible, it is best to first deal with a co-worker directly.

Question 60

By not saying anything you are sending the message that this is acceptable behaviour.

Question 61

Send the message that you will not break the rules. Otherwise, you will endanger both the company's reputation and your own sales potential.

Question 62

This will damage the reputation of the company and encourage the manager to persist in his practices.

Question 63

Talk to a co-worker about problems you are having with their behaviour before bringing in management. Perhaps they are not aware of the harm they are doing.

Question 64
This is confrontational and will only encourage him to continue in his unprofessional behaviour.

Question 65
It is best to deal with the co-worker directly on a problem before bringing in management. Simply asking for help might produce the desired response.

Question 66
This is confrontational and might create a hostile work environment.

Question 67
If possible, it is best to first deal with a co-worker directly.

Question 68
This will not deal with the problem of the co-worker not returning. Rather, it punishes the customers, which makes the company as a whole look bad.

Question 69
If possible, it is best to first deal with a co-worker directly.

Question 70
If you say nothing you are indirectly condoning their behaviour.

Question 71
Showing him the benefits of cooperation will encourage him to work better with others.

Question 72
This will undermine the work of your team and condone his selfish behaviour.

Question 73
Help your co-workers deal with a problem before bringing in management. You shouldn't arbitrarily change procedures or sign them up for training.

Question 74
This condones their behaviour and will cost the company in terms of productivity.

Question 75
There may be an alternative option that will take into account your extenuating circumstances. The best option is to open a dialogue.

Question 76
This could lead to you being reprimanded. You have not given management a chance to help you with your situation.

Question 77
This will give management a chance to work out an alternative for you. Clear communication is always the best option.

Question 78
Not showing up for work, without even talking to anyone for an alternative option, will make you look like an inefficient and unprofessional employee. It will do you more harm in the long run.

Question 79

You have done everything you can for this employee, management now needs to be brought in.

Question 80

Giving up will not solve the problem and will ultimately lessen the productivity of your department.

Question 81

You are legally obligated to accommodate the disabled employee. However, there needs to be a balance between accommodation and his taking advantage of the situation.

Question 82

This does not accomplish anything beyond allowing the employee to not perform his core function. This will make the disabled employee redundant, which will lessen his self-esteem. It might also make his co-workers resentful.

Question 83

If possible, it is best to first deal with a co-worker directly.

Question 84

This might involve him getting hurt and could certainly endanger the lives of others. You should be more proactive than that.

Question 85

It is important to first deal directly with the co-worker with whom you are having the problem.

Question 86

This may keep the peace between the two of you but her actions remain unprofessional and she needs to be made aware of this fact.

Question 87

There is no sign that your co-worker is under performing. You should allow him to work the way he sees fit. If you aren't personally affected, it isn't any of your business.

Question 88

There is no need to go to management about the performance of a co-worker. It is the duty of management to assess performances.

Question 89

It is best if the workers involved in the situation deal with each other directly. If you are not affected by the jokesters, it is not your problem.

Question 90

This will not solve their problem and will just further involve you in the situation.

Question 91

Ask that she make arrangements that abide by the company's policy. It is best to deal with this person directly.

Question 92

This is an extreme option for such a policy violation and there is no indication that you have the authority.

Question 93

Bringing in management should only happen after you first attempt to solve problems with co-workers. It is important to try and stop co-workers from violating company policy.

Question 94

This would condone her breaking of company policy.

Question 95

If possible, it is best to first deal with a co-worker directly.

Question 96

This puts the blame on the callers, which is not good for the company's image. They may not know about the policy. Another option should be used.

Question 97

It is important to try and encourage the co-worker to be honest.

Question 98

Dishonest behaviour like this has no place in the work environment.

Question 99

If possible, it is best to first deal with a co-worker directly.

Question 100

It is never productive to dismiss a co-worker's feelings on any situation.

WCPT

The Written Communication Proficiency Test (WCPT) measures an individual's ability to communicate in writing. These exams are used to assess employees (manager level) or leaders whose position requires them to write clear and concise letters, memos, reports or other documents. The test contains a number of short passages, which have errors and modified paragraphs that have to be corrected. There are a total of 50 multiple-choice questions in the following areas:

· Grammar
· Punctuation
· Fill in the blank
· Ordering sentences
· Reading comprehension

The test takes about 1 hour and 20 minutes to complete. If you are unsuccessful you must wait 180 days before you can rewrite the test.

Only paper, pencils and erasers are allowed - no books, dictionaries, notes, writing paper, calculators, calculator watches or other aids are permitted in the room.

Detach the answer key to take the test.

WCPT ANSWER KEY

	A	B	C	D			A	B	C	D			A	B	C	D	
1)	○	○	○	○	___	11)	○	○	○	○	___	21)	○	○	○	○	___
2)	○	○	○	○	___	12)	○	○	○	○	___	22)	○	○	○	○	___
3)	○	○	○	○	___	13)	○	○	○	○	___	23)	○	○	○	○	___
4)	○	○	○	○	___	14)	○	○	○	○	___	24)	○	○	○	○	___
5)	○	○	○	○	___	15)	○	○	○	○	___	25)	○	○	○	○	___
6)	○	○	○	○	___	16)	○	○	○	○	___	26)	○	○	○	○	___
7)	○	○	○	○	___	17)	○	○	○	○	___	27)	○	○	○	○	___
8)	○	○	○	○	___	18)	○	○	○	○	___	28)	○	○	○	○	___
9)	○	○	○	○	___	19)	○	○	○	○	___	29)	○	○	○	○	___
10)	○	○	○	○	___	20)	○	○	○	○	___	30)	○	○	○	○	___

	A	B	C	D			A	B	C	D	
31)	○	○	○	○	___	41)	○	○	○	○	___
32)	○	○	○	○	___	42)	○	○	○	○	___
33)	○	○	○	○	___	43)	○	○	○	○	___
34)	○	○	○	○	___	44)	○	○	○	○	___
35)	○	○	○	○	___	45)	○	○	○	○	___
36)	○	○	○	○	___	46)	○	○	○	○	___
37)	○	○	○	○	___	47)	○	○	○	○	___
38)	○	○	○	○	___	48)	○	○	○	○	___
39)	○	○	○	○	___	49)	○	○	○	○	___
40)	○	○	○	○	___	50)	○	○	○	○	___

Read the following paragraphs and answer the questions.

Paragraph A

(1)The main concern these citizen's have is the removal of barriers, but this legislation wouldn't provide these citizen's with the remedy _____ long been waiting for. (2)The bill would require municipalities, schools, transit systems, hospitals, universities and colleges to develop plans that identify barriers in their policies and programs. (3)There's no requirement for these bodies to implement their plans or set deadlines to eliminate the barriers.

Paragraph B

(4)Jill Givens pledged more than two-years ago to enact legislation knocking down the barriers that stand in the way of people with disabilities. (5)The bill will be introduced next year. (6)It is a step in the right direction, but it will need _____ amendment to bring about the changes demanded by the 1.6 million Canadians with disabilities. (7)The proposed law would raise public awareness of the many barriers that impede people with disabilities from working, going to school or simply _____ a normal life.

Paragraph C

(8)Nor does the new Disabilities Act go beyond encouraging the private sector to make facilities, and services more accessible. (9)Nothing will happen if moral persuasion fails. (10)Provincial officials and community advocates agree that part of the problem is the lack of common standards to define accessibility. (11)Two new councils will be created to set such standards and advise the government on future initiatives.

Question 1

Which of the following alternatives is the right order of the three paragraphs of the text?

a) A, C, B
b) B, A, C
c) B, C, A
d) C, A, B

Question 2

Which of the following is the most appropriate title for the text?

a) A Final Solution to Disability Issues
b) Total Barrier Elimination
c) Awareness But Not Enough Action
d) Canada's Political Agenda

Question 3

Which of the following rephrases of Sentence 4 is best in terms of style and conciseness?

a) The legislation being knocked down was pledged by Jill Givens two years ago for people with disabilities.

b) People with disabilities pledged more than two years ago to enact legislation knocking down the barriers that stand in their way.

c) Knocking down barriers that stand in the way of people with disabilities by changing legislation has been a promise of Jill Givens for more than two years.

d) Jill Givens enacted legislation more than two years ago knocking down the barriers that stand in the way of people with disabilities.

Question 4

Which of the following words, if inserted in the blank in Sentence 6, would best fit the style of the sentence in the whole text?

a) Substantial

b) Big

c) Infinitesimal

d) Gargantuan

Question 5

Which of the following phrases, if added in the blank in Sentence 7, would best fit the meaning of the paragraph?

a) sharing

b) being

c) leading

d) belonging

Question 6

Which of the following changes is needed in the text?

a) Sentence 6: change the comma after direction to a semicolon.

b) Sentence 1: change citizen's to citizens.

c) Sentence 7: change raise to rise.

d) Sentence 11: replace Two with Too

Question 7

Which of the following changes would improve the text?

a) Sentence 2: add a comma after policies.

b) Sentence 3: remove the apostrophe in the word there's.

c) Sentence 4: add dashes to the words people-with-disabilities.

d) Sentence 8: remove the comma after the word facilities.

Question 8

Where would you most likely find this article?

a) Training Manual

b) Newspaper

c) Design Magazine

d) Sales Brochure

Question 9

Which of the following changes would improve the text?

a) Sentence 4: remove the dash between two-years.

b) Sentence 7: remove the comma after working.

c) Sentence 8: add an apostrophe to the word disabilities.

d) Sentence 11: add an apostrophe to the word councils

Question 10

What is the best word to replace the blank space in sentence 1?

a) that has
b) have
c) they've
d) they're

Read the following three paragraphs and answer the ensuing questions based on what you have read.

Paragraph A

(1) Beset by a troubled administration and serious financial woes that could mean tax hikes or service cuts, Edmonton needs a top _____ who can provide a steady hand on the tiller. (2) A city search committee has unanimously picked Jeff Harris to be the new chief administrative officer. (3) Counsel should enthusiastically endorse this choice; when it debates the issue in counsel this week.

Paragraph B

(4) Harris's former work in the City of Calgary, his term as commissioner of community and neighbourhood services with Edmonton and his most recent job as interim chief administrative officer give him strong qualifications to take on this big job. (5) "He has the mettle and the smarts to manage a city with a $4 billion operating budget and 18,000 employees."

Paragraph C

(6) He has the backbone to make hard decisions and the sensitivity to ensure that the vulnerable _____ not victimized. (7) Harris has earned the respect of staff and counsellors alike and has a good rapport with Mayor Bing, something that his _____, Janet Dawson, never enjoyed, which ultimately led to her departure in March. (8) Unlike someone hired from outside the province, Harris is already well acquainted with the personalities and issues at City Hall. (9) If selected, Harris would take on the job with a "to do" list already filled with tasks.

Question 11

Which of the following words, if inserted in the blank in Sentence 7, would best fit the style of the sentence in the whole text?

a) enemy
b) pal
c) predecessor
d) alias

Question 12

Which of the following words, if inserted in the blank in Sentence 1, would best fit the style of the sentence in the whole text?

a) debater
b) bureaucrat
c) man
d) parliamentarian

Question 13

Which of the following words, if inserted in the blank in Sentence 6, would best fit the style of the sentence in the whole text?

a) are
b) is
c) were
d) can

Question 14

Which of the following alternatives is the right order of the three paragraphs of the text?

a) A, B, C

b) C, A, B

c) B, C, A

d) B, A, C

Question 15

Which of the following would be the best title for the article?

a) Fixing Corruption

b) Searching for Leadership

c) Edmonton Politics

d) A Welcome Change to the Helm

Question 16

Where would this article most likely be displayed in a newspaper?

a) Political Editorial Section

b) Provincial Affairs Section

c) Municipal Affairs Section

d) National Affairs Section

Question 17

Which of the following rephrases of Sentence 2 is best in terms of style and conciseness?

a) Jeff Harris picked himself unanimously as the new chief administrative officer by a city search committee.

b) The new chief administrative officer would best be filled by Jeff Harris.

c) Jeff Harris was unanimously picked by a city search committee as the new chief administrative officer.

d) A city search committee unanimously picked their new chief administrative officer. The new chief administrative officer is going to be Jeff Harris.

Question 18

Which of the following changes is needed in the text?

a) Sentence 4: The word chief should be spelled cheif.

b) Sentence 3: The word counsel should be spelled council.

c) Sentence 5: The words operating budget should be replaced with financing budget.

d) Sentence 7: The word rapport should be replaced with the word report.

Question 19

Which of the following changes would improve the text?

a) Sentence 3: There should be no semi-colon after the word choice.

b) Sentence 4: There should be no apostrophe in the word Harris's.

c) Sentence 4: There should be no comma after the word Calgary.

d) Sentence 5: There should be a comma after the word mettle.

Question 20

Which of the following changes would improve the text?

a) Sentence 7: There should be no comma after Mayor Bing.

b) Sentence 5: There should not be quotation marks around the sentence.

c) Sentence 7: The word March should not be capitalized.

d) Sentence 9: There should be a comma added after the word list.

Read the following paragraphs and answer the questions.

Paragraph A

(1)The commission did however vote to close an Air Force base in Brunswick Maine. (2)Citizens in the area wanted to simply reduce the number of personnel at this location. (3)It was _____ by the commission that the base needed to be closed.

Paragraph B

(4)Many over the past few months have been worried that the plans to scale down the military would leave the New England states _____. (5)Many feel that if the New England areas are _____ down they will not be able to be brought back.

Paragraph C

(6)Two New England locations were kept open during the Pentagon's talks about scaling back military bases. (7)The locations were the shipyard in Kittery, Maine and a submarine base in connecticut. (8)These are considerd the economic backbone of the region by many living there.

Question 21

What would be the most logical order of the paragraphs in this selection?

a) A,B,C
b) B,C,A
c) C,A,B
d) A,C,B

Question 22

Which would be considered the most appropriate title for this selection?

a) New England Punished
b) Pentagon Talks
c) Military Base Closures
d) Storms Hit Hard

Question 23

Where would this selection most likely be found?

a) Newspaper
b) Scientific Journal
c) Textbook
d) Short Story

Question 24

Which of the following rephrases of Sentence 8 is best in terms of style and conciseness?

a) The places are going to be the best ones to keep open.

b) The regions are important economic areas for the country.

c) The places should be left open since people like to visit them so much and tourist dollars are created.

d) The locations are thought by many to be the economic foundation for the region.

Question 25

Which of the following changes would improve the text?

a) Sentence 2: there should be a comma after the word area.

b) Sentence 1: add a comma between Brunswick and Maine.

c) Sentence 6: there should not be an apostrophe on the word Pentagon's.

d) Sentence 8: add an exclamation mark after the word there.

Question 26

Which of the following words, if inserted into the blank in Sentence 3, would best fit the style of the sentence in the whole text?

a) Allowed.
b) Listen.
c) Left.
d) Voted.

Question 27

Which of the following changes would improve the text?

a) Sentence 2: personnel should be replaced with personal.

b) Sentence 2: change the "c" to a lower case in Citizens.

c) Sentence 7: change the "c" to a capital in connecticut.

d) Sentence 8: change the word there to their.

Question 28

Which of the following words, if inserted into the blank in Sentence 4, would best fit the style of the sentence in the whole text?

a) Charged.
b) Vulnerable.
c) Eradicated.
d) Decimated.

Question 29

Which of the following changes would improve the text?

a) Sentence 8: Considerd should be spelled considered.

b) Sentence 1: Commission should be spelled comission.

c) New England should be spelled New – England throughout.

d) Sentence 7: Maine should be spelled Mane.

Question 30

Which of the following words, if inserted into the blank in Sentence 5, would best fit the style of the sentence in the whole text?

a) Replaced.
b) Scaled.
c) Habituated.
d) Relieved.

Read the following three paragraphs and answer the ensuing questions based on what you have read.

Paragraph A

(1)There is a new hurricane brewing in the atlantic ocean. (2)There are sustained winds at: 39 miles per hour and it is moving at 7 miles per hour. (3)Florida is the first location that will be hit.

Paragraph B

(4)The next place the hurricane should make landfall is Louisiana. (5)By this point, it should be a Category 2 storm. (6)People in Louisiana and Texas are _____ to begin taking precautions now.

Paragraph C

(7)Once landfall is made in Louisiana; the storm is expected to wear itself down and not make it much farther north than the middle of Louisiana. (8)Areas north of this location are being _____ to allow evacuees to take up _____ in their towns.

Question 31

Which of the following changes would improve the text?

a) Sentence 8: capitalize the word north.

b) Sentence 7: Wear should be spelled where.

c) Sentence 7: landfall should be two words - land fall.

d) Sentence 1: capitalize the words atlantic and ocean.

Question 32

Which would be considered the most appropriate title for this selection?

a) Death and Fury are Headed This Way.

b) Batten Down the Hatches Georgia.

c) Latest Hurricane in the Atlantic.

d) Ravages of Mother Nature.

Question 33

Which of the following rephrases of Sentence 6 is best in terms of style and conciseness?

a) Citizens preparing for the hurricane of Louisiana and Texas are cautioned that now is the best time to begin hurricane precautions.

b) Citizens of Louisiana and Texas are cautioned that now is the best time to begin hurricane precautions.

c) Citizens of Louisiana and Texas are to begin preparing.

d) Citizens of Louisiana and Texas are cautioned by the mayor and the president, that now is the best time to begin hurricane precautions.

Question 34

Which of the following changes would improve the text?

a) Sentence 2: remove the colon after the word at.

b) Sentence 3: capitalize the "f" in first.

c) Sentence 4: an exclamation mark should be used after Louisiana.

d) Sentence 7: change than to then.

Question 35

In which section of the newspaper would this selection be found?

a) Classified section.
b) Sports section.
c) Business section.
d) Weather section.

Question 36

Which of the following words, if inserted into the blank in Sentence 6, would best fit the style of the sentence in the whole text?

a) Persuaded.
b) Encouraged.
c) Demanded.
d) Discouraged.

Question 37

Which of the following changes would improve the text?

a) Sentence 4: add a comma after the word landfall.

b) Sentence 5: remove the comma after the word point.

c) Sentence 7: replace the semicolon with a comma after the word Louisiana.

d) Sentence 8: add quotation marks around this sentence.

Question 38

What would be the most logical order of the paragraphs in this selection?

a) C,B,A
b) A,B,C
c) A,C,B
d) C,A,B

Question 39

Which of the following words, if inserted into the blanks in Sentence 8, would best fit the style of the sentence in the whole text?

a) Mandated and place.
b) Order and citizenship.
c) Urged and residence.
d) Required and citizenship.

Question 40

Where would this selection most likely be found?

a) Scientific Journal.
b) Short Story.
c) Sales Pamphlet.
d) Newspaper.

Read the following paragraphs and answer the ensuing questions based on what you have read.

Paragraph A
(1) Medicine, communication and leisure are just three areas of our lives that have improved because of computers. (2)The advantages they have brought, in my opinion, far outweigh any disadvantages.

Paragraph B
(3) Computer technology has _____ increased the opportunities that sick and disabled people have to lead normal lives. (4) For example, blind people can now use a laser beam to help them work out how far they are from objects. (5) Computers have also helped people who live in isolated areas to get medical help quickly in an emergency. (6) X-rays and brain scans of patients a long way away can be looked at by specialists in big city hospitals by use of computers linked to modems. (7) They can then give instructions to hospital staff about what to do. (8) Sometimes this can save lives.

Paragraph C
(9) In communication, one of the things that has changed our lives immensely has been the Internet. (10)Businesses these days cannot survive without being connected to the Internet. (11) If someone in an office on the other side of the world needs to send a document to someone in Britain, it would take days without a computer. (12) But thanks to the Internet it can be done in a matter of seconds by email. (13) Email has changed our personal lives too. (14) Even grandparents around the world are "logging-on" to talk to their young grandchildren far away.

Paragraph D
(15) It is difficult for most people to imagine life without computers. (16) Even if we do not have a computer in our homes, computers are now a major part of our lives. (17) Among the many areas where they have brought benefits are medicine, communication and leisure.

Paragraph E
(18) Leisure is another aspect of everyday life that computers have improved. (19) Many children get great enjoyment out of the many interesting and challenging computer games they can play. (20)Although there are many games that involve violence, if the games are chose carefully they can really help children develop thinking skills and quick reflexes. (21) Also when we sit down to watch a sports game on television, it is computers that bring us the many different camera angles, instant action replays and tallies of penalties.

Question 41
Which of the following questions would this essay most likely be addressing?

a) What are some of the advantages and disadvantages of computers?

b) Discuss how computers are taking over our lives.

c) What are the benefits of computers?

d) Discuss some major changes taking place in the medical, communication and leisure industries.

Question 42

Which of the following is an example used in the essay on how disabled people are aided by a computer?

a) Blind people can use laser beams to help guide them.

b) Specialists can view X-rays from long distances using modems.

c) Video games can help improve reflexes.

d) All of the above.

Question 43

This sentence is missing from the text. Where does it belong?
People in wheelchairs can easily drive and control their chairs without help from anyone else.

a) Before the first sentence in Paragraph B.

b) Before the second sentence in Paragraph B.

c) Before the third sentence in Paragraph B.

d) Before the fourth sentence in Paragraph B.

Question 44

Which of the following is a negative aspect of computers mentioned in the essay?

a) Difficulty sending files around the world.

b) Violent video games.

c) Poor communication between generations.

d) Lack of professional people in rural areas.

Question 45

What two areas of life does the essay focus on when discussing changes in communication?

a) Business and email.   b) Business and grandparents.

c) Grandparents and email.   d) Business and personal life.

Question 46

Which sentence of the introduction tells the reader exactly what the paragraphs will be about?

a) First   b) Second

c) Third   d) Fourth

Question 47

Which of the following alternatives is the right order of the five paragraphs of the text?

a) D, E, C, B, A   b) A, C, B, D, E

c) A, B, C, E, D   d) D, B, C, E, A

Question 48
Which of the following rephrases of Sentence 6 is best in terms of style and conciseness?

a) Specialists in big city hospitals can use computers linked to modems to look at X-rays and brain scans of patients a long way away.

b) X-rays and brain scans of patients a long way away can be looked at by specialists in big city hospitals by use of computers linked to modems.

c) In big city hospitals, specialists can use computers to look at X-rays and brain scans of patients a long way away linked to modems.

d) X-rays and brain scans of patients can be looked at by specialists in big city hospitals a long way away by use of computers linked to modems.

Question 49
Which of the following changes need to be made to the essay?

a) Sentence 3 – change opportunities to opportunitie's.

b) Sentence 14 – change grandchildren to grand children.

c) Sentence 17 – add a comma after the word communication.

d) Sentence 20 – change are chose to are chosen.

Question 50
What is the best word to replace the blank space in sentence 3?

a) marginally
b) dramatically
c) progressive
d) substantial

WCPT Answer Key

1) B	26) D
2) C	27) C
3) C	28) B
4) A	29) A
5) C	30) B
6) B	31) D
7) D	32) C
8) B	33) B
9) A	34) A
10) C	35) D
11) C	36) B
12) B	37) C
13) A	38) B
14) A	39) C
15) D	40) D
16) A	41) C
17) C	42) A
18) B	43) C
19) A	44) B
20) B	45) D
21) B	46) C
22) C	47) D
23) A	48) A
24) D	49) D
25) B	50) B

Question 1

The first sentence of paragraph A refers back to the citizens in paragraph B. The opening line in paragraph C continues from the last sentence in paragraph A.

Question 2

"A Final Solution to Disability Issues" and " Total Barrier Elimination" would be inappropriate as the article suggests that people with disabilities are not happy with these initial steps. "Canada's Political Agenda" is too vague of a title.

Question 3

The first sentence is incorrect because legislation is not being knocked down. The second sentence is incorrect because Jill Givens made the pledge. The forth sentence is incorrect because the legislation was not enacted two years ago. Option three is correct because it contains all the pertinent information without being redundant.

Question 4

"Big" is too informal for the article. "Infinitesimal" has an incorrect meaning because the implication is that the changes required are large in nature. "Gargantuan" does not fit the style of the article.

Question 5

"Leading" is the correct answer as it completes the expression appropriately.

Question 6

The word "citizens" in sentence 1 is not expressing ownership and does not require an apostrophe.

Question 7

There is no need for a comma after the word "facilities".

Question 8

The style of the article best resembles that found in a newspaper.

Question 9

There is no need to hyphenate the words two years, as they are separate words.

Question 10

"That has" is incorrect as it would not agree with the verb "waiting". "Have" would not make grammatical or logical sense. "They're" does not agree with the tense of the sentence. "They've" is the best answer.

Question 11

"Enemy" is inappropriate as it is too harsh and probably untrue. "Pal" is too informal for this article. "Alias" would not make sense. "Predecessor" is the best answer.

Question 12

"Debater" is not the position that is being filled. "Man" would be inappropriate and sexist in this article. "Parliamentarian" would be too formal and an incorrect position. "Bureaucrat" is the best answer.

Question 13

"Are" is the grammatically correct word because it agrees with the present tense of the sentence and the plural subject "the vulnerable".

Question 14

A, B, C is the best solution. Jeff Harris is introduced in paragraph A, so it should be the first paragraph.

Question 15

"A Welcome Change to the Helm" is the best answer because it reflects the feeling of the article that the newly-appointed position is well filled.

Question 16

This article is full of opinion, which is typically found in the editorial section.

Question 17

Sentence 1 is incorrect, as Jeff did not pick himself. Sentence 2 is vague about how he was picked. Sentence 4 contains redundant information. Sentence 3 is the best selection.

Question 18

The word "counsel" means advice. The proper word for sentence 3 is "council", meaning political committee.

Question 19

There is no need for a semi-colon after the word "choice". A semi-colon is used to combine two independent clauses. Sentence three has an independent and a dependent clause.

Question 20

Quotation marks around sentence 5 are inappropriate, as the sentence is not a quotation from a speaker in the article.

Question 21

B,C,A is the best solution. The main idea is introduced in Paragraph B. The two locations that were kept open are mentioned in Paragraph C and the closing Paragraph is A.

Question 22

Military Base Closures is the best answer as it sums up the main idea of the article.

Question 23

This article is a current event notice, so it would be found in a newspaper.

Question 24

Option 1 is incorrect because it does not give any of the original information. Option 2 is incorrect as it does not follow the general style of the piece and has inaccurate information. Option 3 is incorrect as it has inaccurate information. Option 4 is correct because it restates the original information accurately.

Question 25

There should be a comma between the city and state.

Question 26

"Voted" is the only action word listed that would complete the sentence to portray the activity that occurred.

Question 27

Option 1 is not correct because New England should be capitalized. Option 2 is not correct because the first letter of a sentence should be capitalized. Option 4 is not correct because Pentagon is a proper name and should be capitalized. Option 3 is correct because Connecticut is a proper name and should be capitalized.

Question 28

"Vulnerable" means susceptible to emotional harm so it describes how the action will affect the people of the area.

Question 29

The past tense of "consider" requires the ending "-ed".

Question 30

"Scaled" is the appropriate word as the expression "scaled down" means reduced.

Question 31

Option 1 is incorrect because "north" is being used as a direction rather than a location. Option 2 is incorrect because "where" indicates a destination. Option 3 is incorrect because "landfall" is one word. Option 4 is correct because Atlantic Ocean is a proper noun and should be capitalized.

Question 32

Options 1 and 4 are too extreme as the hurricane will not be a strong one. Option 2 is not correct because the hurricane is not predicted to hit Georgia. Option 3 is correct because it gives a quick statement about the article's content.

Question 33

Option 1 contains redundant information. Option 3 is vague and doesn't contain enough information. Option 4 contains information that is not included in the original sentence. Option 2 is the correct answer.

Question 34

Option 2 is incorrect because "first" doesn't need to be capitalized. Option 3 is incorrect because no exclamation mark is required. Option 4 is incorrect because "than" is required in a comparison. Option 1 is correct because the colon needs to be used to start a list and there is no list here.

Question 35

Option 4 is correct because it is where the latest weather-related information is found.

Question 36

Option 2 is correct because the article is encouraging people to begin to take some action. The words "persuaded", "demanded" and "discouraged" would not fit the tone of the article.

Question 37

Option 1 is incorrect because there is no need for a comma. Option 2 is incorrect as the comma belongs after the word "point". Option 4 is incorrect as the sentence is not a statement being made by a particular person. Option 3 is correct as the appropriate punctuation mark here is a comma rather than a semicolon.

Question 38

A,B,C is the most logical order because Paragraph A begins by telling where the storm currently is. Paragraph B explains where the hurricane will go next. Paragraph C explains what will happen when it is over land.

Question 39

Option 1 is incorrect because "place" would not fit in with the sentence. Options 2 and 4 are incorrect because evacuees would probably already be citizens. Option 3 is the correct answer because the past tense "urged" and "residence" complete the sentence logically.

Question 40

The selection would be in the newspaper because it is a recent event. The other options are less likely to carry a story that changes so often.

Question 41

Even though the essay focuses on the medical, communication and leisure industries, the main topic of the essay is the benefits of computers.

Question 42

The only disabled people discussed in the text, who use computers with laser beams to determine how far they are away from different objects.

Question 43

The first sentence of the paragraph would be the introductory sentence. The second sentence beginning with "For example" is a good transition from the first and second sentence. The third sentence marks a transition from disabled people to a new issue of rural medicine, so this sentence should be added before the third sentence.

Question 44

The essay states that computers make sending files around the world and communication easier, not more difficult and the article does not discuss computers having an impact on lack of people in rural areas.

Question 45

The two main areas the essay focuses on are business and communication. Grandparents, and email are examples of the personal life.

Question 46

The third sentence states: "…brought benefits are medicine, communication and leisure."

Question 47

The essay should be written with the introduction, followed by paragraphs on medicine, communication, leisure and finally a conclusion according to the introductory paragraph.

Question 48

Answers B and D are both in passive voice and are not as well written as option B. Option C is inappropriate as it confusingly implies that patients, and not computers are linked by modem.

Question 49

The appropriate verb form in sentence 20 is "if the games are chose carefully".

Question 50

An adverb is required describing the verb increased. The essay is discussing the significant gains that computers have created in life, so the word dramatically would be a better fit with the mood of the essay.

GSPAT

The Grammar, Spelling and Punctuation Test (GSPAT) assesses an individual's ability to identify and correct grammar, spelling and punctuation errors. The test consists of 75 multiple-choice questions divided into three categories, which are:

1. Spelling - 30 questions
2. Grammar - 30 questions
3. Punctuation - 15 questions

The test takes 45 minutes and the minimum pass mark is 45/75. If you are unsuccessful you must wait 30 days before you can rewrite the test.

Only paper, pencils and erasers are allowed - no books, dictionaries, notes, writing paper, calculators, calculator watches or other aids are permitted in the room.

Detach the answer key to take the test.

GSPAT ANSWER KEY

	A	B	C	D	E	
1)	○	○	○	○	○	____
2)	○	○	○	○	○	____
3)	○	○	○	○	○	____
4)	○	○	○	○	○	____
5)	○	○	○	○	○	____
6)	○	○	○	○	○	____
7)	○	○	○	○	○	____
8)	○	○	○	○	○	____
9)	○	○	○	○	○	____
10)	○	○	○	○	○	____
11)	○	○	○	○	○	____
12)	○	○	○	○	○	____
13)	○	○	○	○	○	____
14)	○	○	○	○	○	____
15)	○	○	○	○	○	____
16)	○	○	○	○	○	____
17)	○	○	○	○	○	____
18)	○	○	○	○	○	____
19)	○	○	○	○	○	____
20)	○	○	○	○	○	____
21)	○	○	○	○	○	____
22)	○	○	○	○	○	____
23)	○	○	○	○	○	____
24)	○	○	○	○	○	____
25)	○	○	○	○	○	____
26)	○	○	○	○	○	____
27)	○	○	○	○	○	____
28)	○	○	○	○	○	____
29)	○	○	○	○	○	____
30)	○	○	○	○	○	____
31)	○	○	○	○	○	____
32)	○	○	○	○	○	____
33)	○	○	○	○	○	____
34)	○	○	○	○	○	____
35)	○	○	○	○	○	____
36)	○	○	○	○	○	____
37)	○	○	○	○	○	____
38)	○	○	○	○	○	____
39)	○	○	○	○	○	____
40)	○	○	○	○	○	____
41)	○	○	○	○	○	____
42)	○	○	○	○	○	____
43)	○	○	○	○	○	____
44)	○	○	○	○	○	____
45)	○	○	○	○	○	____
46)	○	○	○	○	○	____
47)	○	○	○	○	○	____
48)	○	○	○	○	○	____
49)	○	○	○	○	○	____
50)	○	○	○	○	○	____
51)	○	○	○	○	○	____
52)	○	○	○	○	○	____
53)	○	○	○	○	○	____
54)	○	○	○	○	○	____
55)	○	○	○	○	○	____
56)	○	○	○	○	○	____
57)	○	○	○	○	○	____
58)	○	○	○	○	○	____
59)	○	○	○	○	○	____
60)	○	○	○	○	○	____
61)	○	○	○	○	○	____
62)	○	○	○	○	○	____
63)	○	○	○	○	○	____
64)	○	○	○	○	○	____
65)	○	○	○	○	○	____
66)	○	○	○	○	○	____
67)	○	○	○	○	○	____
68)	○	○	○	○	○	____
69)	○	○	○	○	○	____
70)	○	○	○	○	○	____
71)	○	○	○	○	○	____
72)	○	○	○	○	○	____
73)	○	○	○	○	○	____
74)	○	○	○	○	○	____
75)	○	○	○	○	○	____

Question 1
Identify the errors in the sentences below.

The man fled into the street, then turned the corner quickly. It was better that he fled rather then stayed in the bank and took hostages.

a) into the street
b) quickly
c) rather then
d) hostages

Question 2

"Who cares whether old people can take care of theirselves or not?" asked the young college student as he prepared for his psychology exam.

a) Who
b) can
c) theirselves
d) he prepared

Question 3

The collision happened on account of the brakes were faulty. Had the brakes been functioning properly then she would have been able to stop.

a) happened
b) on account of
c) functioning
d) then

Question 4

I am extremely impressed with your dedication. Since you began training; you have been able to work the entire shift without rest.

a) extremely
b) with your
c) training; you
d) able to work

Question 5

Because she had been married twice, she had two mothers-in-law in her life and she didn't like neither.

a) Because
b) twice
c) mothers-in-law
d) didn't like neither

Question 6

A recent New York University study show that cancer is more prevalent in California than on the east coast.

a) New York University
b) show
c) more prevalent
d) than

Question 7

Several noise complaint originated from a celebration occurring during a street festival promoting jazz music. Noise levels that persisted past 3:00 in the morning infuriated citizens who live in the neighbourhood.

a) complaint originated
b) occurring
c) persisted past
d) who live

Question 8

Of his three brothers, Jamal was the stronger. He could bench press at least 50 pounds more than his nearest sibling.

a) Of his
b) was the stronger
c) at least
d) more than

Question 9

She couldn't have been more happier on her wedding day, even if she had been married in Hawaii.

a) couldn't have
b) more happier
c) day, even
d) had been married

Question 10

My younger brother doesn't have a job right now. Currently he is hoping his quickly typing skills would land him a temporary job.

a) doesn't
b) Currently
c) quickly
d) would land

Select the most appropriate word (s) to complete the sentences below.

Question 11

The movie had already started _____ the film projector broke down.

a) when
b) while
c) since
d) although

Question 12

She couldn't attend the opera _____ she had tickets.

a) or
b) although
c) besides
d) therefore

Question 13

He wasn't certain, _____ he could make an educated guess.

a) therefore
b) but
c) indeed
d) while

Question 14

Janet didn't start the examination _____ she was told to do so.

a) until
b) while
c) during
d) if

Question 15
The figure skaters couldn't finish the jump _____ they hadn't practiced enough.

a) while
b) although
c) because
d) but

Question 16
The colonel has many medals he wears _____ his dress uniform.

a) which
b) in
c) with
d) to

Question 17
_____ their poor image, most politicians are hardworking, loyal and dedicated.

a) Because of
b) Despite
c) Because
d) Through

Question 18
_____ that's the way you feel, I'll try and accommodate you.

a) When
b) Due to
c) Despite
d) If

Question 19
_____ you may dislike skiing, I find it one of life's great joys.

a) Because
b) While
c) Which
d) If

Question 20
He decided to invest in the real estate market _____ his lack of knowledge.

a) because of
b) as a result of
c) during
d) in spite of

Identify the errors in the sentences below.

Question 21
It's going to be a long night. This was to much for a new team to handle in its short lifespan.

a) It's
b) was to much
c) to handle
d) its

Question 22

The government realized it had problems with the legislation, so David Bonton of the Department of Finance were selected to help rework it.

a) government realized
b) had problems
c) of Finance
d) were selected

Question 23

After arriving at a suspicious incident call, the police officer heard a loud noise in the basement while searching the house. The basement was filled with insects and mice, but the officer had to precede into the basement anyway.

a) suspicious incident call
b) while searching
c) was filled
d) had to precede

Question 24

The crews of the construction company was assigned the task of erecting an office tower in Melbourne. The crews performed the task perfectly.

a) of the construction
b) was assigned
c) of erecting
d) crews performed

Question 25

The whether is warmer today than it was yesterday.

a) whether
b) warmer
c) than
d) was

Select the most appropriate word (s) to complete the sentences below.

Question 26

It is simple to build an investment portfolio _____ you have the proper training.

a) condition
b) even though
c) as long
d) if

Question 27

_____ the heavy snow, the ski slopes delayed their opening.

a) Because of
b) Including
c) While
d) Even though

Question 28

I did not say anything _____ I hadn't seen her.

a) because of
b) due
c) unless
d) because

Question 29

He could run well _____ he lacked the swimming skills to get hired as a lifeguard.

a) and
b) because
c) but
d) therefore

Question 30

He felt faint _____ they were talking about his dead mother.

a) while
b) unless
c) during
d) until

Identify which of the following words are misspelled.

Question 31

a) rarety
b) retaliation
c) citizens
d) who
e) None of the above.

Question 32

a) undertook
b) daunting
c) ahead
d) commensed
e) None of the above.

Question 33

a) vicious
b) sibling
c) subdue
d) tranquilizers
e) None of the above.

Question 34

a) demonstrators
b) atrocities
c) foriegn
d) horrible
e) None of the above.

Question 35

a) Psychology
b) sociology
c) criminalogy
d) potential
e) None of the above.

Question 36

a) increasingly
b) campains
c) controversy
d) apolitical
e) None of the above.

Question 37

a) regime
c) receive
e) None of the above.

b) nurishment
d) nocturnal

Question 38

a) celebrations
c) comrade
e) None of the above.

b) dependence
d) eachother

Question 39

a) transferred
c) naudical
e) None of the above.

b) undergo
d) competencies

Question 40

a) inherent
c) psychiatrists
e) None of the above.

b) counselling
d) incountering

Question 41

a) ability
c) compatible
e) None of the above

b) staple
d) specificaly

Question 42

a) corruption
c) unecessary
e) None of the above

b) withdrawal
d) disappearance

Question 43

a) disability
c) gradually
e) None of the above

b) fradulent
d) university

Question 44

a) rehabilitation
c) progresion
e) None of the above

b) grasping
d) negotiable

Question 45
a) front b) government
c) implication d) inspector
e) None of the above

Question 46
a) incapabel b) honesty
c) fulfilment d) engagement
e) None of the above

Question 47
a) distressed b) whisper
c) vocale d) licensing
e) None of the above

Question 48
a) municipel b) monotonous
c) nearby d) noisy
e) None of the above

Question 49
a) allocate b) comment
c) peculiar d) luxurius
e) None of the above

Question 50
a) recommendation b) mechanecal
c) metropolitan d) temperature
e) None of the above

Question 51
a) rationale b) verssion
c) foreseeable d) accidentally
e) None of the above

Question 52
a) absolute b) balance
c) composure d) double
e) None of the above

Question 53

a) furnitur b) independent
c) knocking d) merit
e) None of the above

Question 54

a) offence b) petrol
c) propperty d) recurrence
e) None of the above

Question 55

a) scheme b) superior
c) unreliable d) accesory
e) None of the above

Question 56

a) barrister b) condition
c) duplecate d) genuine
e) None of the above

Question 57

a) indirect b) known
c) middel d) official
e) None of the above

Question 58

a) phrase b) prospect
c) redundent d) scratched
e) None of the above

Question 59

a) suppose b) utilise
c) accuracy d) before
e) None of the above

Question 60

a) fatigue b) immediatly
c) introduction d) malicious
e) None of the above

Indicate any punctuation errors in the sentences below:

Question 61

Before taking the tickets, the teenager must clock in, then she can begin work.

a) taking
b) in, then
c) can
d) work.
e) No correction required

Question 62

When planning an outing with children, remember to bring; activities, snacks, and a first aid kit.

a) children,
b) bring;
c) ,snacks, and a
d) aid kit.
e) No correction required

Question 63

Trips to the zoo, are lots of fun. There are many animals to see and things to do.

a) zoo,
b) fun.
c) are
d) things to do.
e) No correction required

Question 64

What is the answer to the question! I did not study enough and need help.

a) answer to
b) question!
c) enough and
d) help.
e) No correction required

Question 65

Wow, that was a close call? Who can help the young lady learn a better method?

a) Wow! That
b) close call?
c) young lady learn
d) method?
e) No correction required

Question 66

The mail carrier ensures that all letters are delivered on his route. He is courteous and punctual as well.

a) ensures
b) route.
c) and
d) well.
e) No correction required

Question 67

The students have been asked to perform many tasks; They include collecting different species of insects and gathering leaves.

a) been asked
b) tasks;
c) collecting different
d) insects and
e) No correction required

Question 68

Healthcare costs are skyrocketing, this is creating a problem for the public and private sector.

a) skyrocketing, this
b) creating a problem
c) public and
d) sector.
e) No correction required

Question 69

Which type of cheese do you need? There is American Monterey, Cheddar, and Colby.

a) need?
b) is American
c) Monterey, Cheddar,
d) Colby.
e) No correction required

Question 70

Have you acquired the supplies that we need? They are the most important, part of the project.

a) you acquired
b) need?
c) important,
d) project.
e) No correction required

Question 71

Where do you want to go, for lunch? We can have Mexican, Italian, or Indian.

a) go,
b) lunch?
c) Mexican,
d) Indian.
e) No correction required

Question 72

The fire was burning bright: it was very hot. The smores will turn out nicely.

a) The fire
b) bright: it
c) hot.
d) smores will turn
e) No correction required

Question 73

"I want to go to John's Diner for lunch today?" said Billy. "They have the best french fries," he thought to himself.

a) today?
b) Billy.
c) "They have the
d) fries," he
e) No correction required

Question 74

The following are the best deals: fish, shrimp, scallops, and kelp. This seafood market has the freshest items:

a) deals:
b) scallops,
c) seafood market
d) items:
e) No correction required

Question 75

Hello! shouted Paul when he saw some friends he recognized at the beach. He ran over to join their game of volleyball.

a) Hello!
b) friends he
c) beach.
d) to join their
e) No correction required

GSPAT Answer Key

1) C	26) D	51) B
2) C	27) A	52) E
3) B	28) D	53) A
4) C	29) C	54) C
5) D	30) A	55) D
6) B	31) A	56) C
7) A	32) D	57) C
8) B	33) E	58) C
9) B	34) C	59) E
10) C	35) C	60) B
11) A	36) B	61) B
12) B	37) B	62) B
13) B	38) D	63) A
14) A	39) C	64) B
15) C	40) D	65) B
16) C	41) D	66) E
17) B	42) C	67) B
18) D	43) B	68) A
19) B	44) C	69) B
20) D	45) E	70) C
21) B	46) A	71) A
22) D	47) C	72) B
23) D	48) A	73) A
24) B	49) D	74) D
25) A	50) B	75) A

Question 1

"Rather then" is improper use of language. The word "then" is used for instances of time (I will put on my pajamas and then get into bed). The correct term would be "rather than" which is used when making comparisons.

Question 2

There is no such word as "theirselves". The correct word would be "themselves".

Question 3

"On account of" is improper use of the language. The correct word that should be used in this situation is "because".

Question 4

A semicolon is used to separate independent clauses. An independent clause can stand alone as a complete sentence. In this case, the clause "Since you began training" could not stand as an independent clause. Because of this a semicolon is inappropriate punctuation.

Question 5

The phrase "didn't like neither" contains a double negative and is confusing. The phrase should be written "didn't like either".

Question 6

This sentence has a problem with subject / verb agreement. The verb "show" (plural form) should agree with the subject of the sentence "study". The sentence should read: A recent New York University study "shows" that …

Question 7

The word "complaint" does not agree with the article describing it. "Complaint" should be plural as there were "several" of them. The sentence should read: "Several noise complaints originated…"

Question 8

For comparative adjectives, when there are more than two objects or people being compared, you must use the word "strongest". Stronger should only be used for comparing two different people or objects.

Question 9

For comparative adjectives and adverbs, if the word has multiple syllables, you must use the modifying word more or most as opposed to adding the –er / -est ending. You cannot do both. The sentence should read: "She couldn't have been more happy …"

Question 10

The word quickly is an adverb that is describing a noun (skills, not typing). The adjective form of the word should be used (quick). The sentence should therefore read: "… he was hoping his quick typing skills…"

Question 11

"When" is the best answer. If you selected any of the words "while", "since" or "although" the sentence wouldn't make sense as the movie could not start if the projector broke down.

Question 12

"Although" is the best answer. The sentence would not make logical sense if you used any of the other words.

Question 13

The correct answer is the word "but". "Therefore" would be inappropriate because he couldn't make an educated guess because he wasn't certain. "While" and "indeed" would be inappropriate as the sentence would not make sense.

Question 14

"Until" is the most appropriate answer. The answers "while" and "if" are possible answers but make the sentence confusing. Until is the best answer.

Question 15

"Because" is the most appropriate answer. If the words "while", "although" or "but" are used the sentence doesn't make sense.

Question 16

"With" is the best answer. You can't use options "which" or "to" as the sentence would not make sense. "In" is inappropriate, as medals are not worn in a uniform.

Question 17

"Despite" is the best answer. "Because" and "through" make the sentence illogical. "Because of" works grammatically but it does not make as much sense as "despite".

Question 18

"If" is the best solution and makes the most logical sense. "When" and "due to" are possible options, but do not make as much sense as "if".

Question 19

"While" is the best answer. "Because", "which" and "if" would make the sentence less logical.

Question 20

"In spite of" is the best solution. "Because of" and "as a result of" would make grammatical sense, but make the sentence less logical. "During" would make the sentence grammatically incorrect.

Question 21

The incorrect form of "to" was used in this sentence. The word "too" has the following meanings: also, as well, in addition, besides, and excessively. The sentence should read: "This was too much for a …"

Question 22

"Were selected" must agree with the subject David Bonton. It can be confusing when there is a clause between the subject and verb (of the Department of Finance). If you said to yourself "David Bonton were selected" you would realize right away it is incorrect. The sentence should read: … "David Bonton of the Department of Finance was selected to help rework it."

Question 23

The word "precede" means to go ahead. The sentence requires the word "proceed" which means to continue or advance on.

Question 24

The subject "crews" and the verb "was" do not agree with each other. "Crews" is a plural noun while "was" is a verb in the singular tense. The correct form of the sentence would be: "The crews of the construction company were assigned…"

Question 25

The use of "whether" in this sentence is incorrect. "Weather" should be used in this case, meaning climate conditions.

Question 26

"If" is the correct answer. "Condition" and "as long" are incorrect because they would create grammatical errors. "Even though" is incorrect, as it would create a logical contradiction.

Question 27

"Because of" is the best answer. "While" and "even though" are incorrect because they would create grammatical errors. "Including" doesn't make sense.

Question 28

"Because" is the best answer. "Because of" and "due" would be grammatically incorrect and "unless" would not make logical sense.

Question 29

"But" is the best answer. The other options create a sentence that fails to make logical sense.

Question 30

"While" is the best answer. It creates the sentence that makes the most logical sense. "Unless" and "until" would both be grammatically correct, but would not make as much sense as option A.

Refer to the Answer Key for answers to questions 31-60

Question 61

A period is required after the word "in;" otherwise, a run-on sentence is created.

Question 62

A semicolon should not be used to introduce a list.

Question 63

There is a comma that is not required after the word "zoo".

Question 64

A question mark is required after the word "question."

Question 65

"That was a close call" is a statement and does not require a question mark. Either a period or exclamation mark should follow this sentence.

Question 66

There are no punctuation errors in these sentences.

Question 67

There needs to be a period after "tasks." This is correct, but only because the 't' on 'They' is capitalized; otherwise, a semicolon or colon would work as well.

Question 68

There needs to be a period or a semicolon after "skyrocketing."

Question 69

A comma is required after "American."

Question 70

There is no comma required after "important."

Question 71

There is no need for a comma after the word "go".

Question 72

The colon should be replaced with either a semicolon or a period with the word "it" capitalized.

Question 73

The question mark should be replaced with a comma after the word "today".

Question 74

The colon after "items" should be replaced with a period.

Question 75

Opening and closing quotation marks are needed around "Hello!"

Wonderlic

The Wonderlic exam consists of 50 questions that you have to answer as many as you can of inside of 12 minutes. Areas of the exam include:

- Problem Solving
- Matching
- Vocabulary
- Syllogisms (Select the logical conclusion)

Our practice exercises consist of 66 questions. You have 15 minutes to complete as many of the questions as you can. You may only use a pencil and scrap piece of paper. No calculators, counting devices or books are permitted.

Paper, pencils and erasers are allowed - no books, dictionaries, notes, writing paper, calculators, calculator watches or other aids are to be taken into the room.

WONDERLIC ANSWER KEY

	A B C D			A B C D			A B C D	
1)	○ ○ ○ ○	___	23)	○ ○ ○ ○	___	45)	○ ○ ○ ○	___
2)	○ ○ ○ ○	___	24)	○ ○ ○ ○	___	46)	○ ○ ○ ○	___
3)	○ ○ ○ ○	___	25)	○ ○ ○ ○	___	47)	○ ○ ○ ○	___
4)	○ ○ ○ ○	___	26)	○ ○ ○ ○	___	48)	○ ○ ○ ○	___
5)	○ ○ ○ ○	___	27)	○ ○ ○ ○	___	49)	○ ○ ○ ○	___
6)	○ ○ ○ ○	___	28)	○ ○ ○ ○	___	50)	○ ○ ○ ○	___
7)	○ ○ ○ ○	___	29)	○ ○ ○ ○	___	51)	○ ○ ○ ○	___
8)	○ ○ ○ ○	___	30)	○ ○ ○ ○	___	52)	○ ○ ○ ○	___
9)	○ ○ ○ ○	___	31)	○ ○ ○ ○	___	53)	○ ○ ○ ○	___
10)	○ ○ ○ ○	___	32)	○ ○ ○ ○	___	54)	○ ○ ○ ○	___
11)	○ ○ ○ ○	___	33)	○ ○ ○ ○	___	55)	○ ○ ○ ○	___
12)	○ ○ ○ ○	___	34)	○ ○ ○ ○	___	56)	○ ○ ○ ○	___
13)	○ ○ ○ ○	___	35)	○ ○ ○ ○	___	57)	○ ○ ○ ○	___
14)	○ ○ ○ ○	___	36)	○ ○ ○ ○	___	58)	○ ○ ○ ○	___
15)	○ ○ ○ ○	___	37)	○ ○ ○ ○	___	59)	○ ○ ○ ○	___
16)	○ ○ ○ ○	___	38)	○ ○ ○ ○	___	60)	○ ○ ○ ○	___
17)	○ ○ ○ ○	___	39)	○ ○ ○ ○	___	61)	○ ○ ○ ○	___
18)	○ ○ ○ ○	___	40)	○ ○ ○ ○	___	62)	○ ○ ○ ○	___
19)	○ ○ ○ ○	___	41)	○ ○ ○ ○	___	63)	○ ○ ○ ○	___
20)	○ ○ ○ ○	___	42)	○ ○ ○ ○	___	64)	○ ○ ○ ○	___
21)	○ ○ ○ ○	___	43)	○ ○ ○ ○	___	65)	○ ○ ○ ○	___
22)	○ ○ ○ ○	___	44)	○ ○ ○ ○	___	66)	○ ○ ○ ○	___

Question 1

Baseball players or cricket players will use the field.
Sean is a baseball player and will be using the field.

Select the logical conclusion.

a) Sean may play cricket as well.

b) Cricket players will use the field as well.

c) Cricket players will not use the field.

d) None of the above.

Question 2

If found guilty, Kevin will be sent to jail.
No one is going to jail.
Select the logical conclusion.

a) Kevin may be found guilty tomorrow.   b) Kevin was found guilty.

c) Kevin may go to jail.   d) None of the above.

Question 3

If there are 250 electoral vote's and they are equally divided between the 50 states, how many does each state have?

a) 4   b) 5   c) 6   d) 50

Question 4

Indicate whether the following are the same or different:
Harold and Maude_____   Hareld and Maude

a) Same   b) different

Question 5

Ghost and the Darkness_____   Ghost in the Darkness

a) Same   b) different

Question 6

Johnson & Johnson_____   Johnson & Johnson

a) Same   b) different

Question 7

What is the best explanation of the following expression?
Getting the short end of the stick.

a) Being physically punished, with leniency.

b) The inferior part; worse side of an unequal deal.

c) Being mislead and lied to in a transaction.

d) Receiving unequal treatment because of being younger family member.

Question 8

Place the following fragments into the proper order to form a logical sentence:
a) in California than on the east coast
b) a recent New York
c) cancer is more prevalent
d) University study shows that

a) A - C - B – D b) B - A - C - D
c) C - B - A – D d) B - D - C - A

Question 9

Choose the two words that are linked as either synonyms or antonyms.
a) lie   b) deceive   c) position   d) locate

a) a & c   b) c & d   c) a & b   d) b & c

Question 10

Choose the two words that are linked as either synonyms or antonyms.
a) match   b) under   c) local   d) equal

a) b & c   b) a & d   c) c & d   d) a & b

Question 11

There are 4 offspring in the Yang family. They live in 6 different houses. Each offspring is married and has 3 babies. We must give 4 stuffed animals to each baby. How many stuffed animals do we need to buy?

a) 48   b) 50   c) 52   d) 54

Question 12

Carlene needs to save $1,440 in order to take a trip. She works 45 hours a week and earns $8 an hour. How many weeks will she have to work in order to save for the trip?

a) 3   b) 4   c) 5   d) 6

Question 13

A computer software package costs $24.07 at the local store. A customer gives 2 twenty-dollar bills. How much change does the customer receive?

a) $15.83   b) $15.93   c) $16.03   d) $16.13

Question 14

Kent put change in a bottle. He put in 3 pennies, 6 quarters, 3 dimes and 1 nickel. What is the probability of picking out a quarter?

a) 23 %   b) 8 %   c) 33 %   d) 46 %

Question 15

Three games are purchased at $12.35, $9.09 and $6.47. A customer gives 3 ten-dollar bills. How much change does the customer receive?

a) $1.89   b) $1.95   c) $2.09   d) $2.15

Question 16
Which of the following represents fractions arranged in a decreasing order of size?

a) 0.003, 0.02, 0.1   b) 2/3, 1/4, 13/15, 3/5, 5/1

c) 15/16, 7/8, 3/4, 2/3, ½   d) None of the above

Question 17
Simon studied longer than Shelley, but not as long as Kate. Shelley did all of her studying with Claire. Claire then studied with Kate. Who did the least studying?

a) Kate   b) Claire   c) Simon   d) Shelley

Question 18
Solve for "y"   48 - y = 27

a) 23   b) 19   c) 27   d) None of the above.

Question 19
Solve for "y"   15 + 2 (13 + y) - 10 = 89

a) 29   b) 21   c) 33   d) None of the above.

Question 20
How many hours will it take a person to walk 20 km at a rate of 3 km/h?

a) 5 1/3 hours   b) 6 1/3 hours

c) 6 2/3 hours   d) None of the above.

Question 21
521 x 346 =

a) 123 566   b) 150 326   c) 180 266   d) None of the above.

Question 22
How much change would James receive after paying $50.00 for the following products:
6 packets of crackers at $3.54 a packet
5 kg of oranges at $1.95 a kilogram
3 dozen muffins at $3.75 per dozen

a) $42.24   b) $24.16   c) $7.76   d) None of the above.

Question 23
Kevin determined that he could ski at the rate of 6 m in 1/5 of a second. How many meters could Kevin ski in 12 seconds?

a) 360 m   b) 380 m   c) 400 m   d) 420 m

Question 24

No convicts are innocent.
Some men are innocent.

Select the logical conclusion.

a) Some men are not convicts.
b) Only women are convicts.
c) All convicts are men.
d) None of the above.

Question 25

Some cops are athletic.
All cops are human.

Select the logical conclusion.

a) All humans are athletic.
b) Some humans are athletic.
c) All cops are athletic.
d) None of the above.

Question 26

No priests are women.
All students are priests.

Select the logical conclusion.

a) Some students are women.
b) No women are students.
c) Different students are women.
d) None of the above.

Question 27

If there are weapons then there is fighting.
If there is fighting then there is bloodshed.

Select the logical conclusion.

a) If there is bloodshed then there are weapons.
b) There may be weapons without fighting.
c) Fighting can occur without bloodshed.
d) None of the above.

Question 28

Indicate whether the following are the same or different:
W.W.Keaton_____   W.W.Keaton

a) same   b) different

Question 29

Bruce Wayne_____   Bryce Wayne

a) same   b) different

Question 30

Fire and Ice_____   Fire in Ice

a) same   b) different

Question 31

What is the best explanation of the following expression?
Burning the candle at both ends.

a) Upsetting friends and family for your own personal gain.

b) Refusing to get sufficient rest because of too much work.

c) Using up your two most important resources while achieving nothing.

d) Running out of time too quickly as you are burning or doing twice as much.

Question 32

What is the best explanation of the following expression?
Cook the books.

a) To falsify an account of an event, often a financial one.

b) To set fire to books in protest.

c) To immorally destroy art and literature due to political manipulation.

d) To establish or produce a book on culinary interests.

Question 33

Tim needs to fill three 20L barrels with oil. If his oil dispenser flows at 100 mL/s, how long will it take him to fill the 3 containers? (Minutes)

a) 100   b) 75   c) 50   d) 10

Question 34

There was a crime scene where none of the victims involved in the incident were found to be women.
The detective in charge of the case reported that all statements were from women.
Select the logical conclusion.

a) Some statements were from victims.   b) Some men were victims.

c) No victims gave statements.   d) None of the above.

Question 35

The average rainfall in Waterloo has increased at an annual rate of 2%. If the total rain fall was 856mm in 2002. What is the expected rainfall in 2005? (mm)

a) 907.4   b) 908.4   c) 873.12   d) 900

Question 36

James ran 2 miles in 12 minutes. He has to run another 5 miles and wants to average a 7-minute mile over the entire run. What will James have to run the remaining 5 miles in on average to accomplish this?

a) 6.3 min / mile   b) 7.4 min / mile

c) 8.6 min / mile   d) 10.2 min / mile

Question 37

Indicate whether the following are the same or different:
Kelly Incorporated   Kelly Incorporated
a) same   b) different

Question 38

Table and Chairs_____   Table and Chairs
a) same   b) different

Question 39

Single and Loving It_____   Single and Loving It
a) same   b) different

Question 40

What is the best explanation of the following expression?
To toe the line.

a) To line up for the start, or beginning, usually a race.

b) To take a small advantage, or improper lead, usually at the beginning of a race.

c) To create your own path and reach your own conclusion.

d) Follow the group, don't disagree, do what others are doing.

Question 41

Place the following fragments into the proper order to form a logical sentence:
a) attend the
b) unfortunately, I was
c) graduation ceremony
d) not allowed to

a) A - C - B – D   b) B - A - C - D
c) C - B - A – D   d) B - D - A - C

Question 42

Choose the two words that are linked as either synonyms or antonyms.
a) creation
b) similar
c) synonymous
d) dismantle

a) a & d   b) c & d
c) b & c   d) a & b

Question 43

Solve for "y" $3(7-y) - 6 \times 2 = -21$

a) 10   b) 8   c) 16   d) None of the above

Question 44

Solve for "y" $2 + y + 11(y + 1) = 130 - y$

a) 7 b) 9 c) 11 d) None of the above

Question 45

Shane and Indervir were digging a hole in the yard. They were required to remove 1000 lbs of dirt to complete the job. Shane was capable of removing 125 lbs of dirt per hour and Indervir was capable of removing 100 lbs of dirt per hour. How long would it take the two working together to complete the whole?

a) 3.45 hours   b) 4.45 hours

c) 5.40 hours   d) 5.75 hours

Question 46

A man drove for 6 hours. In that time he managed to complete 2/6 of his journey. What is the total length of his journey?

a) 12 hours   b) 14 hours

c) 18 hours   d) 30 hours

Question 47

It is generally accepted among scientists that everything that is in fact alive must breathe using some capacity. Students completing a project found that there were no rocks that drew breathe.
Select the logical conclusion.

a) Some rocks live.   b) Everything that breathes, lives.

c) Some things that are alive, are rocks.   d) None of the above.

Question 48

No trout are mammals.
Some water animals are trout.

Select the logical conclusion.

a) Water animals are not mammals.   b) Some water animals are not mammals.

c) Some water animals are mammals.   d) None of the above.

Question 49

Which of the following images doesn't belong?

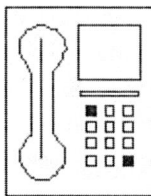 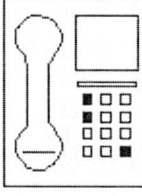 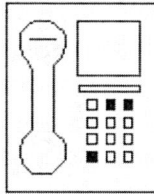 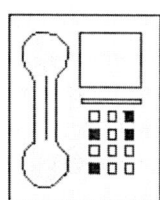

A   B   C   D

Question 50

Which of the following images doesn't belong?

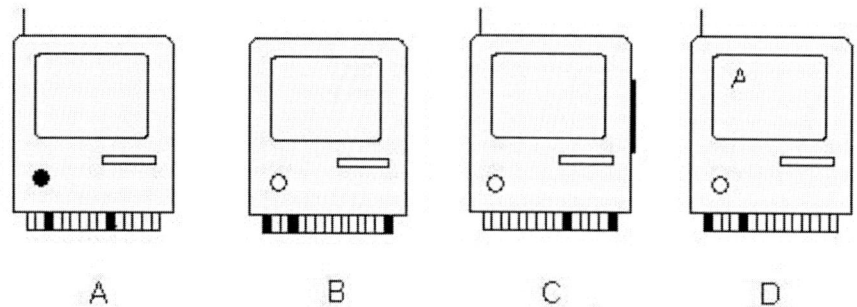

Question 51

Which of the following images doesn't belong?

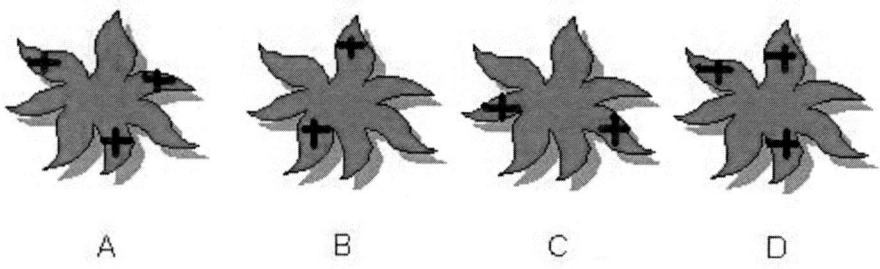

Question 52

What number if doubled, gives you one quarter of 32?

a) 4   b) 8   c) 12   d) None of the above.

Question 53

Shell spent $36 million on an oil refinery and transport tanker. The price of the refinery was twice the price of the tanker. How much did Shell pay for the refinery?

a) $18 million   b) $24 million

c) $30 million   d) None of the above.

Question 54

According to International Law, genocide must be prevented and is never justifiable. There have been wars in recent history that have been recognized by the UN as justifiable.

Select the logical conclusion.

a) Some wars are not genocide.

b) All wars are not genocide.

c) Genocide can be justified if it takes place in a war.

d) None of the above.

Question 55
Indicate whether the following are the same or different:
Travelling Salesman_____ Travelling Salesmen

a) same   b) different

Question 56
High Speed Internet_____ High Speed Intranet

a) same   b) different

Question 57
Cake Mix_____ Cake Mix

a) same   b) different

Question 58
Rolling Stones_____ Rolling Stones

a) same   b) different

Question 59
Bouncing babies_____ Bouncing baby

a) same   b) different

Question 60
Place the following fragments into the proper order to form a logical sentence:
a) summers on record, London police say they have smashed
b) a terrorist group responsible for terrorizing
c) after one of the bloodiest
d) neighbourhoods in the city's northwest end

a) A - C - B – D   b) B - A - C - D
c) C - A - B – D   d) D - C - B - A

Question 61
Choose the two words that are linked as either synonyms or antonyms.
a) variable
b) constant
c) custom
d) replaceable

a) b & d   b) c & d   c) b & c   d) a & b

Question 62
In a pizza eating contest a man can eat an eighth of his own weight in 45 minutes. If the man weighs 80 kg, how much can he eat in 30 minutes?

a) 5 1/3 kg   b) 5 2/3 kg   c) 6 1/3 kg   d) 6 2/3 kg

Question 63

If an orange costs twice as much as an apple, and John buys three apples and three oranges for $2.70, how much is one apple?

a) $0.90 b) $0.60 c) $0.30 d) None of the above.

Question 64

For the past week John jogged every day, and increased his distance by 1.5 km every day. Last Tuesday John ran 2 km but today he ran 6.5 km. What day of the week is it today?

a) Friday b) Saturday c) Sunday d) None of the above.

Question 65

William wanted to paint his floor. Each litre of paint covers 6 square meters of flooring. How many litres would William need to paint the floor with dimensions measuring 8 meters by 3 meters?

a) 6.5 b) 5 c) 4 d) 3.5

Question 66

No candles are glittered.
Some beautiful things are glittered.

Select the logical conclusion.

a) Then some beautiful things are candles.

b) Some glittered things are candles.

c) Some beautiful things are not candles.

d) Then some glittered things are not beautiful.

WONDERLIC ANSWER KEY & DETAILED ANSWER EXPLANATIONS

1) C	23) A	45) B
2) D	24) A	46) C
3) B	25) B	47) D
4) B - Different	26) B	48) B
5) B - Different	27) D	49) C
6) A - Same	28) A - Same	50) B
7) B	29) B - Different	51) D
8) D	30) B - Different	52) A
9) C	31) B	53) B
10) B	32) A	54) A
11) A	33) D	55) B - Different
12) B	34) C	56) B - Different
13) B	35) B	57) A - Same
14) D	36) B	58) A - Same
15) C	37) A - Same	59) B - Different
16) C	38) A - Same	60) C
17) D	39) A - Same	61) D
18) D	40) D	62) D
19) A	41) D	63) C
20) C	42) C	64) A
21) C	43) A	65) C
22) C	44) B	66) C

Question 1
The logic this question follows is:
Either A or B.
A.
Not B.

Question 2
The logic this question follows is:
If A then B.
Not B.
Not A.

Question 3
250 electoral votes divided by 50 states means each state receives 5 votes.

Question 8
A recent New York University study shows that cancer is more prevalent in California than on the east coast.
D - A - C - B

Question 9
Lie and deceive are synonyms.

Question 10
Match and equal are synonyms.
Question 11
4 offspring each having 3 babies means a total of 12 babies (4 x 3 = 12). If each baby had 4 toys, than the total is 48 (4 x 12 = 48).
Question 12
Carlene earns $360 per week (8 x 45 = 360). This means she would need to work 4 weeks to earn the money (1440 / 360 = 4).
Question 13
The change would be $15.93 (40 – 24.07 = 15.93).
Question 14
There are a total of 13 coins (3 + 6 + 3 + 1 = 13) and 6 quarters. That means there is a 46.1% chance of picking a quarter (6 / 13 = 0.461 or 46.1%).
Question 15
The total bill would be $27.91 (12.35 + 9.09 + 6.47 = 27.91), which means there would be $2.09 in change (30 – 27.91 = 2.09)
Question 16
With a common denominator of 48, answer C would be:
15/16, 42/48, 36/48, 32/48 and 24/48.
Question 17
The first sentence would rank the students as: 1) Kate   2) Simon   3) Shelley
The second sentence states: Shelley = Claire
The third sentence states: Claire does more studying than Shelley.
Therefore Shelley does the least amount of studying.
Question 18
48 - y = 27
- y = 27 - 48
-y = - 21
y = 21
Question 19
15 + 2 (13 + y) - 10 = 89
2 (13+y) = 89 – 15 + 10
13 + y = 84 / 2
y = 42 – 13
y = 29
Question 20
It will take 6.67 hours (20 / 3 = 6.6666). The fractions 2/3 works out to 0.666 or 0.67 rounded.
Question 21
521 x 346 = 180,266
Question 22
The products will cost $42.24 ($12.24 + 9.75 + 11.25). If $50 is spent, James will receive $7.76 in change (50 – 42.24 = 7.76).
Question 23
Kevin can ski 30 metres in 1 second (6 x 5 = 30), so in 12 seconds, he can ski 360 metres (30 x 12 = 360).

Question 24
The logic this question follows is:
No A are B.
Some C are B.
Some C are not A.

Question 25
The logic this question follows is:
Some A are B.
All B are C.
Some C are A.

Question 26
The logic this question follows is:
No B are C.
All A are B.
No C are A.

Question 27
The logic this question follows is:
If A then B.
If B then C.
If A then C. (but not necessarily if C then A)

Question 33
First determine volume of three containers [3 x 20L = 60L]. Then convert fill rate from mL/s to L/min. Recall 1L = 1000mL and 60s = 1 minute;
100 / 1000 x 60 = 6L/min];
Then divide total volume by fill rate [60 / 6 = 10 minutes]

Question 34
The logic this question follows is:
No A are B.
All C are B.
No C are A.
If it helps, reorganize the sentences.
All A (statements) are B (from women).
No C (victims) are B (women). No C (victims) gave A (statements).

Question 35
The annual increase in rain fall from one year to the next is 2%;
Starting at 856mm (2002), begin to calculate the rain fall for the following years: 856 x 1.02 = 873.12mm (2003);
Then 873.12 x 1.02 = 890.58mm (2004);
Finally, 890.58 x 1.02 = 908.4 mm (2005).

Question 36
There are two components to James' total run, 2 miles at 6 minutes/mile and 5 miles at "y" minutes/mile. These two numbers when added together and divided by 7 must result in 7.

$$\frac{2(6) + 5(y)}{7} = 7 \qquad \text{therefore:} \qquad \begin{aligned} 12 + 5y &= 49 \\ 5y &= 49 - 12 \\ y &= 37/5 \\ y &= 7.4 \text{ minutes / mile} \end{aligned}$$

Question 41
Unfortunately, I was not allowed to attend the graduation ceremony.
C - A - D - B

Question 42
Similar and synonymous are synonyms.

Question 43
$3(7-y) - 6 \times 2 = -21$
$3(7-y) - 12 = -21$
$3(7-y) = -21 + 12$
$7 - y = -9/3$
$-y = -3 - 7$
$y = 10$

Question 44
$2 + y + 11(y + 1) = 130 - y$
$2 + y + 11(y + 1) + y = 130$
$2 + y + 11y + 11 + y = 130$
$13 + 13y = 130$
$13y = 130 - 13$
$y = 117 / 13$
$y = 9$

Question 45
The two can remove 225 lbs of dirt per hour (100 + 125 = 225). That means they will need 4.45 hours to remove the 1000 lbs. (1000 / 225 = 4.44) You will have to round up to 4.45 hours to make sure all the dirt is removed (4.4 will only remove 990 lbs of dirt).

Question 46
The 6 hour hours completed represents 2/6 of the journey. The entire trip would therefore take 18 hours (6 x 6 / 2 = 18 hours).

Question 47
The logic this question follows is:
All A are B.
No C are B.
No C are A.

Question 48
The logic this question follows is:
No A are B.
Some C are A.
Some C are not B.

Same logic as:
No A are B.
Some C are B.
Some C are not A.

Question 49

C - Only phone with button used in middle row.

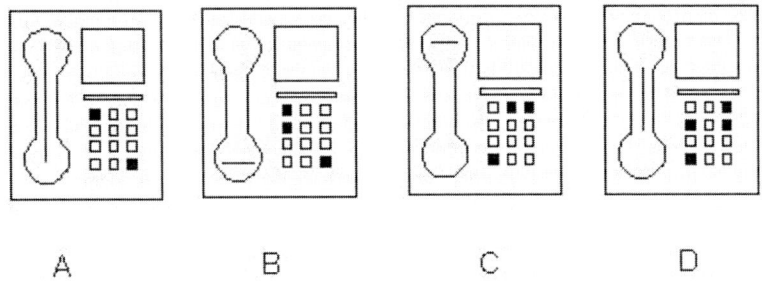

Question 50

B - Only object with two unique features (3 strips at bottom and no antenna).

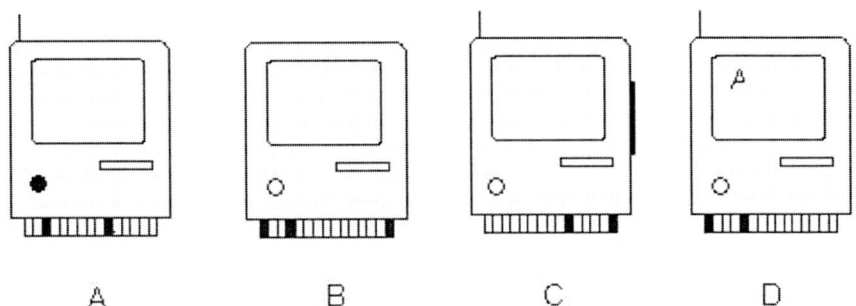

Question 51

D - Only plant with mark on two side-by-side leaves.

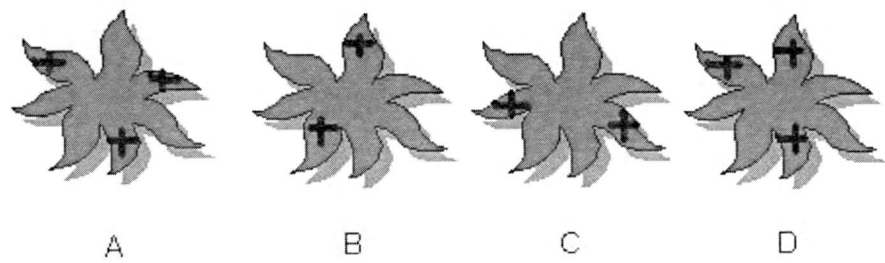

Question 52

One quarter of 32 is 8 (32 / 4 = 8). The number that is doubled to give you 8 is 4 (8 / 2 = 4).

Question 53

The cost of the tanker is "y" and the cost of the refinery would therefore be "2y" as it is twice as much. 2y + y = 36 million. 3y = 36 million so "y" the price of the tanker must be $12 million, and the refinery $24 million.

Question 54

The logic this question follows is:
No A is B.
Some C are B.
Some C are not A.

Question 60
After one of the bloodiest summers on record, London police say they have smashed a terrorist group responsible for terrorizing neighbourhoods in the city's northwest end.
C - A - B - D

Question 61
Variable and constant are antonyms.

Question 62
In 45 minutes the man can eat 10 kgs (80 / 8 = 10). 30 is 2/3 of 45 so in order to solve the problem, you have to multiply 2/3 and 10 kgs. 10 x 2/3 = 20 / 3 = 6.66 or 6 2/3 kgs.

Question 63
The cost of the apple is "y" and the cost of the orange would be "2y". Therefore:
3(y) + 3x2(y) = $2.70
3y + 6y = $2.70
9y = 2.70
y = 0.30 or $0.30, the price of one apple.

Question 64
John has increased by 4.5 km (6.5 – 2 = 4.5) which means 3 days have elapsed (4.5 / 1.5 = 3). This would make today Friday.

Question 65
The area of the floor is 24 square metres (8 x 3 = 24). Next dived the area of the flooring by the amount of area that one litre of paint will cover 24 / 6 = 4 litres required.

Question 66
The logic this question follows is:
No A are B.
Some C are B.
Some C are not A.

WSE-MCT ANSWER KEY

Spelling Component

A B C D E
1) ○ ○ ○ ○ _____
2) ○ ○ ○ ○ _____
3) ○ ○ ○ ○ _____
4) ○ ○ ○ ○ _____
5) ○ ○ ○ ○ _____
6) ○ ○ ○ ○ _____
7) ○ ○ ○ ○ _____
8) ○ ○ ○ ○ _____
9) ○ ○ ○ ○ _____
10) ○ ○ ○ ○ _____
11) ○ ○ ○ ○ _____
12) ○ ○ ○ ○ _____
13) ○ ○ ○ ○ _____
14) ○ ○ ○ ○ _____
15) ○ ○ ○ ○ ○ _____
16) ○ ○ ○ ○ ○ _____
17) ○ ○ ○ ○ ○ _____
18) ○ ○ ○ ○ ○ _____
19) ○ ○ ○ ○ ○ _____
20) ○ ○ ○ ○ ○ _____
21) ○ ○ ○ ○ ○ _____
22) ○ ○ ○ ○ ○ _____
23) ○ ○ ○ ○ ○ _____
24) ○ ○ ○ ○ ○ _____
25) ○ ○ ○ ○ ○ _____
26) ○ ○ ○ ○ ○ _____

Punctuation Component

A B C D E
1) ○ ○ ○ ○ ○ _____
2) ○ ○ ○ ○ ○ _____
3) ○ ○ ○ ○ ○ _____
4) ○ ○ ○ ○ ○ _____
5) ○ ○ ○ ○ ○ _____
6) ○ ○ ○ ○ ○ _____
7) ○ ○ ○ ○ ○ _____
8) ○ ○ ○ ○ ○ _____
9) ○ ○ ○ ○ ○ _____
10) ○ ○ ○ ○ ○ _____
11) ○ ○ ○ ○ ○ _____
12) ○ ○ ○ ○ ○ _____
13) ○ ○ ○ ○ ○ _____
14) ○ ○ ○ ○ ○ _____
15) ○ ○ ○ ○ ○ _____
16) ○ ○ ○ ○ ○ _____
17) ○ ○ ○ ○ ○ _____
18) ○ ○ ○ ○ _____
19) ○ ○ ○ ○ _____
20) ○ ○ ○ ○ _____
21) ○ ○ ○ ○ _____
22) ○ ○ ○ ○ _____
23) ○ ○ ○ ○ _____
24) ○ ○ ○ ○ _____

Grammar Component

A B C D
1) ○ ○ ○ ○ _____
2) ○ ○ ○ ○ _____
3) ○ ○ ○ ○ _____
4) ○ ○ ○ ○ _____
5) ○ ○ ○ ○ _____
6) ○ ○ ○ ○ _____
7) ○ ○ ○ ○ _____
8) ○ ○ ○ ○ _____
9) ○ ○ ○ ○ _____
10) ○ ○ ○ ○ _____
11) ○ ○ ○ ○ _____
12) ○ ○ ○ ○ _____
13) ○ ○ ○ ○ _____
14) ○ ○ ○ ○ _____
15) ○ ○ ○ ○ _____
16) ○ ○ ○ ○ _____
17) ○ ○ ○ ○ _____

WSE-MCT ANSWER KEY

Sentence Component

	A	B	C	D	
1)	○	○	○	○	___
2)	○	○	○	○	___
3)	○	○	○	○	___
4)	○	○	○	○	___
5)	○	○	○	○	___
6)	○	○	○	○	___
7)	○	○	○	○	___
8)	○	○	○	○	___
9)	○	○	○	○	___
10)	○	○	○	○	___
11)	○	○	○	○	___
12)	○	○	○	○	___
13)	○	○	○	○	___
14)	○	○	○	○	___
15)	○	○	○	○	___
16)	○	○	○	○	___
17)	○	○	○	○	___
18)	○	○	○	○	___

Punctuation Component

	A	B	C	D	E	F	
1)	○	○	○	○			___
2)	○	○	○	○			___
3)	○	○	○	○			___
4)	○	○	○	○			___
5)	○	○	○	○			___
6)	○	○	○	○			___
7)	○	○	○	○			___
8)	○	○	○	○			___
9)	○	○	○	○			___
10)	○	○	○	○			___
11)	○	○	○	○			___
12)	○	○	○	○			___
13)	○	○	○	○	○	○	___
14)	○	○	○	○	○	○	___
15)	○	○	○	○	○	○	___
16)	○	○	○	○	○	○	___
17)	○	○	○	○	○	○	___
18)	○	○	○	○	○	○	___
19)	○	○	○	○	○	○	___
20)	○	○	○	○	○		___
21)	○	○	○	○	○		___
22)	○	○	○	○	○	○	___
23)	○	○	○	○	○		___
24)	○	○	○	○	○		___
25)	○	○	○	○	○		___
26)	○	○	○	○	○	○	___
27)	○	○	○	○	○		___

Writing Skills in English Multiple Choice Test (WSE-MCT)

The Writing Skills in English – Multiple-Choice Test (WSE-MCT) is designed to assess levels 1, 2 and 3. The following is a description of each level:

Level 1: Basic skills in spelling, capitalization and punctuation.
Level 2: Basic skills in the above plus vocabulary, grammar, and sentence construction.
Level 3: Ability to write while respecting the mechanical principles of writing.

There are a total of 112 questions and there is a 90-minute time limit. The test is broken into 5 books.

Book 1 – 26 spelling questions.

Book 2 – 24 questions covering punctuation, grammar and capitalization.

Book 3 – 17 grammar questions.

Book 4 – 18 sentence ordering questions.

Book 5 – 27 vocabulary questions.

Spelling Component

Question 1

Which of the four words above is spelled incorrectly in the sentences below?

There were thousands of <u>demonstraters</u> at Parliament Hill protesting the <u>atrocities</u> committed by <u>foreign</u> governments with <u>horrible</u> human rights records.

a) demonstraters
b) atrocities
c) foreign
d) horrible

Question 2

Before leaving for work each morning, Constable Channey <u>exercises</u> by completing a half hour of <u>resistance</u> training, on top of a half hour of <u>aerobics</u>. She feels that if she maintains this <u>disipline</u> she will perform her duties as a police officer more effectively.

a) exercises
b) resistance
c) aerobics
d) disipline

Question 3

Constable Gordon <u>initiated</u> a foot pursuit as his prime suspect for a <u>domestick</u> assault fled through the back yard. The <u>perpetrator</u> was eventually <u>apprehended</u> several blocks away.

a) initiated
b) domestick
c) perpetrator
d) apprehended

Question 4

Mr. Carling is a well-known champion of <u>generic</u> drug <u>manufacturers</u>, and many other politicians and countless <u>commentaters</u> agree with him. They want to shorten or, in some cases, do away with the <u>patent</u> protection of serious pharmaceutical companies.

a) generic
b) manufacturers
c) commentaters
d) patent

Question 5

Several noise complaints <u>originated</u> from a celebration occurring during a street <u>festival</u> promoting jazz music. Noise levels that persisted past 3:00 in the morning <u>infurriated</u> citizens who live in the <u>neighbourhood</u>.

a) originated
b) festival
c) infurriated
d) neighbourhood

Question 6

Glass blowing is a traditional <u>Celctic</u> art. This skill has been passed down from each generation. The largest misgiving is that glass blowing is a dead art.

a) blowing
b) Celctic
c) misgiving
d) traditional

Question 7

Penguins live in Antarctica. They are notcurnal animals. This means that they move about more during the night hours. This allows them an advantage over the whales that hunt in the daytime.

a) notcurnal
b) penguins
c) Antarctica
d) advantage

Question 8

Lightening storms can produce great spectacles. The ultimate power of these storms has long been studied by scientists. Their power can be harnnesed for electrical power to heat homes.

a) spectacles
b) lightening
c) scientists
d) harnnesed

Question 9

When preparing for testing, the student should find a quite place to study. This should include seclution from outside noises and telephones.

a) telephones
b) seclution
c) preparing
d) student

Question 10

The rookie officers undertook extensive training and development programs in order to prepare them for the daunting tasks that would lie ahead of them as they commensed their police duties.

a) undertook
b) daunting
c) lie ahead
d) commensed

Question 11

Stress is an inherent nature of the job as a police officer. In order to help deal with stress police associations across Canada have arranged counselling with psychiatrists, and mandatory leave after incountering life threatening situations.

a) inherent
b) counselling
c) psychiatrists
d) incountering

Question 12

The emergency task force seconded several officers as a result of the September 11 attacks. City Council was concerned with the potential of another attack and felt that increased vigilance was required in these frigtening times.

a) emergency
b) seconded
c) vigilance
d) frigtening

Question 13

The rookie officers undertook extensive training and <u>development</u> programs in order to prepare <u>themeselves</u> for the <u>daunting</u> tasks that would lie ahead of them as they <u>commenced</u> their police duties.

a) development
b) themeselves
c) daunting
d) commenced

Question 14

There are several <u>academic</u> courses available at both <u>univercity</u> and college level that would be <u>beneficial</u> to potential <u>applicants</u> wishing to obtain a position with a police force.

a) academic
b) univercity
c) beneficial
d) applicants

Question 15

Identify which of the following words is misspelled in the following questions.

a) simpathy
b) verge
c) actual
d) borrowed
e) None of the above

Question 16

a) courage
b) emphasis
c) guidence
d) initiative
e) None of the above

Question 17

a) legitimate
b) module
c) ordeal
d) pligt
e) None of the above

Question 18

a) punishment
b) rellapse
c) sentence
d) tactic
e) None of the above

Question 19

a) vigur
b) adequate
c) broken
d) cultural
e) None of the above

Question 20

a) encounter
b) harbour
c) innocent
d) leverage
e) None of the above

Question 21

a) monopoly
b) organiseation
c) policing
d) pursue
e) None of the above

Question 22

a) release	b) seargeant	c) technical
d) vital	e) None of the above

Question 23

a) adolecent	b) building	c) critical
d) enforce	e) None of the above

Question 24

a) hazard	b) instalment	c) licence
d) motion	e) None of the above

Question 25

a) burgluries	b) daughter	c) enormous
d) height	e) None of the above

Question 26

a) decicive	b) environment	c) history
d) insurance	e) None of the above

Punctuation Component

Question 1

Indicate any punctuation errors in the sentences below:
Before taking the tickets, the teenager must clock in, then she can begin work.

a) taking					b) in, then					c) can

d) work.					e) No correction required

Question 2

When planning an outing with children, remember to bring: activities, snacks, and a first aid kit.

a) children,				b) bring:					c) , snacks, and a

d) aid kit.					e) No correction required

Question 3

Trips to the zoo, are lots of fun. There are many animals to see and things to do.

a) zoo,						b) fun.						c) are

d) things to do.			e) No correction required

Question 4

What is the answer to the question! I did not study enough and need help.

a) answer to				b) question!				c) enough and

d) help.					e) No correction required

Question 5

Wow! That was a close call? Who can help the young lady learn a better method?

a) Wow! That				b) close call?				c) young lady learn

d) method?					e) No correction required

Question 6

The mail carrier ensures that all letters are delivered on his route. He is courteous and punctual as well.

a) ensures					b) route.					c) and

d) well.					e) No correction required

Question 7

The students have been asked to perform many tasks; They include collecting different species of insects and gathering leaves.

a) been asked				b) tasks;					c) collecting different

d) insects and				e) No correction required

Question 8

Healthcare costs are skyrocketing, this is creating a problem for the public and private sector.

a) skyrocketing, this   b) creating a problem   c) public and

d) sector.   e) No correction required

Question 9

Which type of cheese do you need? There is American Monterey, Cheddar, and Colby.

a) need?   b) is American   c) Monterey, Cheddar,

d) Colby.   e) No correction required

Question 10

Have you acquired the supplies that we need? They are the most important, part of the project.

a) you acquired   b) need?   c) important,

d) project.   e) No correction required

Question 11

Where do you want to go, for lunch? We can have Mexican, Italian, or Indian.

a) go,   b) lunch?   c) Mexican,

d) Indian.   e) No correction required

Question 12

The fire was burning bright: it was very hot. The smores will turn out nicely.

a) The fire   b) bright: it   c) hot.

d) smores will turn   e) No correction required

Question 13

"I want to go to McDonald's for lunch today?" said Billy. "They have the best french-fries," he thought to himself.

a) today?   b) Billy.   c) "They have the"

d) french-fries," he   e) No correction required

Question 14

The following are the best deals: fish, shrimp, scallops, and kelp. This seafood market has the freshest items?

a) deals: b) scallops,   c) seafood market

d) items?   e) No correction required

Question 15

Hello! shouted Paul when he saw some friends he recognized at the beach. He ran over to join their game of volleyball.

a) Hello!   b) friends he   c) beach.

d) to join their   e) No correction required

Question 16

Where is Charlene? I told her she could go to the movies, the football game, or the soda shop, where is she?

a) movies,   b) game,   c) shop,

d) she?   e) No correction required

Question 17

What has to be done for this work? There are several steps, collect all of the materials together, mix the first two ingredients, preheat the oven, and flour a pan.

a) steps,   b) together,   c) ingredients,

d) oven   e) No correction required

Question 18

"Which of the following is the best decision for the problem at hand!" shouted the manager. "I need a decision made before any of you are allowed to leave!"

a) "Which of   b) hand!"   c) manager. "I

d) leave!"   e) No correction required

Question 19

Which of the following punctuation adjustments should be made to create logical sentences?
instances of retaliation for testifying in court are very rare despite this officers should be vigilant suspects may attempt to intimidate witnesses

a) place a period after the word "vigilant"

b) place a comma after the word "retaliation"

c) place a period after the word "rarity"

d) place a comma after the word "should"

Question 20

who cares whether old people can take care of themselves or not asked the young college student as he prepared for his psychology exam

a) place a question mark after the word "exam"

b) place a comma after the word "not"

c) place quotation marks around "Who...asked"

d) place a question mark after the word "not"

Question 21

the suspect fled into the street then turned a corner quickly it was better that he fled rather than staying in the bank and taking hostages

a) add a comma after the word "suspect"

b) add a period after the word "quickly"

c) add a semi-colon after the word "rather"

d) add an apostrophe to the word "fled"

Question 22

the collision happened because the brakes were faulty had the brakes been functioning properly she would have been able to stop she should have had them fixed earlier

a) place a hyphen after the word "functioning"

b) place a question mark after the word "earlier"

c) place a comma after the word "she"

d) place a period after the word "faulty"

Question 23

because she had been married twice she had two mothers in law in her life she didnt like either of them

a) add hyphens to "mothers-in-law"

b) add an apostrophe to "mother's"

c) add a comma after the word "two"

d) add an exclamation mark after the word "either"

Question 24

I am extremely impressed with your dedication said Susan she was referring to the amount of time Jim was spending in the gym

a) add quotation marks around the words "I...impressed"

b) add a hyphen after the word "impressed"

c) add a comma after the word "referring"

d) add a comma after the word "dedication"

Grammar Component

Choose the sentence that is most clearly written and grammatically correct in the following questions.

Question 1

a) Because she had been married twice, she had two mother-in-laws in her life, and she didn't like either.

b) Because she had been married twice, she had two mothers-in-law in her life, and she didn't like either.

c) Because she had been married twice, she had two mother's-in-law in her life, and she didn't like either.

d) Because she had been married twice, she had two mothers-in-laws in her life, and she didn't like either.

Question 2

a) Between him and his brother, Jamal was the stronger. He could bench press at least 50 pounds more than his sibling.

b) Between him and his brother, Jamal was the strongest. He could bench press at least 50 pounds more than his sibling.

c) Between him and his brother, Jamal was the more stronger. He could bench press at least 50 pounds more than his sibling.

d) Both 1 and 3 are correct.

Question 3

a) My younger brother don't have a job right now. He hopes his quick typing skills will land him a temporary job.

b) My younger brother don't have a job right now. He hopes his quickly typing skills will land him a temporary job.

c) My younger brother doesn't have a job right now. He hopes his quickly typing skills will land him a temporary job.

d) My younger brother doesn't have a job right now. He hopes his quick typing skills will land him a temporary job.

Question 4

a) The government realized it had a problem with the legislation so David Boothby and Michael Duncan of the Association of the Chiefs of Police were selected to help rework it.

b) The government realized it had a problem with the legislation so David Boothby and Michael Duncan of the Association of the Chiefs of Police is selected to help rework it.

c) The government realized it had a problem with the legislation so David Boothby and Michael Duncan of the Association of the Chiefs of Police was selected to help rework it.

d) The government realized it had a problem with the legislation so David Boothby and Michael Duncan of the Association of the Chiefs of Police selected to help rework it.

Question 5

a) The basement was filled with insects and mice, but the officer had to precede into it anyway.

b) The basement was filled with insects and mouses, but the officer had to proceed into the basement anyway.

c) The basement was filled with insects and mice, but the officer had to proceed into it anyway.

d) The basement was filled with insects and mouses, but the officer had to precede into the basement anyway.

Question 6

a) My little brother, a dedicated martial artist, he is fantastic for his age.

b) My little brother is a dedicated martial artist and is fantastic for his age.

c) My little brother, is quite a dedicated martial artist for his age.

d) My little brother, for his age is quite a fantastically dedicated martial artist.

Question 7

a) Mark Twain's novels, like many writers, are largely autobiographical.

b) Mark Twain's novels, like those of many novelists, are largely autobiographical.

c) Mark Twain's novels, like those of many writers, are largely autobiographical.

d) Mark Twain's novels, like so many other writers, are largely autobiographical.

Question 8

a) If the room would have been brighter, I would have been able to read for a while before bedtime.

b) If rooms are brighter, I would have been able to read for a while before bedtime.

c) If the room could have been brighter, I would have been able to read for a while before bedtime.

d) If the room had been brighter, I would have been able to read for a while before bedtime.

Question 9

a) Fewer rainfall means less traffic accidents, according to several experts on highway safety.

b) Less rainfall means less traffic accidents, according to several experts on highway safety.

c) Less rainfall means fewer traffic accidents, according to several experts on highway safety.

d) Fewer rainfall means less traffic accidents, according to several experts on highway safety.

Question 10

a) The photographer wanted to take the picture, the child wasn't smiling.

b) The photographer wanted to take the picture but the child wasn't smiling.

c) The photographer wanted to take the picture: the child wasn't smiling.

d) Either A or C

Question 11

a) After the accident occurred, the victims called the police. They showed up in less than 5 minutes.

b) The victims called the police, after the accident and showed up in less than 5 minutes.

c) The Police were called, after the accident and arrived in less than 5 minutes.

d) Less than 5 minutes after the police arrived the accident occurred.

Question 12

a) When the weather changed so rapidly, the ships crew can only tie down the sails and ride out the storms.

b) When the weather changes so rapidly, the ships crew could only tie down the sails and ride out the storm.

c) When the weather changed so rapidly, the ships crew can only tie down the sail and rode out the storm.

d) When the weather changes so rapidly, the ship's crew can only tie down the sails and ride out the storm.

Question 13

Indicate which underlined portion contains an error in the following questions.

Kelly of Deloitte and Touche and Sean, a student of Concordia, are applying for positions with the Victoria Police Department. Their recruiting officers name is Constable Shaw.

a) are applying b) positions

c) Their d) recruiting officers

Question 14

If they are unsuccessful and don't get past the interview stage, their going to have to reapply after waiting six months.

a) they are unsuccessful b) past

c) their going d) reapply after

Question 15

The previous rules posted encourages people to break the new rules.

a) previous b) posted

c) encourages d) break

Question 16

Much of the potential applicants fail to realize all the skills that are required as a police officer. Mathematics, including addition, subtraction, multiplication and division, are primary skills required for accident reconstruction, and general-purpose investigations.

a) Much of the potential b) that are required as a

c) are primary skills d) general-purpose

Question 17

The cost of graffiti and vandalism in both human and financial terms has been considerable. Many of the residents were frightened, angry and the neighbourhood was getting ruined.

a) cost of graffiti b) in both human

c) has been d) frightened, angry and the neighbourhood

Sentence Ordering Component

Select the proper order of the following sentences so that the paragraphs make sense.

Question 1

(A) Robert was not as nervous as Louise since he had been married before. (B) Louise was nervous which was expected since this was her first and only wedding. (C) The two made it through the ceremony just fine once it was started. (D) The big day had come for Louise and her fiancé Robert.

a) BDAC	b) DBAC	c) DACB	d) BACD

Question 2

(A) This build-up allows the water to erode the shoreline without actually making it less protected. (B) The local people have discovered a way to protect themselves from the natural threat that is ingenious. (C) Flooding is a large problem for many people who live and work in London. (D) They build up the shoreline of the city two inches each year with left over landscaping materials and construction site remains.

a) BDAC	b) ABDC	c) DCAB	d) CBDA

Question 3

(A) He has petitioned the government to subsidize his crops to ensure he brings in the same amount of money each year despite his crop size. (B) Farmers constitute less than 2% of the total working population in the United Kingdom today. (C) Fred is a corn farmer who is having a hard time making ends meet. (D) Due to the relatively small number of farmers however his voice is not heard and his request goes unnoticed.

a) BCAD	b) BCDA	c) ADCB	d) ABCD

Question 4

(A) He is also disenchanted about the fact that he is making it possible for large companies to pollute the Earth everyday. (B) When he accepted the position he thought he would be making a difference in the world. (C) As it turns out his main function is paperwork for companies that do not want to complete it themselves. (D) James has taken on a new job in Environmental Engineering.

a) CBAD	b) BADC	c) DBCA	d) ADBC

Question 5

(A) Medication is available to help alleviate some of the adverse effects of the condition. (B) Diabetes is a serious condition that affects many people in different ways. (C) The increased insulin release allows the person to function normally with a sensible diet. (D) The medication blocks neural pathways that inhibit the release of insulin within the body.

a) CDBA	b) BADC	c) ABCD	d) CBAD

Question 6

(A) She has gone from one poorly equipped school to another. (B) Finally she has found a school that is geared towards competition and eventually the Olympics. (C) She is very pleased with the way the new school is molding her to do her best and win at competitions. (D) Amber has been in gymnastics for almost 3 years.

a) DABC	b) CBAD	c) BADC	d) DBCA

Question 7

(A) A survey has been handed out to the patrons over the past month to determine what the public thinks. (B) The museum's director is trying to determine if another exhibit should be put in its place while the work is being done. (C) The largest exhibit in the museum needs to be resurfaced and cleaned up a bit. (D) The results of the survey have sent the director looking for something to replace the main attraction at his museum.

a) DABC   b) CBAD   c) CADB   d) CDAB

Question 8

(A) Potential students must complete the 20-page application. (B) The Imperial College of London has a very strict and stringent admissions process. (C) Finally a letter from the student themselves needs to be created which states why the college should accept them as a student. (D) A letter of recommendation needs to be received from three independent sources.

a) BCAD   b) CBAD   c) CADB   d) BADC

Question 9

(A) The sport of rugby has a rich and interesting history and origin. (B) The general consensus however is that the game of rugby dates back to 1037 when a group of natives where playing a game of Caid and were seen by an affluent young London boy. (C) Others would argue this was not true at all but that the first game of football dates back to 1173 when a London born monk wrote about the game in his journal. (D) Many would say it was first started when William Webb Ellis first picked up the football and ran with it in his arms in 1823.

a) ADCB   b) CABD   c) CBAD   d) CDAB

Question 10

(A) This hike has lead to many of the upper class to become irate and annoyed. (B) The tax system is going through an overhaul this next term. (C) They feel that they are being punished for the sole reason that they were more able to make a good living. (D) The vote has been to increase the tax on luxury items so that necessary ones are not out of reach of the common man.

a) BCAD   b) CDBA   c) BDAC   d) ABCD

Question 11

(A) The findings indicate that despite the massive consumption of mushrooms in the UK, many people suffer from a deficiency. (B) Scientists have reported recently that mushrooms can be an excellent source of the needed vitamin. (C) New research indicates that you can fulfill your daily requirements for Vitamin D in a never before thought of place. (D) The mushrooms must be fresh and uncooked for the full benefit, but a minor benefit is still received if they are included in sauces.

a) CBAD   b) CABD   c) BADC   d) DBAC

Question 12

(A) The nursing staff performs a secondary procedure that will question the surgeon before starting the surgery. (B) Finally the surgical chart is on display in the operating room at all times for reference. (C) It is a person's worst nightmare to go in for surgery and come out with the wrong procedure being performed. (D) Many things have been done to correct this problem such as requiring the patient to identify for the surgeon what procedure they are in the hospital for.

a) CDAB   b) DBAC   c) BACD   d) BCAD

Question 13

(A) It could be a good thing for you to get your daily dose of white chocolate Harvard scientists are now reporting. (B) Like all things you should not over-consume in an effort to lower your blood pressure and you should follow the advice of your physician if you have high blood pressure. (C) They have found a correlation between a moderate intake of white chocolate and lowered blood pressure. (D) Everyone seems to love to eat chocolate as a comfort food.

a) DACB   b) DBCA   c) CABD   d) DCAB

Question 14

(A) She is a nurse in a nursing home intensive care unit and knows at this point in her career that things can get crazy. (B) She likes to be able to take a moment or two to orient herself with her caseload and relax before her hectic shift. (C) She loves her job despite the ups and downs of it and the wild schedule. (D) Leslie arrives at work a few minutes early as she always does.

a) ABCD   b) DBAC   c) CABD   d) BADC

Question 15

(A) Areas that are in their path have done many things to deter the birds from taking up residence in their town. (B) Some have put down chicken wire in fields that have been used as nesting areas in the past. (C) Other places have gone as far as to poison the birds to cut down their numbers. (D) The Egret birds can be a nuisance when they migrate in large numbers.

a) DCBA   b) BADC   c) DABC   d) DBAC

Question 16

(A) Then they checked the weather at their destination to ensure they packed the most appropriate clothing for skiing and hiking. (B) They packed enough food for the drive to the mountains from their home in the city. (C) The Dewitt family was planning on a vacation into the Black Mountains. (D) When all of their things were packed in the car they loaded in the children and headed off for a full week of fun.

a) CBAD   b) BDAC   c) CDBA   d) CABD

Question 17

(A) Deep below the Earth's crust is a river of molten rock. (B) This produces a lot of steam and pressure. (C) At the surface, cracks and pressure vents can be created due to the constant pressure. (D) At times the molten rock superheats water that can escape through these cracks and vents in the form of a geyser.

a) DACB   b) BADC   c) ABCD   d) DCBA

Question 18

(A) When a volcano forms it can take one of three forms, which are listed from least to most dangerous. (B) The cinder cone forms by streaming gases that carry lava blobs into the atmosphere. (C) The composite volcano is formed by multiple eruptions and is seen by scientists as the most dangerous and treacherous of all volcano types. (D) The shield volcano has a large summit with low-sloping sides.

a) ACBD　　　　b) CDBA　　　　c) BACD　　　　d) ADBC

Vocabulary Component

Question 1
Culpability means:
a) Exasperate   b) Blame   c) Annoy   d) Exonerate

Question 2
Potent means:
a) Malevolent   b) Vicious   c) Stagnant   d) Intoxicating

Question 3
Prudent means:
a) Insecure   b) Dominant   c) Resourceful   d) Careful

Question 4
Wanton means:
a) Invigorated   b) Zestful   c) Reckless   d) Shameful

Question 5
Gravitate means:
a) Float   b) Settle   c) Stimulate   d) Challenge

Question 6
Recess means:
a) Interrogate   b) Depression   c) Philanthropy   d) Interrupt

Question 7
Geyser means:
a) Natural Spring   b) Elderly   c) Radiation Detector   d) A Plant

Question 8
Libel means:
a) Courtship   b) Plagiarism   c) Rumour   d) Defamation

Question 9
Valiant means:
a) Succumb   b) Civilian   c) Gallant   d) Sufficient

Question 10
Emphatic means:
a) Irritable   b) Empathy   c) Holistic   d) Insistent

Question 11
Expendable means:
a) Able to Grow   b) Disposable   c) Careful   d) Watchful

Question 12
Abominable means:
a) Hateful   b) Snowman   c) Violent   d) A bomb

Question 13

Which two words have the same meaning?
| a) Hot | b) Cold | c) Wet | d) Damp |

a) a & b b) a & c c) a & d
d) b & c e) b & d f) c & d

Question 14

Which two words have the opposite meaning?
| a) Hot | b) Wet | c) Cold | d) Damp |

a) a & b b) a & c c) a & d
d) b & c e) b & d f) c & d

Question 15

Which two words have the same meaning?
| a) Bear | b) Bare | c) Naked | d) Lamp |

a) a & b b) a & c c) a & d
d) b & c e) b & d f) c & d

Question 16

Which two words have the opposite meaning?
| a) Shy | b) Careful | c) Honest | d) Outgoing |

a) a & b b) a & c c) a & d
d) b & c e) b & d f) c & d

Question 17

Which two words have the same meaning?
| a) Mad | b) Sad | c) Angry | d) Happy |

a) a & b b) a & c c) a & d
d) b & c e) b & d f) c & d

Question 18

Which two words have the opposite meaning?
| a) Neat | b) Messy | c) Warm | d) High |

a) a & b b) a & c c) a & d
d) b & c e) b & d f) c & d

Question 19

Which two words have the same meaning?
| a) Decode | b) Magnify | c) Enlarge | d) Quiet |

a) a & b b) a & c c) a & d
d) b & c e) b & d f) c & d

Question 20
Which two words have the opposite meaning?
a) Brave b) Honest c) Careful d) Cowardly
a) a & b b) a & c c) a & d
d) b & c e) b & d f) c & d

Question 21
Which two words have the same meaning?
a) Shirt b) Shoes c) Pants d) Trousers
a) a & b b) a & c c) a & d
d) b & c e) b & d f) c & d

Question 22
Which two words have the opposite meaning?
a) Thoughtful b) Large c) Inconsiderate d) Impressive
a) a & b b) a & c c) a & d
d) b & c e) b & d f) c & d

Question 23
Which two words have the same meaning?
a) Odd b) Kind c) Troublesome d) Strange
a) a & b b) a & c c) a & d
d) b & c e) b & d f) c & d

Question 24
Which two words have the opposite meaning?
a) Crazed b) Original c) Duplicate d) Energetic
a) a & b b) a & c c) a & d
d) b & c e) b & d f) c & d

Question 25
Which two words have the same meaning?
a) Savage b) Natural c) Wild d) Enormous
a) a & b b) a & c c) a & d
d) b & c e) b & d f) c & d

Question 26
Which two words have the opposite meaning?
a) Receive b) Donate c) Create d) Challenge
a) a & b b) a & c c) a & d
d) b & c e) b & d f) c & d

Question 27
Which two words have the same meaning?
a) Careful b) Polite c) War d) Civil
a) a & b b) a & c c) a & d
d) b & c e) b & d f) c & d

WSE- MCT ANSWER KEY & DETAILED ANSWER EXPLANATIONS

Spelling	Punctuation	Grammar	Sentences	Vocabulary
1) A	1) B	1) B	1) B	1) B
2) D	2) B	2) A	2) D	2) D
3) B	3) A	3) D	3) A	3) D
4) C	4) B	4) A	4) C	4) C
5) C	5) B	5) C	5) B	5) B
6) B	6) E	6) B	6) A	6) B
7) A	7) B	7) C	7) B	7) A
8) D	8) A	8) D	8) D	8) D
9) B	9) B	9) C	9) A	9) C
10) D	10) C	10) B	10) C	10) D
11) D	11) A	11) A	11) A	11) B
12) D	12) B	12) D	12) A	12) A
13) B	13) A	13) D	13) A	13) F
14) B	14) D	14) C	14) B	14) B
15) A	15) A	15) C	15) C	15) D
16) C	16) C	16) A	16) A	16) C
17) D	17) A	17) D	17) C	17) B
18) B	18) B		18) D	18) A
19) A	19) A			19) D
20) C	20) D			20) C
21) B	21) B			21) F
22) B	22) D			22) B
23) A	23) A			23) C
24) E	24) D			24) D
25) A				25) B
26) A				26) A
				27) E

Punctuation Test

Question 1
A period is required after the word "in"; otherwise, a run-on sentence is created.

Question 2
A colon should not be used before a series introduced by a verb or preposition.

Question 3
There is a comma that is not required after the word "zoo".

Question 4
A question mark is required after the word "question".

Question 5
"That was a close call" is a statement and does not require a question mark.

Question 6
There are no punctuation errors in these sentences.

Question 7

A period is required after "tasks".

Question 8

A period is required after "skyrocketing".

Question 9

A comma is required after "American".

Question 10

There is no comma required after "important".

Question 11

There is no need for a comma after the word "go".

Question 12

The colon should be replaced with either a semicolon or a period and the word "it" should be capitalized.

Question 13

The question mark should be replaced with a comma after the word "today".

Question 14

The question mark after "items" should be replaced with a period.

Question 15

Opening and closing quotation marks are required around "Hello!"

Question 16

The comma after the word "shop" should be replaced with a semicolon or a period. The word "where" would have to be capitalized to indicate the start of a new sentence.

Question 17

A colon is required after the word "steps".

Question 18

A question mark is required at the end of the question.

Question 19

Instances of retaliation for testifying in court are very rare. Despite this, officers should be vigilant. Suspects may attempt to intimidate witnesses.

Question 20

"Who cares whether old people can take care of themselves or not?" asked the young college student as he prepared for his psychology exam.

Question 21

The suspect fled into the street then turned a corner quickly. It was better that he fled rather than staying in the bank and taking hostages.

Question 22

The collision happened because the brakes were faulty. Had the brakes been functioning properly she would have been able to stop. She should have had them fixed earlier.

Question 23

Because she had been married twice, she had two mothers-in-law in her life. She didn't like either of them.

Question 24

"I am extremely impressed with your dedication," said Susan. She was referring to the amount of time Jim was spending in the gym.

Grammar Test

Question 1

The correct plural form of "mother-in-law" is "mothers-in-law".

Question 2

When a comparative adjective is used between two parties, the correct ending is "-er". If a modifier is used, it becomes redundant (more stronger) and is inappropriate.

Question 3

The correct verb tense for "do not" with a third person singular subject is "doesn't". "Quick" as opposed to "quickly" has to be used to describe skills, as it is an adjective describing a noun.

Question 4

The correct tense to use for third person plural is "were". All other sentences use an incorrect verb tense.

Question 5

The correct plural form of "mouse" is "mice", not "mouses". The word "proceed" means to "continue on", while the word "precede" means "to go before".

Question 6

Sentence #1 is redundant, as the word "he" is not required. There is an extra comma in sentence #2. Sentence #3 is obscure and doesn't make sense.

Question 7

The middle clause has to properly refer to the first clause. "Those" replaces "novels", so the sentence could be written "Mark Twain's novels, like the novels of many writers…"

Question 8

Sentence #4 has the proper tense of the verb for the sentence.

Question 9

The correct adjective for rainfall is "less" (rainfall can't be counted) and the correct adjective for accidents is "fewer" (accidents can be counted).

Question 10

The two clauses have to be combined with a conjunction (but). A comma or colon is inappropriate.

Question 11

Option A is the correct answer. Option B is confusing and vague as to who showed up in less than 5 minutes (victims or police). Option C has an improperly placed comma, and option D should have a comma added and is confusing.

Question 12

Options A and C are incorrect as "changed" is in past tense and "can" is in present tense. The present tense of "changes" requires "can". Option B requires an apostrophe on the word "ship's".

Question 13

In this sentence the word "officers" is plural as opposed to possessive. The sentence should read: "Their recruiting officer's name is Constable Shaw."

Question 14

In this sentence "their" is used incorrectly. What the sentence is stating is that "they are going to have to reapply…" The contraction form of "they are" is "they're".

Question 15

This is another example of subject verb agreement. The subject in this sentence is plural "rules" and has to agree with the verb in number. The correct form of this sentence would be: "The previous rules posted encourage people to break the rules."

Question 16

The word "much" should generally be used for amounts that cannot be easily counted, for instance "much of the dirt" or "much of the water" etc. If the amount could easily be counted you must use the word "many", for instance "many of the people" or "many of the countries" etc. The correct form of this sentence would be: "Many of the potential applicants fail…"

Question 17

There is an incomplete list in the second sentence. There is a list of adjectives "frightened, angry" that is broken up with a new clause "and the neighbourhood was getting ruined". The list has to be completed first before a new clause can be incorporated into the sentence. The sentence could read either:

"Many of the residents were frightened and angry and the neighbourhood was getting ruined."
or
"Many of the residents were frightened and angry. The neighbourhood was getting ruined."

Sentence Ordering Test
Question 1

The big day had come for Louise and her fiancé Robert. Louise was nervous which was expected since this was her first and only wedding. Robert was not as nervous as Louise since he had been married before. The two made it through the ceremony just fine once it was started.

Question 2

Flooding is a large problem for many people who live and work in London. The local people have discovered a way to protect themselves from the natural threat that is ingenious. They build up the shoreline of the city two inches each year with left over landscaping materials and construction site remains. This build-up allows the water to erode the shoreline without actually making it less protected.

Question 3

Farmers constitute less than 2% of the total working population in the United Kingdom today. Fred is a corn farmer who is having a hard time making ends meet. He has petitioned the government to subsidize his crops to ensure he brings in the same amount of money each year despite his crop size. Due to the relatively small number of farmers however his voice is not heard and his request goes unnoticed.

Question 4

James has taken on a new job in Environmental Engineering. When he accepted the position he thought he would be making a difference in the world. As it turns out his main function is paperwork for companies that do not want to complete it themselves. He is also disenchanted about the fact that he is making it possible for large companies to pollute the Earth everyday.

Question 5

Diabetes is a serious condition that affects many people in different ways. Medication is available to help alleviate some of the adverse effects of the condition. The medication blocks neural pathways that inhibit the release of insulin within the body. The increased insulin release allows the person to function normally with a sensible diet.

Question 6

Amber has been in gymnastics for almost 3 years. She has gone from one poorly equipped school to another. Finally she has found a school that is geared towards competition and eventually the Olympics. She is very pleased with the way the new school is molding her to do her best and win at competitions.

Question 7

The largest exhibit in the museum needs to be resurfaced and cleaned up a bit. The museum's director is trying to determine if another exhibit should be put in its place while the work is being done. A survey has been handed out to the patrons over the past month to determine what the public thinks. The results of the survey have sent the director looking for something to replace the main attraction at his museum.

Question 8

The Imperial College of London has a very strict and stringent admissions process. Potential students must complete the 20 page application. A letter of recommendation needs to be received from three independent sources. Finally a letter from the student themselves needs to be created which states why the college should accept them as a student.

Question 9

The sport of rugby has a rich and interesting history and origin. Many would say it was first started when William Webb Ellis first picked up the football and ran with it in his arms in 1823. Others would argue this was not true at all but that the first game of football dates back to 1173 when a London born monk wrote about the game in his journal. The general consensus however is that the game of rugby dates back to 1037 when a group of natives where playing a game of Caid and were seen by an affluent young London boy.

Question 10

The tax system is going through an overhaul this next term. The vote has been to increase the tax on luxury items so that necessary ones are not out of reach of the common man. This hike has lead to many of the upper class to become irate and annoyed. They feel that they are being punished for the sole reason that they were more able to make a good living.

Question 11

New research indicates that you can fulfill your daily requirements for Vitamin D in a never before thought of place. Scientists have reported recently that mushrooms can be an excellent source of the needed vitamin. The findings indicate that despite the massive consumption of mushrooms in the UK, many people suffer from a deficiency. The mushrooms must be fresh and uncooked for the full benefit, but a minor benefit is still received if they are included in sauces.

Question 12

It is a person's worst nightmare to go in for surgery and come out with the wrong procedure being performed. Many things have been done to correct this problem such as requiring the patient to identify for the surgeon what procedure they are in the hospital for. The nursing staff performs a secondary procedure that will question the surgeon before starting the surgery. Finally the surgical chart is on display in the operating room at all times for reference.

Question 13

Everyone seems to love to eat chocolate as a comfort food. It could be a good thing for you to get your daily dose of white chocolate Harvard scientists are now reporting. They have found a correlation between a moderate intake of white chocolate and lowered blood pressure. Like all things you should not over-consume in an effort to lower your blood pressure and you should follow the advice of your physician if you have high blood pressure.

Question 14

Leslie arrives at work a few minutes early as she always does. She likes to be able to take a moment or two to orient herself with her caseload and relax before her hectic shift. She is a nurse in a nursing home intensive care unit and knows at this point in her career that things can get crazy. She loves her job despite the ups and downs of it and the wild schedule.

Question 15

The Egret birds can be a nuisance when they migrate in large numbers. Areas that are in their path have done many things to deter the birds from taking up residence in their town. Some have put down chicken wire in fields that have been used as nesting areas in the past. Other places have gone as far as to poison the birds to cut down their numbers.

Question 16

The Dewitt family was planning on a vacation into the Black Mountains. They packed enough food for the drive to the mountains from their home in the city. Then they checked the weather at their destination to ensure they packed the most appropriate clothing for skiing and hiking. When all of their things were packed in the car they loaded in the children and headed off for a full week of fun.

Question 17

Deep below the Earth's crust is a river of molten rock. This produces a lot of steam and pressure. At the surface, cracks and pressure vents can be created due to the constant pressure. At times the molten rock superheats water that can escape through these cracks and vents in the form of a geyser.

Question 18

When a volcano forms it can take one of three forms, which are listed from least to most dangerous. The shield volcano has a large summit with low-sloping sides. The cinder cone forms by streaming gases that carry lava blobs into the atmosphere. The composite volcano is formed by multiple eruptions and is seen by scientists as the most dangerous and treacherous of all volcano types.

Discard